Encounter Ireland

GW00728941

ENCOUNTER IRELAND

A combined course and workbook for Advanced-level English

Jennifer Sweeney

Gill and Macmillan

Published in Ireland by
Gill and Macmillan Ltd
Goldenbridge
Dublin 8
with associated companies throughout the world

© The Language Centre of Ireland 1992
0 7171 1857 6
Designed by Duo Design
Print origination by Seton Music Graphics, Bantry, Co. Cork
Printed by Criterion Press, Dublin

DEDICATION

I would like to thank the Language Centre of Ireland for giving me the opportunity to write *Encounter Ireland*, my colleagues for their invaluable help in piloting the material and my friends, including many ex-students, for their encouragement and moral support.

Jennifer Sweeney

ACKNOWLEDGMENTS

For permission to reproduce copyright material, grateful acknowledgment is made to the following:
The Irish Times for 'Inventing a Sense of Being Irish' by Fintan O'Toole; *The Sunday Tribune* for 'Teenage Drinking' by Liz McManus; The Blackstaff Press for 'Enemy Encounter' by Padraic Fiacc from *Poetry of the North* edited by Frank Ormsby; Faber and Faber Ltd, for 'Dublin Made Me' by Donagh McDonagh from *The Hungry Grass*; 'Dublin' by Louis MacNeice from *Collected Poems* and 'Digging' by Seamus Heaney from *Death of a Naturalist*; The Bodley Head for an extract from *The Ballroom of Romance* by William Trevor; The O'Brien Press Ltd for the extract from 'How Cuchulainn got his name' from *The Ulster Cycle* (C.D.U. publication); Routledge for two drawings (on page 124) from *Irish Folkways* by E. Estyn Evans.
'To Hunt or not to Hunt' is from *Animal Watch, the magazine of the Irish Council against Blood Sports* (Summer 1990); the passage on the Dublin Horse Show is from *Horse and Hound* (September 1990) and the passage by Maeve Binchy is from *Irish Life and Traditions* by Sharon Gmelch (O'Brien Press).

The publishers have made every effort to trace copyright holders, but if they have inadvertently overlooked any they will be pleased to make the necessary arrangements at the first opportunity.

For permission to reproduce photographs grateful acknowledgment is made to the following:
Bord Fáilte; Northern Ireland Tourist Board; Camera Press; Guinness Ireland Ltd; Tim Severin and Nathan Benn/Brendan Archive; *The Irish Times*; Rod Tuach; Source Photographic Archives; Terry Thorp; Hulton-Deutsch; RTE; Lenmen; Office of Public Works; Sportsfile.

The songs on the *Encounter Ireland* cassette were recorded at the Abbey Tavern, Howth.

CONTENTS

NOTE FOR TEACHERS

This book comprises (*a*) ten basic units, each of which presents and develops a particular aspect of Irish culture or history, with exercises and activities designed to develop the linguistic skills of post-intermediate language learners, (*b*) unit 11 which revises and assesses the linguistic and cultural content of units 1 to 10, (*c*) a section dealing with specific grammar points occurring in each of the basic units of the book, (*d*) an answer key to units 1 to 11 and the grammar exercises, and (e) an accompanying cassette that includes both authentic and specially prepared listening material for six of the units, and five songs. Listening comprehension questions and the words of the songs are provided in the book.

The suggested order of units 1 to 10 is the best one because of the historical theme, which is developed as follows:

> Unit 2: prehistory to the Celts
> Unit 4: Early Christian Ireland
> Unit 6: from the Vikings to Georgian Dublin
> Unit 10: the nineteenth century to 1916

From the point of view of language learning, however, this order is not essential, since each unit is self-contained. And indeed, apart from unit 1, which is the best introduction, teachers should feel free to approach the remaining units in whatever order best suits them and their students.

While opportunities for oral communication have been exploited to the maximum throughout the book, each unit gives practice in all four skills, the emphasis being dictated by appropriateness of approach to a particular theme. So, although there is no attempt to follow a rigid pattern, the following basic guidelines regarding the composition of each unit will be helpful.

SPEAKING

The theme of each unit is introduced by an oral activity, which relates as far as possible to the student's own knowledge and experience. Thereafter there are ample opportunities for practice in speaking English through pair or group work, class discussion and debate, and role play. Note that the instructions given are simply suggestions: the size of your class and the interest of your students will indicate to you how faithfully they should be followed. In a small, well-integrated class, for example, it may sometimes be better to bypass the pair or group work and involve everybody immediately.

LISTENING

Units 2, 4, 6, 8, 10 and 11 have listening activities, i.e. questions on the authentic and specially prepared talks, conversations, lectures etc. on the accompanying cassette. While in each case the instructions indicate that the taped material is to be played twice, in the manner of Cambridge examinations, these activities should not be considered as tests but as aids to improving listening skills. Replaying the tape with frequent pauses to focus on pitch and intonation, idiomatic language etc. can be a valuable exercise.

Units 1, 3, 5, 7 and 9 include the words of well-known Irish songs. These are also recorded on the cassette.

READING The nucleus of each unit is a substantial reading passage that presents and develops the theme. There is also a secondary, thematically related text. As much of the reading as possible should be done as out-of-class work, to give students the opportunity for individual preparation, dictionary work, etc. The pre-reading questions are designed to elicit basic information about the subject matter, and answers to these can be usefully discussed in pairs or groups or as a class. Similarly, multiple-choice questions should be answered individually and then discussed before the key is resorted to. While the more searching open-ended questions (which focus on the use of language, syntax, tone, style, and register) can be given orally, such students as prospective examination candidates will benefit from answering them in writing.

WRITING Guidance and practice is given in discursive, narrative, descriptive and practical writing in each unit. While short-term summer students often prefer to spend their time outside class on less formal methods of improving their English, others have particular reasons for wanting to develop their ability to write good English. The oral preparation and the interest of the topics themselves should prove motivating to everybody—even if the result in some cases is only a short paragraph! For this reason the number of words required is generally not stipulated, the emphasis being on interest and enjoyment rather than on producing work of a specified length.

VOCABULARY PRACTICE AND CLOZE PASSAGES Each unit concludes with a vocabulary practice exercise, which revises lexical items, idioms and phrasal verbs encountered in the unit, and a thematically related cloze passage. These are best done individually as out-of-class work, with time given for students to compare and discuss their answers in pairs or groups.

GRAMMAR The grammar section in no way attempts to be comprehensive, and the students, as well as having their own grammar reference-books, should have access to further practice materials to deal with other problems as they arise.

The aim is, through explanations, examples, and exercises, to (*a*) revise and practise particular areas of grammar that tend to continue to cause difficulty at post-intermediate level—these include certain tenses, modals and conditionals, and defining and non-defining relative clauses—and (*b*) introduce and practise new or less familiar structures that are, nevertheless, in common current usage. Included here are 'might as well' and 'it's time' + the subjunctive (as compared with 'it's time' + the infinitive).

The points focused on in each unit of the grammar section occur naturally in the related unit of the book. The reasons for keeping the section separate are to make reference and comparison easy and to facilitate self-study.

KEYS Keys to the units and grammar are included in the book so that students can use it for self-study where necessary. Most students at this level are mature enough not to misuse answer keys by taking short-cuts, but it may be worth reminding them that maximum learning value will only be achieved by their first answering the questions individually and then, where possible, comparing and discussing their answers in pairs or groups. Teachers, of course, will be better equipped to deal with difficulties in understanding if they too answer the questions before referring to the keys!

The key to the units includes (*a*) answers to all questions that require a specific answer (e.g. multiple-choice questions), (*b*) brief suggested answers to open-ended comprehension questions, and (*c*) answers to the cloze passages. Where more than one answer is possible here, the word in the original text appears first. It should be noted that while students may offer other answers that are grammatically correct, these will probably be less appropriate, for reasons of style and register.

The key to the grammar section provides either the correct answer where only one is possible or desired or suggested responses and alternatives where there is no specifically correct answer.

Finally, it should be stressed that the approach to and treatment of the themes in *Encounter Ireland* are simply suggestions on the author's part. Teachers can and should adapt them to the needs and interests of a particular class, and indeed should exploit their own knowledge, skills and resources to supplement the exercises and activities provided. There will undoubtedly be times when a short story, a newspaper article or a video can be used to advantage. Feel free to use the book in whatever way suits you and your students best.

UNIT 1

ON BEING IRISH

WHO ARE THEY?

Here are six people, either Irish born and bred or of Irish extraction, who have, for one reason or another, made an impact on the world.

A

B

C

D

E

F

1. Working in pairs or small groups, see how many you can identify and if you can say why they are famous.

2. Were you aware that all these people can, or could, lay claim to being Irish?

WHAT MAKES A PERSON IRISH?

Or, for that matter, French, German, Japanese, or Indian? In other words—

1. Apart from the obvious qualifications of place of birth and/or parentage, what entitles a person to a particular nationality?

2. With your partner or group, make a list of what you think are legitimate *definitions of nationality*.

3. Discuss your ideas with the rest of the class and try to produce a final list you all agree on.

INVENTING A SENSE OF BEING IRISH

Read the following passage (by Fintan O'Toole, from the *Irish Times*, 10 January 1991); then, with your partner or group, answer the questions.

QUESTIONS

1. What are the four different ways in which the writer defines the relationship between the individual and nationality?

2. How many of these definitions can you apply to your own country? Are any of them peculiar to Ireland?

3. How do the writer's definitions compare with the ones you made?

We don't choose our parents and, on the same principle, most of us tend to feel that we don't choose our country either. A nationality, like a mole on the left cheek or an aptitude for mathematics, is something you are born with. There is a lot of truth in this notion, but it is not the whole
5 truth, at least not in Ireland. Many people who are born on this island choose not to regard themselves as Irish. And almost all of us, at some stage in our lives, have to choose whether or not to remain Irish, in the sense of living and working in this country, of bringing up our own kids, if we have any, here. Lots of Irish people, because of emigration, choose,
10 with varying degrees of freedom, to become Americans or Australians or, more commonly, to belong to that curious floating island inhabited by many emigrants, the ex-isle of Erin. It isn't just exotic hybrid people with

far-flung ancestry who have to make up their minds whether or not to choose Irish nationality. We all have to choose it, since we all, in a sense, have far-flung ancestry, scattered around the continents.

15

When you look back on it, from the vantage of the contradictory country we now inhabit, it sometimes seems that the Ireland we have lived through was one invented by half-outsiders, by people who had to invent an Ireland in order to invent themselves. Dev was born in America of a Hispanic father and an Irish mother. Jim Larkin was a Liverpudlian, James Connolly a Glaswegian. Mícheál Mac Liammóir, who could walk on stage as a living, breathing embodiment of the country with his extraordinary accent and his beautiful Gaelic, was utterly and completely English by birth and upbringing, with no Irish connections at all. And the funny thing is that the revelation makes Mac Liammóir, on the eve of 1992, seem more, not less Irish, a purer version of the invention we all have to cope with.

20

25

NOTES

Dev (Éamon de Valera): played a key role in the struggle for Irish independence, founder and leader of Fianna Fáil, Taoiseach for over twenty years, and President of Ireland from 1959 to 1973.

James Larkin: organiser of the trade union movement at the beginning of the century.

James Connolly: one of the leaders of the Easter Rising, 1916.

Mícheál Mac Liammóir: well-known actor and writer and founder of the Gate Theatre, Dublin.

MULTIPLE-CHOICE QUESTIONS

Now read the passage again and decide which is the best answer to each of the following multiple-choice questions.

1. The writer compares a nationality to 'a mole on the left cheek' because they are both
   (a) unwanted
   (b) unavoidable
   (c) unnecessary
   (d) unsightly.

2. The 'ex-isle of Erin' he refers to (line 12) is in fact
   (a) a curious floating island
   (b) a figment of his imagination
   (c) Ireland itself
   (d) England.

3. According to the writer, Irish nationality is something
   (a) we have no control over
   (b) few people have a right to
   (c) we have to make a decision about
   (d) emigrants have to give up.

5. The discovery that Mac Liammóir was English by birth and upbringing
   (a) was only made at the end of 1991
   (b) has an ironic result
   (c) disqualifies him from Irish nationality
   (d) was difficult for the writer to come to terms with.

4. In what sense is the 'country we now inhabit' (lines 16–17) contradictory?
   (a) It conflicts with the Ireland invented by half-outsiders.
   (b) It seems to have been invented by people who were not native Irish.
   (c) There is disagreement over whether or not Dev, Larkin and Connolly were really Irish.
   (d) It is so different from 'the Ireland we have lived through'.

THE IRISH AND IRISHNESS

Work with your partner or small group to answer the following questions.

1. Look at the remarks below and decide what each of them tells you about the speaker's attitude towards his or her Irishness.

(a) I'm Irish and proud of it!

(b) Help—I have an identity problem!

(c) I don't give a damn what I am.

(d) You can reject your country but not your identity.

(e) I put my Irish background to good use.

(f) It gives me a kick to despise my Irishness.

(g) Ireland is like the man you once divorced but will never stop loving.

(h) Home is where the heart is!

2. Now read and discuss what some well-known Irish people have said on the subject. Which of the above remarks most appropriately summarises the attitude each person conveys?

7

You may find that more than one answer is possible in each case. The important thing is to be able to give reasons for your choice.

Compare your answers with the other members of the class. You might like to do this by writing the answers on the blackboard. Where there is disagreement, try to resolve it by arguing your case and listening to different points of view.

JAMES JOYCE

Possibly the greatest novelist of the twentieth century, who spent most of his life in self-imposed exile. 'I will not serve that in which I no longer believe, whether it call itself my home, my fatherland, or my church.'

Another writer had this to say on Joyce's death in 1941: 'Joyce was before all an Irishman … Ireland had entered him: it was the grit in his oyster shell.'

BOB GELDOF

'Boomtown Rats' singer, called 'a true Brit' by Margaret Thatcher and knighted for his work with Live Aid. 'I'm not at all nationalistic. It makes no difference to me whether she calls me a true Brit or a true Chinaman.' But when he heard that Ireland had contributed more to Live Aid than any other country, he admitted to 'a small trickle of racial pride.'

JOHN F. KENNEDY

Before President Kennedy visited Ireland in 1961 he became so involved in things Irish that an adviser remarked: 'He's getting so Irish, the next thing we know he'll be speaking with a brogue.'

Writing about Kennedy's reception in Dublin, his biographer, Lord Longford, says: 'Kennedy had nothing to bring the Irish people except himself, and himself as profoundly Irish, in all respects one of them. He felt it, they felt it, they felt that he felt it; he felt the rapport was total and beyond comparison or description.'

NORTHERN PROTESTANTS

The sociologist Edward Moxon-Browne says: 'When someone in Northern Ireland states his or her national identity, their statement is a subjective reflection of basic political allegiances. When outside Northern Ireland, many Protestants are prepared to accept (and are usually accorded) an Irish identity, but within Northern Ireland they will strongly assert their "Britishness".'

EDNA O'BRIEN

Contemporary (and often controversial) woman writer from Co. Clare, who has lived in London since her twenties. 'Leaving Ireland was no wrench at all. England had nothing to recommend it but I had got away. That was my victory. I thought of how Ireland had warped me, and those around me, and their parents before them, all stooped by a variety of fears.'

But, she says, 'Irish? I would not want to be anything else. It is a state of mind as well as an actual country. It is being at odds with other nationalities, having quite a different philosophy about pleasure, about punishment, about life and about death. At least it does not leave one pusillanimous.'

GEORGE BERNARD SHAW

One of the most important and prolific dramatists in English, he left Ireland at the age of twenty and rarely returned. 'Like all Irishmen, I dislike the Irish … on instinct. Every Irishman who felt that his business in life was on the higher planes of the cultural professions felt that his first business was to get out of Ireland.'

VISITORS TO IRELAND

According to the historian Brian Inglis, 'it may happen that the visitor is so delighted with what he finds in Ireland that he decides to make his home here. Traditionally it will not be long before he begins to think of himself as Irish: often he becomes more Irish than the Irish themselves.'

WRITING

Your task is to write a debate speech, the motion being,

'Feelings of national pride are counterproductive to world unity.'

The important thing to keep in mind is that what you write is going to be *spoken* in front of an audience, tomorrow or on whichever day you choose to have the debate. The language you use, while not being quite as colloquial as conversational English, should not be as formal as a discursive essay.

As far as possible, form two equal teams, one to speak for and the other against the motion. Remember, it can be much more rewarding and a lot more fun persuading people to accept a point of view you don't actually believe in than convincing them of your sincerely held convictions!

Working with your team, make a list of all the ideas you can think of that will promote your argument, then distribute them among the members of the team. If there are more ideas than students, reduce the number of the former by finding a logical connection between two or more points.

As an individual, for homework, write a debate speech of not more than 200 words. Try to make the speech as interesting and lively as possible by making maximum use of illustrative examples, anecdotes—even jokes!

And a last bit of advice: it is reasonably safe to say that, if you enjoy what you write or say, people will enjoy reading or listening to it. But if you are bored . . . , (there are no prizes for guessing how the sentence ends!)

WHAT LOOKS CAN TELL

How far is it possible to identify a person's nationality by his or her looks?

1. Test yourself by deciding where you think these six people come from. Then discuss your decisions, and your reasons for them, with the rest of the class.

A

B

C

D

E

F

Now turn to page 262 to find out what their nationalities really are. Were there any surprises? What conclusions can you draw?

2. Make a quick list of any features (skin, eyes, hair, etc.) you automatically associate with Irish people. Compare your list with the rest of the class to see what points you agree on.

. . . AND CHARACTER?

A person's physical features may tell us something, but not everything, about where he or she comes from. Can character and behaviour tell us any more? All countries have their national stereotypes, but how valid are they? To find out:

1. On a page, make a quick list of any character traits and behaviour you think are typical of your nationality—but don't state what your nationality is. Hand in your folded page to the teacher, who will then mix up all the lists and redistribute them to the class. As each student reads out his or her new list, the rest of the class should decide which nationality is being described.

How easy was it to identify the different nationalities? Where there was more than one representative of a certain nationality, did the descriptions agree? What conclusions can you draw?

2. What characteristics do you associate with the Irish? Discuss your ideas with the rest of the class.

A GOOD SALAD

Read the following passage, then, with your partner or group, answer the questions, and compare your answers with the rest of the class.

QUESTIONS

1. What is the significance of the title?

2. What answer is given to the opening question?

3. What does the passage tell you about the character of the Irish?

4. To what extent do the views you expressed earlier agree with the writer's?

What does the average Irish person look like? According to ancient mythology, Ireland was the destination of a succession of invaders who came here from all arts and parts of the known world. Among them were the Fir Bolg*, small, wiry people with Mediterranean features, colouring and temperament. Hardly surprising since, we are told, they came from Greece by way of the Iberian peninsula. After them came the Tuatha Dé Danann* (the people of the goddess Dana), who were said to have been tall and fair-skinned, with red hair and green eyes. These, and other tribes, eventually gave way to their historical counterparts: the Celts, the Vikings, the Normans and a whole hotch-potch of more recent arrivals.

Racially, therefore, Irish people are very much like a good salad, with a little bit of every European people in them. In a general way they can be said to be tall and, perhaps because of having lived for so long under cloudy skies, to have pale complexions and light-coloured eyes; in fact about half the population have blue eyes. Contrary to popular belief, however, only 4 per cent have red hair, the predominating colour being mid to dark brown. The most distinguishing genetic feature of the Irish is the high frequency of blood group O, higher than in any other European country but a feature shared by such similarly isolated people as the Scots, Icelanders, and Basques.

Over a period of years the writer and journalist Dervla Murphy conducted an experiment during visits to London. 'Studying faces in public places,' she says, 'I spot someone who looks Irish and test my hunch by asking them the way. In 95 per cent of cases they speak with a brogue. Yet there is no longer—if there ever was—an Irish physical type. My recognitions have nothing to do with features, colourings, physiques; they depend only on facial expressions (often "the look in the eye")—that is, on what shows through of the essence within.' What that essence is is hard to

f'ir' boləg

5

'tuəhə de: danən

10

15

20

25

encapsulate in words. Dervla Murphy sees the human history of a nation
like a jig-saw laid out on a tray. 'In most countries, where the tray has not
been joggled too often or too roughly, the pieces eventually adhere
permanently to one another and an integrated picture, known as a
"national identity", replaces all the bits.' In Ireland, she theorises,
because the bits never had a chance to stick together, a straightforward
national identity was never formed. What we have is much more subtle,
intangible, elusive—a national essence.

It comes back to the salad business, really. Throw into a bowl a variety of
ingredients, each one with its own distinctive shape, texture, colour, and
flavour, and you have an uninspiring motley mixture. But toss it well in a
dressing composed of liberal helpings of time, climate, geography and a
pinch of something only the gods can supply, and abracadabra, you have
something quite different, quite distinctive, quite unique. It's that
enigmatic composition Dervla Murphy calls the 'national essence' and
which, by its very nature, defies description. For every person who
describes the Irish as friendly, outgoing, confident and full of fun you will
find another person declaring they are hard to get to know, reticent,
diffident, and moody.

The truth is we Irish are such a nation of paradoxes that we can confuse
ourselves as much as other people. A classic case is J. M. Synge's drama
The Playboy of the Western World, in which a young man, Christy Mahon,
becomes the hero of the hour after supposedly killing his 'da'. When the
play was first performed in 1907, it took five hundred policemen to control
the rioting audience screaming, 'Kill the author!' Synge is now one of the
literary heroes of the century, and his *Playboy* is revived with monotonous
regularity in theatres all over the country. The ambiguity has been honed
to the point of absurdity by the ubiquitous Kerry joke. Did you hear, for
example, about the Irishman who died while on holiday in Spain? A
friend, paying his last respects to the sun-bronzed corpse, remarked,
'Man, didn't his holiday do him a power of good!' Or did you know that an
Irish homosexual is a man who prefers women to drink? 'Nobody loves
like an Irishman,' went the words of a popular song a few decades ago, yet
a well-known Dublin journalist is quoted as saying, 'An Irishman is the
only man in the world who will clamber over the bodies of a dozen naked
women in order to get to a bottle of stout.' An American going home after a
business trip to Dublin once said, 'The people I saw hadn't the slightest
intention of doing what they said they'd do—though they gave me a good
time while they were saying it.' And what other country but Ireland could
boast of being the least neurotic in the world, as a recent international
survey shows, yet with the world's highest rate of chronic psychosis? Beat
that for confusion.

13

NOTES

Kerry joke: Because of their isolation in the south-west of Ireland, people from Co. Kerry at one time had the reputation of being slow and stupid, hence the jokes making fun of them. Although Kerry people have long since proved themselves to be quite the opposite, such jokes continue to be made!

man: here an interjection expressing admiration.

MORE QUESTIONS

Now read the passage again and answer these questions as precisely as you can. You may do this orally with your partner and/or in writing as homework.

1. Pick out the words or phrases in the paragraphs indicated whose meanings are given here:

Paragraph 1

lean, strong, and agile: ....

a confused mixture: ....

Paragraph 4

of many different types: ....

a small amount: ....

Paragraph 3

notice: ....

an instinctive idea: ....

Irish accent: ....

shaken: ....

Paragraph 5

sharpened: ....

going to see a person who has died to show one's regard for him: ....

had a beneficial effect: ....

climb awkwardly: ....

proudly claim to be: ....

2. Of the many mythological inhabitants of Ireland, why do you think the writer particularly chose to describe the Fir Bolg and the Tuatha Dé Danann?

3. Whom does 'their' refer to in line 9, and in what sense are the people mentioned their 'historical counterparts'?

4. What is suggested by the fact that Ireland and certain other countries have a high frequency of blood group O? Does this appear to be contradictory, and if so, can you offer a possible explanation?

5. What is the analogy between Dervla Murphy's 'jig-saw' and the writer's 'good salad'?

6. What 'defies description' (line 44), and how is this illustrated?

7. What is Synge's play a 'classic case' of, and why?

8. Which sentence do the examples given in the last paragraph illustrate? How successful do you think each example is?

IDENTIFY THESE!

Do you know who any of these Irish people are?

A   B   C

D   E

F

G

H

I

1. Working with a partner or small group, see if you can identify any of these people from their photographs.

2. Do you need help? Here are short descriptions of each person. You should be able to recognise some of them!

(i)   Lawyer and senator; elected President of Ireland in 1990.

(ii)   Founder-member of Amnesty International, and Nobel Peace Prize winner.

(iii) Worked for the cause of Irish independence, inspired a famous poet, and was a parent of number 1.

(iv) Writer and Dublin character, notorious for his drinking and wit.

(v)   Co-founder of the National Theatre and a supporter of the Irish literary revival.

(vi)   Northern politician and cleric; a big person with a big voice, renowned for making big trouble!

(vii) A superb actor—on and off stage!

(viii) Singer and member of a famous rock band.

(ix)   Leading twentieth-century Irish statesman; name isn't Irish, though.

3. By now you may have been able to identify some of the people from their descriptions, and you may even have been able to put some of the names to the correct photographs. There will, no doubt, be some photographs and descriptions still unidentified. Your homework is to find out who these people are and, if possible, more information about them.

A: ....   B: ....

C: ....   D: ....

E: ....   F: ....

G: ....   H: ....

I: ....

VOCABULARY PRACTICE

Choose the word or phrase that best completes the sentence.

This exercise is designed to remind you of and to revise words and phrases you have come across in unit 1. Be warned, however, that the correct word or phrase is not always the one you have already met!

1. My cousins were born in Ireland but the family emigrated when they were very young so they were .... up in England.

(*a*) grown   (*b*) brought   (*c*) reared   (*d*) educated

2. When it comes to politics, he and his father are always at .... with each other; they never stop arguing.

(*a*) differences   (*b*) conflict   (*c*) disagreement   (*d*) odds

17

3. He got a bit of .... in his eye and had to take out his contact lens to dislodge it.

      (*a*) grit   (*b*) gravel   (*c*) grain   (*d*) dust

4. When she finished school she .... off for America with the intention of getting a summer job before starting university.

      (*a*) made   (*b*) went   (*c*) set   (*d*) flew

5. She spent such a lovely afternoon .... her neighbours' dog while they were at a wedding that she decided to get a dog of her own.

   (*a*) coping with   (*b*) looking after   (*c*) seeing to   (*d*) dealing with

6. A mule is a .... between a male donkey and a female horse.

      (*a*) combination   (*b*) mixture   (*c*) hybrid   (*d*) cross

7. Looking .... now, I realise I had a very happy upbringing.

      (*a*) back on it   (*b*) back at it   (*c*) backward   (*d*) backwards

8. After Live Aid, Bob Geldof's fame spread to the most .... corners of the globe.

      (*a*) far-fetched   (*b*) far-reaching   (*c*) far-gone   (*d*) far-flung

9. Because of their light skin colouring, a lot of Irish people have .... in the summer.

      (*a*) spots   (*b*) moles   (*c*) blemishes   (*d*) freckles

10. My family are .... all over the world: I have two brothers in Canada, one sister in Australia, and another in South America.

      (*a*) scattered   (*b*) spread   (*c*) distributed   (*d*) flung

11. There's nothing I'd like more than a long holiday in the sun right now, but we're so busy in the office I simply can't get ....

      (*a*) away   (*b*) off   (*c*) out   (*d*) free

12. Don't leave that record on top of the radiator or it'll get ....

    (*a*) curved   (*b*) twisted   (*c*) distorted   (*d*) warped

13. On her first day back at work after maternity leave she found it a terrible .... leaving her little son with a baby-minder.

    (*a*) parting   (*b*) sorrow   (*c*) wrench   (*d*) difficulty

14. No, that perfume's rather too strong for my liking; I want something a little more ....

    (*a*) subtle   (*b*) odourless   (*c*) indefinable   (*d*) refined

15. The .... crowd broke through the police barriers and started throwing petrol bombs at the embassy.

    (*a*) rioting   (*b*) revolting   (*c*) misbehaving   (*d*) disorderly

CLOZE

The following passage summarises the views on nationality expressed earlier in the unit. Fill each of the twenty numbered spaces with one suitable word.

It is generally accepted .... [1] a person's nationality depends .... [2] the country in which he or she was born and, more often .... [3] not, bred. When it comes to the question of .... [4] makes a person Irish, however, this definition is altogether too limiting. There are, after .... [5], far more people living .... [6] Ireland, most of .... [7] have never set foot on Irish soil, who can .... [8] claim to being Irish than there are Irish citizens. An obvious .... [9] of this is the number of American presidents in this century alone who have considered .... [10] an honour to be called Irish. Moreover, some people, ... [11] Mícheál Mac Liammóir, who hadn't a drop of Irish .... [12] in his veins, willingly adopt Irish nationality and, in many respects, become more Irish than the Irish .... [13]. On the .... [14] hand there are those .... [15] ancestors have lived here .... [16] hundreds of years but who will vehemently .... [17] their Irishness for political reasons. Finally, many young people today, ... [18] they are forced to emigrate in .... [19] to make a .... [20], consciously decide to abandon the nationality they were born with.

Here are the words of Dublin's best-known and best-loved street ballad. When precisely Molly Malone lived is hard to say, but she was obviously at one time a faimiliar character in the streets of Dublin. And, as the song says, she can still be seen selling fish from her barrow. Do you know where you can find her?

Listen to the song on the cassette and then sing along with it.

MOLLY MALONE

In Dublin's fair city, where the girls are so pretty,
I first set my eyes on swcct Molly Malone,
As she wheeled her wheelbarrow through streets broad and narrow
Crying, 'Cockles and mussels, alive, alive O!'

Chorus
Alive alive O, alive alive O!
Crying, 'Cockles and mussels, alive alive O!'

2.
She was a fishmonger, but sure 'twas no wonder,
For so were her father and mother before.
And they each wheeled their barrow through streets broad and narrow
Crying, 'Cockles and mussels, alive alive O!'

Chorus

3.
She died of a fever, and no one could save her,
And that was the end of sweet Molly Malone;
Now her ghost wheels her barrow through streets broad and narrow
Crying, 'Cockles and mussels, alive alive O!'

UNIT 2

BEGINNING AT THE BEGINNING

What do you know about the beginnings of civilisation in your own country? Discuss these questions with a partner or small group, and then compare your answers with the rest of the class. Don't worry if you can't answer all the questions! The important thing is to compare whatever information you have.

1. Who were the first people to inhabit your country? Where did they come from?

2. Have they left any traces of their culture behind them (monuments, tools, weapons, ornaments)? What do these tell you about their way of life?

3. Can you say anything about the earliest known language (or languages) spoken in your country?

THE MELTING-POT

Read the following passage; then, with your partner, answer the questions.

QUESTIONS

1. What categories are the pre-Celtic people who inhabited Ireland divided into, and what is known about each of them?

2. Why is it difficult to say exactly when Ireland became Celticised?

3. What difference is implied between the Roman and the Celtic ways of life?

4. What happened to the Celtic languages before, during and after the Roman occupation of Britain?

Ireland is a melting-pot, an island invaded and settled by many different people with different cultures who all, to a greater or lesser extent, left their mark on the country. To have a reasonable understanding of the

Irish today it is essential to know what went into the melting-pot and what
influenced the mixing of the ingredients.

If we make the journey through time, we find that the first settlers arrived
here via Scotland about nine thousand years ago. Although archeologists are
regularly making new discoveries, little is known about these Mesolithic (or
Middle Stone Age) people, except that they were hunters and food-gatherers
and that the Irish owe their high frequency of blood group O to them.

They were followed by waves of Neolithic colonists, farmers of
Mediterranean stock, who used flint tools to clear the forests and cultivate
the soil. Their greatest legacy is the Megalithic monuments they constructed,
many of which have survived till today in various parts of the country. The
tombs they built, which served not only as burial sites but also as shrines to
ensure the continuity of nature and the maintenance of fertility, can be
classified into three main types: the simple 'court cairn' (probably the work
of immigrants from the Loire Estuary in France); the more impressive 'portal
dolmen' (huge standing-stones topped by a cap-stone); and the highly
sophisticated 'passage grave', a complex construction of which Newgrange in
the Boyne valley is the most impressive example.

Round about 2000 BC the Bronze Age was heralded by the arrival of the
Beaker Folk, so called because of the distinctive beaker-like pots they
made. Trade with other countries evidently flourished at this time; apart
from the need to import the tin essential to bronze-making, gold, copper
and bronze artefacts made by Irish metal-workers have been found as far
away as Denmark, France, and the eastern Mediterranean.

Dolmen, Co. Donegal

The Celts, who were the first civilisation in Europe to appear north of the Alps, probably started arriving in Ireland as early as the sixth century

30 BC. When precisely Ireland became Celticised, however, is difficult to say, because of the lack of written records. While classical writers have described the Celtic civilisation on the European continent in great detail, and the Romans recorded what they saw when they invaded Britain in AD 55, we cannot assume that such descriptions are applicable

35 to contemporary Ireland. From an archeological point of view it can be said that the country took on a distinctively Celtic character in the last centuries BC. This was marked by a decorative style known as La Tène, named after the site on Lake Neuchâtel in Switzerland, where a Celtic settlement was excavated in the nineteenth century.

40 The Romans, of course, never got round to conquering Hibernia; so while they were imposing their centralised administrative and legal system on Britain, Ireland was establishing for itself a Celtic, or Gaelic, identity that has remained through the centuries as its essential 'Irishness'. The basic unit of society was the extended family, and the unit of exchange was the

45 cow. The country was divided into 150 or so *tuatha* or little kingdoms, each with its own king, while there were five provinces (four of which still survive) with overkings, and a 'high king', whose seat was at Tara. Succession to the kingship was determined not by primogeniture but by election, which, while it endeavoured to ensure that the best man got the job, was often the cause of

50 serious faction-fighting. Despite this, the country was united by a common culture and language. Features of the former worth mentioning are the druidic religion, the elaborate code of legislation interpreted by professional lawyers known as 'brehons', and the great respect for learning demonstrated by the high position in society of the *file* or poet.

55 With regard to language, by the time the Romans conquered Britain the Celts were already divided linguistically into what are now called the P (British) Celts and the Q (Irish) Celts. How this division developed is not certain, but with the British Celts being pushed further west into Wales, the effect of the Roman occupation was to make the distinction

60 essentially one between Irish and Welsh. When the Romans pulled out of Britain five hundred years later and the country was eventually taken over by Germanic tribes (the Angles, Saxons, and Jutes), the Celts who were not assimilated by the new culture fled again to the extremities of Britain—Wales, Cornwall, and Scotland—and also to Brittany in northern

65 France. Of the Celtic languages surviving today—Irish, Gaelic, Welsh, and Breton—Irish is the only one with an independent state to support it.

MORE QUESTIONS

Now read the passage again and answer these questions as precisely as you can. You may do this orally with a partner, and/or in writing as homework.

1. Explain what is meant by 'ingredients' in line 5.

2. What is the essential difference between the Mesolithic and Neolithic people?

3. If 'Mesolithic' refers to the Middle Stone Age, what do you think 'Neolithic' refers to?

4. Why did the Neolithic people build tombs?

5. How can it be proved that there was contact between Ireland and continental Europe during the Bronze Age?

6. What is the connection between 'classical writers' (line 31) and 'the Romans' (line 33)?

7. What does 'this' refer to in line 50?

8. What are the features mentioned in lines 51–54 examples of?

9. What effect on the native population of Britain is shared by the Romans and the Germanic tribes?

10. What distinction is made between Irish and other surviving Celtic languages?

LISTENING

You are going to hear Clare Tuffy, an expert on prehistoric monuments, giving a guided tour of Newgrange, the ancient burial site in Co. Meath, about fifty kilometres from Dublin.
Look at the diagrams and questions in your book and be prepared to answer them. Then listen to the piece twice.

1. Which of the following is the correct plan of Newgrange?

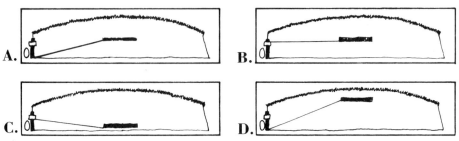

A.   B.

C.   D.

2. Which of these illustrations is the correct front view of Newgrange?

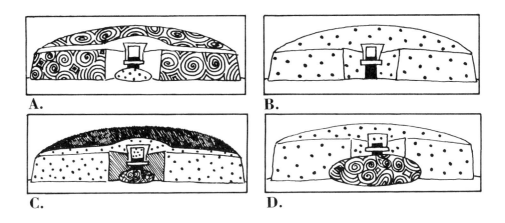

A.

B.

C.

D.

3. Which of these the correct cross-section of Newgrange?

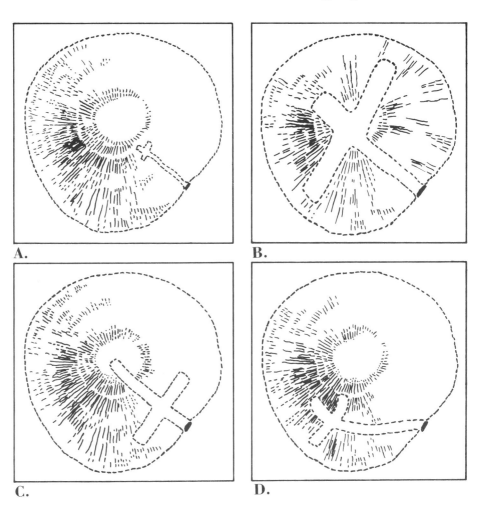

A.

B.

C.

D.

4. How many of the following patterns were used to decorate the stones of Newgrange?

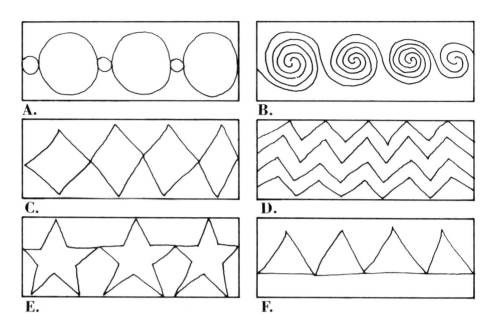

A.

B.

C.

D.

E.

F.

5. Say whether the following statements are true or false.

    a.   Newgrange is about 3,000 years old.

    b.   Since the restoration of the outside in the 1960s, Newgrange looks exactly the way it did in the stone age.

    c.   The roof-box was a way of marking the new year on the stone age calendar.

    d.   The chamber is completely dry because the roof was built without cement.

    e.   The basin stones in the three recesses held the ashes and the jewellery of the dead people.

    f.   Stone Age people evidently thought the world of the spirits was a happy, carefree place.

WRITING

Some extracts from the diary of a Stone Age man or woman.

1. Using the information you have gained about prehistoric Ireland, and of course your imagination, jot down some ideas about what life must have been like at that time. Think about

    —the pattern of daily life;

    —important occasions;

    —the significance of the seasons.

Keep in mind that a diary, in the sense in which the word is used here, does not just record events but also expresses the thoughts and feelings of the diarist.

2. Share your ideas with the rest of the class. This will help you to see whether yours are valid, as well as giving you the opportunity to hear what other people think.

3. For homework, choose any two or three days of your life as a Stone Age man or woman to write about. They can be consecutive or spread over a period of years. The length of each entry will naturally depend on what happened that day, but you should limit yourself to about 300 words altogether.

THE CELTIC WORLD

The map of present-day Europe on page 28 shows how great the extent of the Celtic world was at one time. Work with a partner or group to answer the following questions, then compare your answers with the rest of the class.

1. Which European countries were once partially or totally occupied by the Celts?

2. In which countries are Celtic languages still spoken?

THE CELTIC
WORLD

Area occupied
by Celts

Celtic
speaking
areas today

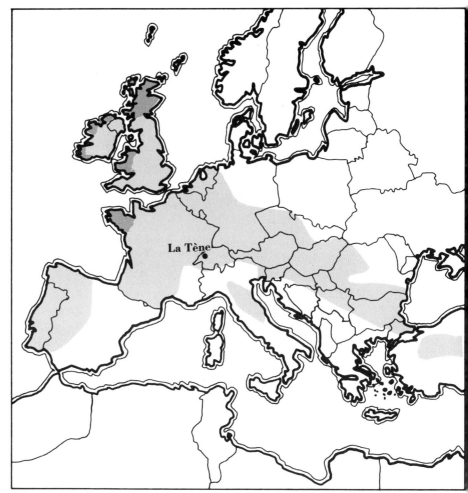

La Tène

WHAT'S IN A LANGUAGE?   *The Celtic World*

There are two official languages in Ireland. Everybody can speak English,
but, although all children learn Irish at school, very few people use it in
their daily lives. Only in the Gaeltacht areas (see map) is it used as the
everyday vernacular, by about 40,000 people.

Fir   Mná   Sláinte   An lár   Oifig an phoist

These are Irish words you are sure to be confronted with! What do they
mean? Which one of them are you more likely to hear than see?

There are several organisations that endeavour to promote Irish. There is
a radio station (Raidió na Gaeltachta) that broadcasts only in Irish, and a
small percentage of television is in Irish. Anybody working in the public
sector must have a qualification in Irish. But, despite the efforts made to
revive it and the fact that you can see and hear it all around you, Irish is a
dying language.

1. What is the situation in your own country? Is there more than one language?

2. Are all the languages used given official recognition? Are they taught in schools, are they needed for jobs, are they used on radio and television?

3. Do you think the time, effort and money spent on trying to preserve minority languages is worth while?

THE IRISH AND IRISH

What do Irish people think of the Irish language? To what extent do they use it? Do they care if it eventually dies out?

Conduct a survey to find out. You can decide to do this as a class, or divide into smaller groups and then compare your findings. Each student should ask three Irish people questions about the Irish language, and report back to the class or group. You should then discuss and collate the information and write a short report.

1. First of all you need to decide who you're going to talk to. The simplest method will probably be to categorise people according to their age (schoolboy or girl, 20 to 40-year-old, and somebody older), but you might also take into consideration the person's occupation, where he or she was brought up (country, city, etc.), and anything else that might be relevant.

2. The next step is to make out a questionnaire. Here are some suggested questions. You may like to change them and/or add questions of your own.

(*a*)	How good is your Irish?
	—non-existent　　　—fair
	—poor　　　　　　—good
	—fluent
(*b*)	Did you (or do you) enjoy learning Irish at school?
	If not, why not?
(*c*)	How often do you speak or write it?
	—never
	—seldom
	—sometimes
	—frequently
	—as a first language
(*d*)	Should there be a separate television channel for Irish?
(*e*)	Would you like to see more being done to promote Irish? If so, what?

3. When you are collating your information, look out for total agreement, majority attitudes, marked differences between different categories of people (e.g. the young and the old). Were there any interesting or surprising comments made by the people you talked to?

4. Now summarise your conclusions by writing a report (about 200 words) for your local newspaper, beginning, 'According to a recent survey on attitudes of Irish people to the Irish language …'

LAWS IN ANCIENT IRELAND

This passage tells you something about the elaborate code of legislation known as the brehon laws. Read and answer the multiple-choice questions that follow. Then check and discuss your answers with a partner before comparing them with the rest of the class.

The legal system of ancient Ireland was something totally different from what we know today. The laws, which were passed on orally from at least the first century BC and were eventually written down in the seventh century, grew from the customs of the early Gaelic tribes, and were
5   interpreted by professional lawyers known as *brehons*. The elaborate code of legislation was based on the government unit (the *tuath* or kingdom), which was small enough to ensure that respect was maintained for the old customs. When a case arose, the brehons decided what the right course of action should be, but responsibility for the enforcing of their decision was
10   left to the family of the aggrieved person. There were no prisons and, even for the crime of murder, there was no capital punishment. Instead, each person had a fixed honour-price directly related to his social status and, if a crime was committed against him, the penalty was calculated in accordance with its seriousness and his rank and worth in society. Since
15   not to pay the penalty decided on by the brehons and demanded by the plaintiff's family would mean being deprived of honour and normal society (an ancient form of boycott, in effect), the defendant generally complied with the judicial decision.

It is worth noting the 'liberated' attitudes to women and their high status
20   in Celtic Ireland, especially when compared with their position under the Romans. They were educated, had equal rights with men, and could divorce their husbands for a large number of reasons, ranging from rape to not being given what they wanted to eat! An interesting custom, which vividly demonstrates the Indo-European origin of the Celts, and which is
25   practised in Ireland even today, is that of fasting. If a person was in debt to another, the latter had the right to sit outside the debtor's house daily and fast in order to embarrass him into paying up.

Although there was much conflict when the Normans arrived hundreds of years later and tried to impose their own, totally different, legislative code on the Irish, the brehon laws survived almost unchanged right up to the seventeenth century, when the last areas where they were still observed finally fell into the hands of the English.

30

MULTIPLE-CHOICE QUESTIONS

1. It was the job of the brehons to
   (a) make sure penalties were paid
   (b) pronounce judgments
   (c) boycott those who refused to obey the law
   (d) fix each person's honour-price.

2. Decisions about the penalties to be paid were influenced by
   (a) the defendant's rank in society
   (b) what the plaintiff's family demanded
   (c) what the accused person had done
   (d) whether the plaintiff had any social status.

3. The word 'liberated' (line 19) is enclosed in quotation marks
   (a) for emphasis
   (b) because its use is not strictly accurate here
   (c) because, compared with later ages, women at that time were really oppressed
   (d) to show the difference between the status of women in Ireland and their Roman counterparts.

4. It can be inferred that
   (a) people in Ireland still fast outside debtors' houses to get them to pay up
   (b) the Celts have an Indo-European origin
   (c) fasting was an interesting custom
   (d) fasting is a method used in modern Ireland to demand one's rights.

5. The brehon laws continued to be used
   (a) even after another legal system was introduced
   (b) despite the fact that they were written down in Irish
   (c) because they were passed on orally for so long
   (d) throughout the country for about 1,700 years.

THE BREHON LAWS

Now here is a sample of the brehon laws for you to look at and comment on. Read them, and then discuss your answers to these questions with a partner or group.

QUESTIONS

1. What aspects of society do these laws cover? One example is women's rights; what other categories can you see?

2. What picture do they give you of the society they catered for? For example, they reveal the hierarchical system and the respect for rank.

1. Husband and wife retain individual rights to all the land, flocks and household goods each brings to the marriage.

2. Children shall be sent at an early age to distant members of the tribe to be reared in the hereditary professions of law, medicine, poetic composition, or war, or of tilling the soil and wifeliness. Foster-children shall be returned to their parents at the marriage age: fourteen for girls and seventeen for boys.

3. It is illegal to give someone food in which has been found a dead mouse.

4. The chief poet of the tribe shall sit next to the king at a banquet. Each shall be served the choicest cut of meat.

5. If a woman makes an assignation with a man to come to her in a bed or behind a bush, the man is not considered guilty even if she screams. If she has not agreed to a meeting, however, he is guilty as soon as she screams.

6. If the doctor heals your wound but it breaks out anew because of his carelessness, neglect, or gross want of skill, he must return the fee you paid. He must also pay you damages as if he himself had wounded you.

7. The blacksmith must rouse all sleeping customers before he puts the iron in the fire. This is to guard against injuries by sparks. Those who fall asleep again will receive no compensation for injuries.

8. If a pregnant woman craves a morsel of food and her husband withholds it through stinginess or neglect, he must pay a fine.

9. When you become old, your family must provide you with one oat-cake a day, together with a container of sour milk. They must bathe you every twentieth night and wash your head every Saturday.

10. The first of February is the day on which husband or wife may decide to walk away from the marriage.

11. No fools, drunks or female scolds are allowed in the doctor's house where a patient is healing there. No bad news is to be brought, and there must be no talking across the bed. There must be no grunting of pigs or barking of dogs outside.

12. Whoever comes to your door, you must feed him, with no questions asked.

13. The poet who overcharges for a poem shall be stripped of half his rank in society.

3. How many of these laws can be translated easily into modern terminology, and how many of them are totally obsolete? Are any of them worth reviving? Find out by taking it in turns to be a brehon who miraculously finds himself transported into the modern world and wants to have his laws reintroduced. He has to put his case to the legislature of today—the other student (or students)—who should ask him questions, argue with him, and make a decision.

Take law 9, for example.

Brehon: This is a very important way of ensuring that people are properly cared for when they're old.

Legislature: But we don't need a law like that today. Old people get state pensions. They don't have to depend on their families.

Brehon: And what if they can't look after themselves?

Legislature: Oh, well, in that case the state will provide any help that's needed. And in really bad cases there are hospitals and old people's homes …

Brehon: But why can't their families take care of them? It must be very lonely for old people to be taken away from their homes and familiar surroundings …

How would you continue the debate?

THE HOUND OF ULSTER

ta:n' bo: kuəl'n'ə

ku: xol'ən'

Although there are no written records of life in Celtic Ireland, there is a rich body of myths and legends that survived by oral tradition until they were eventually written down by the scribes of the Early Christian era. One of the best known is the epic 'Táin Bó Chuailne'* ('The Cattle Raid of Cooley'), which tells the story of a protracted war between Connacht and Ulster and features Ireland's greatest legendary hero, Cú Chulainn*.

In this extract from the 'Táin' you learn the legendary explanation of how he came to be called Cú Chulainn. Read it and discuss what heroic qualities the young boy displays. (This version of the story is taken from *Celtic Society: the Celtic Way of Life and the Ulster Cycle*, published by O'Brien Press, 1976. If you would like to read about the further exploits of Cú Chulainn you will find them in that book or in *The Táin: the Great Celtic Epic* by Liam Mac Uistín, also published by O'Brien Press.)

Note: 'Cú' is the Irish for 'hound' (hunting dog), but in personal names probably meant 'warrior'. Hurling is a game, still very popular in Ireland, played with a stick (hurley) and a ball.

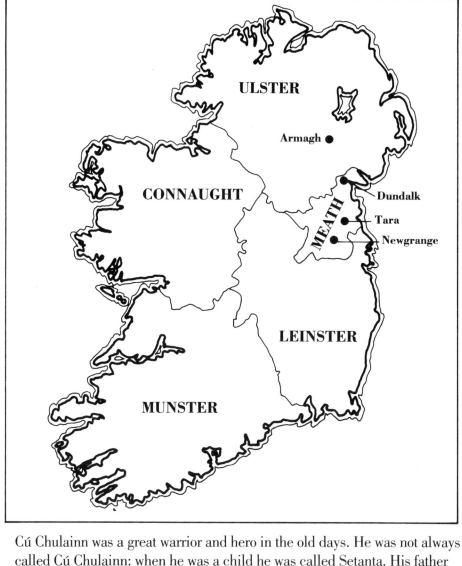

Cú Chulainn was a great warrior and hero in the old days. He was not always called Cú Chulainn: when he was a child he was called Setanta. His father was chieftain of Muirtheann*, an area stretching from Dundalk in Co. Louth, southwards into Co. Meath. When he was seven years old he was sent away to be trained as a warrior (like many other young boys of his age). Even then he was unusual. When Setanta was young there was a very famous sword-maker in Ulster called Culann the Smith. Culann earned his living by making swords. He did not own land or property, and he was not as rich as the princes and chieftains. One day Culann decided to have a feast. He invited King Conor, who was Setanta's foster-father, and some of his followers as well. He didn't want too many people, as he wasn't a rich man, so he asked Conor not to bring many followers with him. Conor decided to bring only fifty chariots full of the highest and mightiest of his champions. This was considered a small number in those days.

On the way to Culann's feast, Conor visited the Boys' House where Setanta was at school. He saw Setanta in the playing-fields playing ball against 150 boys and winning all the games. They were playing a game called Shoot-the-Goal. Setanta was able to get his ball into the goal even though there were 150 boys against him. When it was the other boys' turn to shoot at the goal, Setanta defended the goal so well that not one ball got in. When they had finished playing this game it was time to wrestle. Setanta was better than all the others at wrestling, and he overthrew all 150 of them. But they could not throw Setanta even when they all tried together. King Conor was amazed when he saw all this. He realised that Setanta was a very strong boy, and he decided to bring him to the feast in Culann's house. He called Setanta out of the crowd in the playing-field and said to him, 'Will you come with me to the feast?' But Setanta didn't want to be disturbed from his games. 'I haven't finished playing yet,' he said. 'I'll follow you when I'm ready.'

Conor went ahead to Culann's house with his fifty chariots full of warriors. When they had all arrived, Culann said to Conor, 'Is everybody here?' 'Yes,' said Conor, forgetting that Setanta had said he would follow. 'In that case,' said Culann, 'I will lock the gates and let my guard dog free to protect the house and my belongings. He's a very savage dog—it takes three chains to hold him, with three men on each chain.'

Soon afterwards Setanta arrived at Culann's house. He had run all the way from the Boys' House, playing with his hurley and ball. He was tossing his ball and throwing his hurley after it and hitting it. Then he would throw his javelin after both the ball and the hurley and catch it before it fell. When he arrived at Culann's house, the dog raced towards him, but Setanta continued playing. From a safe distance in the house, Conor and his followers were watching. They realised that Setanta was in great danger. They were sure that the dog would kill him, but they were too far away to do anything to help. However, as the dog jumped to attack him, Setanta threw down the hurley, the ball and the javelin and tackled it with his two hands. He put one hand around the dog's throat and the other on his back. He lifted the dog and threw it against the nearest pillar with such strength that it was killed instantly.

When King Conor and his followers saw this, they cheered and ran out and carried him shoulder-high. They were delighted that Setanta, who was the son of the king's sister, had escaped. But Culann was not so happy. Although he was glad that Setanta had not been killed, he was very sad that his great guard dog was dead. 'My life is empty and my household defenceless now that I have lost my dog. He protected and sheltered our belongings and animals—we are lost without him,' he said.

'I will be your hound,' said Setanta. 'Until I have reared you a new pup from the same pack, I will protect you and your possessions. I will be your dog.'

'Then we will call you Cú Chulainn, the Hound of Culann,' said Fergus McRoy, one of the king's followers. And they carried the boy into the house shouting his new name after him. 'Cú Chulainn! Cú Chulainn!' And from that day on, everybody called him Cú Chulainn.

PHRASAL AND PREPOSITIONAL VERBS

These are all verbs you have met in this unit. Choose one of them to complete each of the following sentences. (One is used twice.)

pull	name
strip	bring
embarrass	comply
cater	impose
take (2)	

1. RTE [the national radio and television service] tries to .... for a wide variety of tastes by putting on everything from serious documentaries to American 'soap operas'.

2. The night club soon .... on a different atmosphere after it was completely revamped by the new owner.

3. She was .... after St Brigid because she was born on 1 February, which is that saint's day.

4. He .... her into paying for the drinks by pretending he couldn't find his wallet.

5. If you are not prepared to .... with the rules of the club I shall have no choice but to ask you to leave.

6. When it was discovered that he had been involved in the scandal, the officer was .... of his rank.

7. I hope I'm not .... on you by staying the night, but I just couldn't face driving home in that snow.

8. Unless you can guarantee that there will be no political interference, we will .... out of the competition.

9. When the present government .... over after the last general election, they immediately introduced a new budget.

10. He was .... up by a guardian, because his parents were killed in a plane crash when he was only three.

VOCABULARY PRACTICE

In each case choose the word that best completes the sentence, but keep in mind that the word you have come across earlier in this unit is not necessarily the right answer!

1. That customs regulation is only .... people who come from EC countries.

  (*a*) relevant to   (*b*) applicable to   (*c*) appropriate to   (*d*) suitable for

2. When he sold his ancestral home to be turned into a luxury hotel, he .... the right to use the estate for exercising his horses.

  (*a*) retained   (*b*) regained   (*c*) maintained   (*d*) held up

3. It's about time you .... your own living and stopped relying on your parents for financial support!

  (*a*) made   (*b*) did   (*c*) gained   (*d*) earned

4. You can be fined up to £500 or put in prison if you're caught not paying your bus ....

  (*a*) ticket   (*b*) fee   (*c*) bill   (*d*) fare

5. Just go off and enjoy your holiday! You know you can depend on me to cope with any problems that might .... while you're away.

(*a*) arise   (*b*) rise   (*c*) raise   (*d*) rouse

6. The .... is alleged to have stolen the car because he wanted to impress his girl-friend. The case continues tomorrow.

(*a*) criminal   (*b*) guilty   (*c*) plaintiff   (*d*) defendant

7. Of course, the cut won't .... if you insist on keeping it covered up with a plaster all the time!

(a) heal   (b) cure   (c) get well   (d) get over

8. Right, let's .... a coin to see who's going to do the washing up.

(*a*) spin   (*b*) toss   (*c*) throw   (*d*) hurl

9. Ah, there you are .... ! Where on earth have you been? I've been waiting for you for hours!

(*a*) at least   (*b*) at last   (*c*) eventually   (*d*) finally

10 .... a large part of Europe was at one time occupied by the Celts, Celtic languages are spoken by only a very small minority today.

(*a*) Despite   (*b*) Notwithstanding   (*c*) Although   (*d*) Even

11. I agree with you up to a(n) ...., but I have to say I find some of your views a bit irrational.

(*a*) extent   (*b*) degree   (*c*) point   (*d*) limit

12. The province of Ulster .... from Malin Head in Co. Donegal to Co. Cavan in the south.

(*a*) extents   (*b*) spreads   (*c*) covers   (*d*) stretches

13. I had a great time in Connemara, except for the first night, when I was kept awake for hours by a donkey .... in the field outside our cottage!

(*a*) barking   (*b*) grunting   (*c*) bleating   (*d*) braying

14. Oh, her husband is notorious for his .... He even makes a mark on the whiskey bottle to show how much is left before he puts it back in the drinks cupboard!

   (*a*) economy   (*b*) thrift   (*c*) stinginess   (*d*) greed

15. Although the .... was only finally abolished in Ireland in 1990, it had not been enforced for over thirty years.

      (*a*) death penalty   (*b*) death punishment
      (*c*) capital punishment   (*d*) capital penalty

CLOZE

The following passage is a brief outline of the story of Cú Chulainn as told in the 'Táin Bó Chuailne'. Choose one suitable word to put into each of the twenty spaces.

The Táin goes on to tell .... [1], ... [2] the age of sixteen, Cú Chulainn went to another feast, this time at Tara, the home of the high king of Ireland. There he met a beautiful girl .... [3] Emer and immediately .... [4] in love with her. Some time .... [5], Cú Chulainn drove to her house in his chariot and asked her to marry him but, ... [6] she didn't .... [7] him outright, she said that he .... [8] have to prove that he was a great warrior first. Cú Chulainn, determined to .... [9] Emer his wife, ... [10] off for the land of Shadows (an island .... [11] the coast of Scotland, thought to be the Isle of Skye) .... [12] Scatha, a mighty woman warrior and a very good teacher, lived. There he not .... [13] learnt the arts of war .... [14] also made friends with Ferdia, son of the king of Connacht and another pupil of Scatha's. Before Cú Chulainn left the Land of Shadows, Ferdia and he swore to be blood brothers and to be faithful to each .... [15] as long as they lived. .... [16] of the dreadful conflict between Queen Maeve of Connacht and King Conor of Ulster, however, the two friends later found .... [17] in single combat against each other. Filled with grief after slaying Ferdia, Cú Chulainn himself eventually died in single-handed defence of Ulster .... [18] the armies of Connacht. In true heroic style, he tied .... [19] to a large upright stone .... [20] that he could die honourably, on his feet.

Unit 3

GUINNESS AND GAS

1. Spend a few minutes answering this questionnaire. You are being asked to make generalisations about the habits of people in your own country. This is not always easy, as habits can vary from one region to another, and they may depend on age, the time of year, and other factors, so make notes of any comments which you feel are relevant.

2. Compare your answers with the rest of the class. To do this, appoint one student to record everybody's answers on the blackboard by writing the nationalities represented across the top and the numbers 1 to 10 down the side. You will then be able to see clearly what similarities and differences there are.

3. Discuss any of the answers you find interesting, unexpected, puzzling, etc. Can reasons be given for them? What do they reveal about the nationalities concerned?

4. What general conclusions can you draw about the way people in different countries spend their free time and about their drinking habits?

(a) How do people spend their free time (i) in the evenings after work, (ii) at the weekend?

(b) Where do people usually meet their friends?

(c) And where do they go if they actually want to make friends?

(d) How and where are special occasions (birthdays, anniversaries, etc.) usually celebrated?

(e) Is there a bar or café in the area where you live that is frequented by the locals? If the answer is yes, (i) how do customers spend their time there, (ii) when is it busiest, and (iii) has it got set opening and closing times?

(f) What do people normally drink at meal times?

(g) What is the most popular alcoholic drink in your country?

(h) Is alcoholism a problem in your country?

(i) How strict are the authorities about drinking and driving?

(j) Is there a tendency for young people to drink too much?

DRINK TALK

1. Here are some colloquial words and expressions used in connection with drinking. Check their meaning, and use them to fill in the numbered spaces in the dialogue below. (One of them is used twice, as indicated.)

under the influence
a hair of the dog
to drink (somebody) under the table
to twist (somebody's) arm
to knock back
to have hollow legs

hangover
plonk
jar (2)
short
plastered
barred

—Oh lord, I have the mother and father of a .... [1] this morning. Brian asked me to go for a .... [2] after work yesterday to celebrate his promotion, you know.

—Good old Brian! So what happened?

—We had a few pints in the pub next to the office, and then about nine o'clock we were starving so we tried that new seafood restaurant up the street.

—And what was it like?

—Oh, the food was great, but the wine wasn't as good as the .... [3] I get for cooking, only it was three times more expensive.

—So you didn't drink it …?

—Well, we just had a bottle each. And then Brian insisted on stopping at his local on the way home. By this stage I really didn't want any more, but you know Brian, he kept .... [4].

—Yeah, and I know you! How much did you have?

—Oh, just a couple of pints each. And Brian had a couple of .... [5] as well.

—Typical! I don't know anybody who can .... [6] whiskey the way he can! He seems to have .... [7]!

41

—I know; it doesn't seem to have any effect on him! Remember all the nights he's .... [8]. We're hardly able to stand up, but he's as sober as a judge!

—Yeah. Do you remember the night we got so .... [9] in the Cock Tavern they wouldn't serve us?

—Last Christmas, right? We behaved so badly we nearly got .... [10]! And Brian drove us home. I don't know how he did it!

—One of these days he's going to get caught for driving .... [11].

—It's a wonder he hasn't been caught before now! Ouch, my head! You haven't got any aspirins, have you?

—Listen, what you need is .... [12]. Come on, it's after opening time. Let's nip across to the pub and have a quiet .... [13]. It'll do you all the good in the world. Anyway, I could do with a drink myself.

2. Colloquialisms and idiomatic expressions connected with drinking and, in particular, referring to various degrees of intoxication are endless! Is the same true in your own language? As a class, make a brainstorm of all the ones you know in English.

GUINNESS AND GAS Read the following passage; then, with your partner or group, discuss your answers to the questions.

QUESTIONS

1. What is paradoxical about the Irish and drink?

2. What are the prevailing attitudes towards alcohol of those who frequent pubs?

3. What is suggested as the main reason for Irish people liking drink? And what proof is given of this?

4. What is paradoxical about Irish writers and drink?

'Work is the curse of the drinking classes,' says a character in one of George Bernard Shaw's plays. And the fact that Shaw was an Irishman is not without significance. Drink has long been considered the curse of the Irish nation.

Here is another of those ubiquitous Irish paradoxes. A recent survey shows that, while we are *the* tea-drinkers of Europe, the most enthusiastic dog-lovers, and the keenest cinema-goers, when it comes to the consumption of alcohol per capita we are well down the list. The reason is that a significant percentage of the population rarely or never 'touch a drop,' and traditionally the consumption of drink has not been allied to the consumption of food. Although this latter situation has changed considerably in recent years and most pubs now serve food, serious drinking is still considered an activity quite separate from eating. Not so long ago an acquaintance of mine refused to go for a pre-dinner drink with his pals until he'd 'had his tea,' on the grounds that it was 'safer to have cocktails' after eating than before. And while wine has soared in popularity since the booming sixties, when holidays in the sun became more accessible, it costs so much for a bottle of plonk the French wouldn't even use for cooking that wine drinking is reserved for special occasions.

In short, most people who drink in this country do their drinking in the pub, and the six-pints-a-night man may well not keep any liquor at home. It is both a serious business—foreign students who occupy precious seats in popular city pubs lingering over a single glass of coke are severely frowned upon—and a national pastime. A street advertisement for a well-known beer recently bore the caption, 'Are you coming for a pint?' The paste was barely dry on the hoarding when a smart-aleck graffitist had added the equally ridiculous truism, 'Is the Pope a Catholic?' The high tolerance of drinking is borne out by the fact that men are frequently measured by their intake, so that the fellow who can drink his mates under the table is looked up to while the one who skips a drink is derided for his weakness.

Consumption rises significantly the moment the call for 'last drinks' is heard, and it is a not uncommon sight to see a drinker with a pint in his hand and two full ones in front of him in the last few minutes before all good law-abiding customers should be conspicuous by their absence. Refusals of invitations to have a 'jar' are usually interpreted as polite requests for a little gentle persuasion, to which the stock response is, 'Well, if you're twisting my arm …' Despite intensive campaigns in recent years to cut down on drunken driving, especially during the critical Christmas season, the man under the influence is still regularly to be found behind the wheel. The inevitable hangover is a cornucopia of conversation in the pub the morning after the night before, and of all the possible cures, 'a hair of the dog' (the classical remedy that works on fashionable homeopathic principles) is widely accepted as the most reliable.

Excessive drinking is only part of the picture, however, and while there is a disturbing growth of alcohol abuse among young people today, Ireland is by
45 no means unique in this regard. On the positive side, the pub is the centre of social and cultural life for most of the people who go there. Our climate makes us an indoor society with an insatiable need for a bit of 'crack' or 'gas' (inadequately translated as 'fun' in standard English) to keep us going. In fact, right from the start the Irish were no slouches at finding ways to cheer
50 themselves up, turning the Egyptian discovery of alcohol distillation for perfume making to better uses; hence *uisce beatha*, the 'water of life', or whiskey, the result of a clear preference for Jameson 10 to Chanel No. 5. And in 1722 Ireland made one of its greatest contributions to the world by inventing Guinness. Another product of Irish ingenuity is *poitín**, an
pot'í:n'
55 explosively potent form of illicit alcohol made from barley or potatoes. This lethal mountain dew is distilled in various parts of the country and sold in lemonade bottles to discerning natives and not-so-discerning visitors.

But when Shaw pronounced work to be the curse of the drinking classes, he forgot to add 'Irish writers excluded.' Despite medical evidence to the
60 contrary, drink has long been considered an essential aid to the creative muse, witness the number of Dublin hostelries dubbed 'literary pubs'. The mind boggles as to how many pages of Joyce's *Ulysses* would have remained forever blank if it hadn't been for the author's intimate knowledge of pub interiors. A typical 'literary' story is told about two
65 writers, Patrick Kavanagh and Brendan Behan, who met on Baggot Street Bridge one day. Having agreed that a jar was in order, it was merely a question of naming the pub. 'How about Mooney's?' says Kavanagh. 'No good, I'm barred there,' replies Behan, suggesting the Crooked Bawbie. 'That's out,' returns Kavanagh. 'I'm barred there.' After naming half a
70 dozen or so more pubs, from which either one or the other is barred, the two give up and go their separate ways. The Irish muse is not exclusive, of course; the American writer J. P. Donleavy once declared, 'When I die, I want to decompose in a barrel of porter and have it served in all the pubs of Dublin'; and the last word on the pint goes to Behan's Welsh twin,
75 Dylan Thomas, who claimed, 'I once drank forty-nine Guinness straight off and came home on top of a bus.' Good man yourself, Dylan.

NOTE

porter: a slightly lighter beer once made by Guinness (originally 'porter's beer'); now the name is sometimes used to mean stout (originally 'stout beer').

MULTIPLE-CHOICE QUESTIONS

Choose the best answer in each case.

1. Which statement most appropriately completes the sentence?
   Although drink is blamed for all their troubles, Irish people
   (a) are extremely fond of dogs
   (b) drink more tea than anybody else in Europe
   (c) enjoy going to the cinema
   (d) consume comparatively little alcohol.

2. The point of the anecdote about an acquaintance of the writer's is that
   (a) cocktails are normally drunk after dinner
   (b) it is unwise to drink on an empty stomach
   (c) it illustrates a particular attitude to drinking
   (d) it shows how much Irish people drink without eating.

3. The graffiti on the advertisement suggests that the most appropriate answer to the question 'Are you going for a pint?' is
   (a) 'Yes, I am.'
   (b) 'Don't ask stupid questions.'
   (c) 'Thanks very much.'
   (d) 'That's a good idea.'

4. According to the passage, how do people usually react when they are being persuaded to have a drink?
   (a) They give in.
   (b) They refuse politely.
   (c) They expect physical force.
   (d) They twist somebody's arm.

5. 'A hair of the dog' (line 40) is the short form of a common idiom. Which phrase completes it?
   (a) that bit you
   (b) you drank so much of
   (c) that made you feel so bad
   (d) you are so fond of.

6. The tone the writer uses when explaining the origin of whiskey could best be described as
   (a) ironic
   (b) neutral
   (c) complimentary
   (d) censorious.

7. According to what the writer says in the last paragraph, it has been proved that
   (a) Irish writers belong to the drinking classes
   (b) drink dulls the imagination
   (c) many Irish writers depend on drink for their creativity
   (d) drink is not considered a curse.

8. 'Literary' is enclosed in quotation marks in lines 61 and 64 because
   (a) the writer wants to stress it
   (b) it is not being used in its proper sense
   (c) it is a word used by Irish writers
   (d) the writer is being sarcastic.

HOMAGE TO THE PINT

The following poem, written by a connoisseur par excellence, Flann O'Brien, is probably the best homage ever paid to the 'pint'. O'Brien can also lay claim to fame as a scholar, a wit, a satirist and a writer. His first book, *At Swim-Two-Birds* (from which this poem is taken), has been called 'the only true successor to Joyce's *Ulysses*,' and indeed it was greatly admired by Joyce.

45

1. The following rhyme words are missing from the poem:
   change, bare, right, get, can, pan, life.
   Read the poem, aloud if possible, to get a sense of the rhythm and rhyme, and decide where the missing words belong. The rhyme scheme is a very regular *a*, *b*, *a*, *b*—so regular, in fact, that the poet happily (and humorously) abandons good grammar for its sake. Can you point out where?

2. 'Plain' here means stout. But can you suggest any other ways of expressing the meaning and tone of the phrase 'is your only man'?

3. What picture does the poem paint of the pint drinker?

A PINT OF PLAIN IS YOUR ONLY MAN

When things go wrong and will not come .... [1],
Though you do the best you .... [2],
When life looks black as the hour of night—
A pint of plain is your only man.

When money's tight and is hard to .... [3]
And your horse has also ran,
When all you have is a heap of debt—
A pint of plain is your only man.

When health is bad and your heart feels strange,
And your face is pale and wan,
When doctors say that you need a .... [4]—
A pint of plain is your only man.

When food is scarce and your larder .... [5],
And no rashers grease you .... [6],
When hunger grows as your meals are rare—
A pint of plain is your only man.

In time of trouble and lousy strife,
You have still got a darling plan,
You can still turn to a brighter .... [7]—
A pint of plain is your only man.

NOTES

larder: a place in older houses, usually a room off the kitchen, where food is kept.
rashers: thin slices of bacon for frying.

MORE DRINK TALK

On pages 49, 51, 53 and 54 you will find cartoons with part of the captions missing. The missing words are given below. *But don't look at any of the cartoons until it is your turn to do so!*

A   'This is a great place for a glass of wine'. 'You can drink as much as you like and they won't throw you out.'
B   'Don't be talkin'!'
C   'I enjoyed your Guinness. I am a racing motor cyclist. I shall not be back.'
D   'Pay no attention. It's just the drink talking.'

1. Divide into groups of four. Each student should take it in turn to describe one of the cartoons in detail to the other three, who, without conferring, decide which words belong to each cartoon. Only when all four cartoons have been described should you compare your answers.

2. Do you agree? If not, discuss your choice with each other. You should be able to explain what the humour in each cartoon is.

3. When you have reached complete agreement, you may look at the correct answers (on page 266). Were you right?

TEENAGE DRINKING

These two passages appeared in different newspapers in the same month. (The first (A) is by Liz McManus, from the *Sunday Tribune*, 24 March 1991; the second (B) is by Mary Cummins, from the *Irish Times*, 4 March 1991). They both deal with the growing problem of drinking among young people in Ireland. Read them, then discuss what they tell you about teenage drinking and the reasons for it.

A.

The image of the drunken Irish was endemic in the early '60s ... but our serious drinking only got going in the mid-60s and 70s when the consumption of alcohol in Ireland shot up. Between 1970 and 1980 it increased by 50%. Not that we were on our own in lashing into the hard
5   stuff when times got good ... even at our most dissolute we were still modest drinkers when measured beside the French and the Germans. Austria and Luxembourg are even worse drinkers—or better, depending on your viewpoint—which has to be some kind of blow to our national pride.

10　Once the economic boom was over the level of drink consumption started
　　to drop … although different people had started to drink for the first
　　time—young people and women. In the early '60s you never saw a 15-
　　year-old girl inside a pub but you were forever falling over old male
　　drunks sicking up on the pavement.

15　Nowadays the roles are likely to be reversed, especially on the night the
　　Inter Cert results come out and no serious drinker over 40 would be seen
　　dead in a city centre pub. Schoolchildren can be sophisticated drinkers
　　with a penchant for beer and wine and an aversion to cider. They drink
　　illicitly or openly and are governed by the attitudes of their peer group.
20　Parental influence has some bearing on teenage drinking but it is limited
　　and not always helpful.

　　After addressing a parents' group once, I listened with amazement to a
　　parent explain how every time he had a drink he felt obliged to offer his
　　nine-year-old daughter one too. Confusion on the matter abounded among
25　the parents until a priest spoke. He wanted parents to stop giving
　　children pocket money. A wonderful idea, although pigs will fly before we
　　get to that happy state.

　　　　*　　*　　*　　*　　*　　*　　*　　*　　*

B.　The average child who drinks is now starting at the age of twelve,
　　according to a study published in Galway.

　　The survey, carried out by Combined Action, a Galway-based group
　　responding to alcohol and substance abuse, showed that boys take their
　　first drink at 12.2 years, girls at 12.8 years.

　　Other disturbing trends shown are:

　　—50 per cent of fifteen-year-old girls who drink abuse alcohol

　　—50 per cent of fifteen-year-old boys who drink took their first drink to
　　get drunk

　　—55.6 per cent of fifteen-year-old girls who drink have taken spirits at
　　some time.

　　One of the most startling findings was that over two-thirds (67.5 per cent)
　　had never received any formal advice or education on alcohol.

QUESTIONS

Now read the passages again and answer these questions. You may do this orally with your partner, and/or as homework.

Passage A

1. According to Liz McManus, how did Irish drinking habits change between the 1960s and 1980s, and for what reason?

2. What changes have taken place since the 1980s, and what does she attribute these to?

3. Explain in your own words what she means by the phrase 'Nowadays the roles are likely to be reversed' (line 15).

4. Who, in the writer's opinion, has the strongest influence on teenage drinking habits?

5. What was the writer's attitude to the priest's solution to the problem? Quote to support your answer.

6. What can you say about the writer's style and tone? To answer this question, examine her use of the following words and phrases:

   shot up (line 3)
   lashing into (line 4)
   are even worse drinkers—or better … (line 7)
   the economic boom (line 10)
   sicking up on the pavement (line 14)
   no serious drinker over 40 would be seen dead … (line 16)
   a penchant for … and an aversion to … (line 18)
   A wonderful idea, although pigs will fly … (line 26)

Passage B

7. In one sentence, say what cause for concern the Combined Action survey revealed; and in another sentence, say what was surprising about its results.

8. What can you say about Mary Cummins's style and tone? Compare her treatment of the subject with the previous writer's.

WRITING

The greatest problems facing young people in my country today.

1. Alcohol abuse is only one of the problems prevalent among the young in Ireland today. Drug abuse, from glue-sniffing by very young children to heroin addiction, is another. Teenage crime, covering everything from shop-lifting and vandalism to car theft, assault, robbery, and even rape, is on the increase. Undoubtedly a high unemployment rate and a low standard of living are partly to blame for such problems. Can you suggest other possible reasons?

Discuss your answers to these questions with a partner or group and make notes of interesting ideas as you're talking.

2. Do the problems mentioned above exist in your country? Can you add to the list? (*a*) What reasons can you suggest for them? (*b*) What is being done to solve the problems? Could more be done?

3. You may have discovered that while many problems are shared by different countries, some are particular to or worse in yours. Does this help you to focus more specifically on the situation in your own country?

4. Use the notes you have made as the basis for your composition plan. Planning, paragraph by paragraph, is essential in order to present a logical, coherent argument.
    What is your approach going to be? You could decide to deal with (*a*) the problems, (*b*) the reasons, and (*c*) the solutions. Alternatively, you could take three or four problems and deal with each one in turn. These are simply suggestions. You may think of a different approach.

5. Always keep in mind when you're writing that you're communicating with a reader. How do you feel when you have to read a series of unrelieved facts, generalisations, and abstractions? You can make your writing much more interesting and effective by giving examples to illustrate your points. Make good use of your own experience, and other people's!

6. Your opening sentence can win or lose the reader. Look at these five possible beginnings to this composition, and rate them from A (for the most interesting) to E (for the utterly boring).

    (*a*) There are many problems facing young people in my country today.

(b) Out of my class at school last year, one died from an overdose of drugs, one committed suicide, and another contracted AIDS.

(c) The first thing we must do is define our terms: i.e. what we mean by 'young people' and what we mean by 'problems'.

(d) Schooldays are said to be the happiest days of your life.

(e) Young people everywhere inherit the problems that the older generation has created.

7. According to the proverb, 'the proof of the pudding is in the eating.' Let the other members of your group read your composition and tell you if they (a) understood your argument and (b) found it interesting. Unless there is a very obvious spelling mistake or slip of the pen, they should not attempt to correct your English. (That's the teacher's job!)

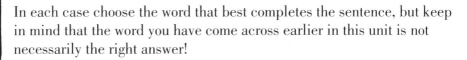

VOCABULARY PRACTICE

In each case choose the word that best completes the sentence, but keep in mind that the word you have come across earlier in this unit is not necessarily the right answer!

1. That was a(n) .... idea of yours to take the phone off the hook! Now nobody can disturb me while I'm watching my favourite programme on television.

    (a) ingenious   (b) ingenuous (c) disingenuous (d) genius

2. I was .... to hear that most premature deaths in Ireland are the result of drink-related diseases.

    (a) startling   (b) surprised   (c) boggled   (d) disillusioned

3. We'll have to produce something better than our usual bottle of plonk for dinner tonight. Tom is very .... when it comes to wine, you know.

(a) discriminatory   (b) discreet   (c) distinctive   (d) discerning

4. I love cooking with garlic. The only trouble is that the taste tends to .... in your mouth for hours after you've eaten.

(a) wait   (b) delay   (c) keep   (d) linger

5. If only there was a tunnel between Ireland and England! Just think how .... it would be to reach the Continent then.

(a) available   (b) accessible   (c) easy   (d) near

6. While they couldn't actually forbid their eighteen-year-old daughter to go to the pub so often, they showed that they .... of it.

(a) disapproved   (b) disliked   (c) disagreed   (d) frowned

7. So you forgot about the meeting yesterday! Well, you were certainly .... by your absence; everybody wondered where you were.

(a) obvious   (b) conspicuous   (c) noticed   (d) noted

8. Business has been .... since the government reduced VAT.

(a) blooming   (b) booming   (c) blossoming   (d) raising

9. He's ashamed of his alcoholic father, but he looks .... his mother, because she brought up the family all by herself.

(a) up   (b) upon   (c) up to   (d) up at

10. The economic situation may have some .... on teenage alcohol abuse, but it's by no means the only reason for it.

(a) relation   (b) relevance   (c) connection   (d) bearing

11. I'm so hungry I could eat a horse! I had to .... breakfast this morning because I overslept.

(a) pass up   (b) pass over   (c) skip   (d) leave

12. The only way to lose weight is to reduce your daily .... of calories.

    (*a*) ingestion   (*b*) intake   (*c*) amount   (*d*) diet

13. They had the patient's blood pressure well under control, but it .... dramatically as soon as his wife came into the room.

    (*a*) arose   (*b*) raised   (*c*) soared up   (*d*) shot up

14. I'm really looking forward to having dinner with you tonight. I had a very .... lunch so I'm warning you, I'll be absolutely starving!

    (*a*) little   (*b*) weak   (*c*) moderate   (*d*) modest

15. He may come bottom of the class every term, but he's certainly no .... at soccer.

    (*a*) slouch   (*b*) dunce   (*c*) fool   (*d*) slob

CLOZE

The following passage on Guinness advertising is adapted from *The Stout Book* by Brendan O'Brien. In it he deals with every conceivable aspect of the subject: from how Guinness is made to the best cure for a hangover.

Read the passage, then fill each of the numbered spaces with one suitable word.

Guinness advertising has .... [1] been colourful and imaginative. In 1954, ... [2] of their campaigns .... [3] floating 150,000 bottles in the world's major ocean. .... [4] each bottle was an invitation to the prospective finder to reply to Guinness. Those .... [5] did included a Mexican prisoner and an Eskimo boy. Times have changed; the sophisticated commercials you now see on .... [6] are obviously more appropriate to an age preoccupied with conservation.

For a long time stout had the reputation of being beneficial .... [7] the health. So when the slogan 'Guinness is good for you' first appeared in 1928, it was .... [8] so much an original idea .... [9] a reinforcement of .... [10] stout drinkers already wanted to believe. .... [11] provided the perfect answer to the pro-temperance, anti-pleasure lobby. Stout lovers .... [12] quite happily drink their pints knowing they were only doing it for the good of their health; .... [13], of course, because they were enjoying it!

And the slogan was corroborated by the .... [14] profession; miniature .... [15] of Guinness were given to nursing mothers and convalescents in hospital .... [16] to the 1970s. But it was the consumers .... [17] who gave it most credibility by claiming miraculous cures for all .... [18] of ailments. Stout benefited .... [19] from constipation to depression; it calmed nerves, aided digestion, improved blood and even increased virility!

It's .... [20] wonder, then, that half the beer consumed in Ireland is Guinness.

There is certainly no shortage of Irish songs associated with drink—its pleasures and, less frequently, its pains. Here is a popular ballad about a fellow who confesses to having spent too much time and money in the pub. He vows to mend his ways and be a good boy. Does he sound convincing?

Listen to the song on the cassette and then sing along with it.

THE WILD ROVER

I've been a wild rover for many a year,
And I spent all my money on whiskey and beer.
Ah, but now I'm returning with gold in great store,
And I never will play the wild rover no more.

Chorus

And it's no nay never, no nay never no more,
Will I play the Wild Rover,
No never, no more.

2.

I went into an ale house I used to frequent,
And I told the landlady my money was spent.
I asked her for credit, she answered me nay,
Such a custom as yours I can have any day.

Chorus

3.

I then took from my pockets ten sovereigns bright,
And the landlady's eyes opened wide with delight.
She said I have whiskey and wines of the best,
And the words that I told you were only in jest.

Chorus

4.

I'll go home to my parents, confess what I've done,
And I'll ask them to pardon their prodigal son.
And when they caress me, as oft' times before,
Sure I never will play the Wild Rover no more.

Chorus

GUINNESS for STRENGTH

Unit 4

WHY …

—are there no snakes in Ireland?
—is the shamrock a national symbol?
—do the Irish all over the world celebrate the seventeenth of March?
If you don't know, read on and find out!

**A LAND OF
SAINTS AND
SCHOLARS**

Ireland has the reputation of being a devoutly religious country. How and why did this happen? This passage deals with the Christianisation of the country and the unique way in which it developed. Read it and discuss your answers to these questions with a partner.

QUESTIONS

1. Why is the period described known as Ireland's Golden Age?

2. What do you learn from the passage about the life and character of St Patrick?

3. What is said about the information we have of St Patrick today?

4. What two distinctive features are mentioned about the development of Christianity in Ireland?

57

Although Christianity became the official religion of the Roman Empire in the fourth century, when the Romans left Britain almost a hundred years later it all but disappeared in England, as did the other elements of their culture. Yet it was at the same time that this was happening across the Irish Sea that the seeds of Christianity were being planted in Ireland, seeds that were to flourish so vigorously that they blossomed into what has been called Ireland's Golden Age. Indeed, while the rest of Europe was plunged in the Dark Ages after being overrun by barbarian tribes, Ireland was gaining renown as a country rich in learning and culture, including the most brilliantly successful art of that period.

The inspiration behind it all was a Romanised Celt called Patrick, who grew up somewhere on the west coast of Britain, probably near Bristol. According to his autobiographical work, the *Confessio*, he was captured by pirates at the age of sixteen and sold into slavery in Ireland, where for six years he tended his master's flocks of sheep on Slemish Mountain in Co. Antrim. He eventually succeeded in escaping, but no sooner had he gained his freedom than he heard 'the voice of the Irish' begging him to go back to the country of his captors and spread the gospel among them. In 432, under the commission of Pope Celestine and after spending twenty years in France (or Gaul, as it was then called) preparing for his great mission, Patrick returned to Ireland, and by the time he died thirty-three years later the whole island was effectively Christianised.

Although Patrick humbly refers to himself as a man of little learning, his ability to convert so many people without creating a single martyr is ample proof of his talents; besides being a shrewd diplomat, he had a deep respect for the ancient traditions of the Celtic people and a sympathy for their mysticism, which enabled him to win over the all-powerful druids and bardic poets. In many cases the old religious practices of druidism continued under the auspices of Christianity, which is why the church in Ireland developed in a different way from the system in continental Europe. One instance of this is Croagh Patrick, a mountain in Co. Mayo, once an object of worship in honour of a pagan god but which even today is a place of pilgrimage for the thousands who climb it (many in their bare feet) every year on the last Sunday in July.

The stories about St Patrick are legion, ranging from the purely mythical, such as his banishing the snakes from Ireland, through the popular (his use of the shamrock to explain the doctrine of the Holy Trinity), to the completely authentic. There is no doubt, for example, that he established the primatial archdiocese of Ireland at Armagh, interestingly enough situated only two miles from Eamhain Mhacha*, the royal fort of the kings of Ulster and the place so closely associated with the great hero Cú

auən' vaxə   40

Chulainn. Apart from the survival of so many legends and customs concerning his travels throughout the country, however, the fact that there are over two thousand cathedrals and churches in the world today
45 dedicated to his name is living proof of his influence on posterity.

By the end of the sixth century, monasticism, more suited to the unurbanised, uncommercial, semi-nomadic way of life in Ireland, where the family was the pattern for society, was flourishing and the church was essentially missionary in its function. As the famous German monk
50 Walafridus Strabo wrote, 'Going on pilgrimages to foreign parts has become, for Irish monks, second nature.' It is estimated that, between the fifth and tenth centuries, the number of 'wanderers' who left the monastic settlements like Clonmacnoise, Glendalough and Bangor for foreign parts can be counted in thousands. The most celebrated of these was Colm
koləm kilʹə 55 Cille* (or Columba), a prince of the O'Donnells from Ulster, who founded a monastery in what is now the city of Derry; as he wrote in one of his many poems,

> My Derry, my little oak-grove,
> My dwelling and my little cell.

60 Colm Cille also founded a community on Iona, an island off the coast of Scotland, which was a mainspring of Christian teaching for centuries, while Aidan, one of his monks, set up the sanctuary at Lindisfarne in Northumbria in the north of England, from where the gospel travelled the length of that country. Another disciple, Colmán (or Columbanus),
65 travelled to the Continent in about 590 to establish monasteries at Luxeuil in France and Bobbio in Italy, while his companion, St Gall, was the inspiration for the monastic settlement near Lake Constance in Switzerland. The list of monks who literally invaded the Europe of the Dark Ages looking like, according to one writer, 'spiritual hippies'
70 because of their long hair and hand-made sandals, is endless. One of them, however, is noted for braving the seas in the opposite direction; long before the time of Columbus, St Brendan the Navigator set off across the Atlantic in a currach and, it is alleged, was the first European to set foot on American soil by landing on Newfoundland.

MORE QUESTIONS

Now read the passage again and answer these questions as precisely as you can. You may do this orally, with a partner, and/or in writing as homework.

1. Pick out the words or phrases in the paragraphs indicated whose meanings are given here:

Paragraph 1

   was in a benighted state ....

Paragraph 2

   imploring ....

Paragraph 3

   gain the support of by persuasion ....

Paragraph 4

   numerous ....

Paragraph 5

   a matter of course ....

Paragraph 6

   people who live an unconventional life....................

2. What word could replace 'all but' in line 3?

3. What does 'this' refer to in line 4?

4. What is the relationship between the Dark Ages and Ireland's Golden Age?

5. What four stages can St Patrick's life be divided into?

6. Why was Patrick able to convert the Irish to Christianity 'without creating a single martyr'?

7. What does 'which' refer to in line 29?

8. What is significant about the Croagh Patrick pilgrimage?

9. The writer puts the stories about St Patrick into different categories. What are they, and what example is given of each?

10. In your own words, explain why monasticism was the way the Christian church developed in Ireland.

11. Why do you think the word 'wanderers' is enclosed in quotation marks in line 52?

12. Apart from the fact that they were missionary monks, what is the apparent relationship between saints Aidan, Columbanus, and Gall?

13. What is implied by the phrase 'it is alleged' in line 73?

LISTENING

According to legend the sixth century St Brendan, popularly known as Brendan the Navigator, sailed across the Atlantic in a curragh and, after many wonderful adventures, landed at Newfoundland. In 1976 Tim Severin, an Englishman who now lives in Co. Cork, set out to prove whether or not the Brendan voyage was actually possible. You are now going to hear an interview with Tim.

Study this map of the North Atlantic and look at the questions. Then listen to the interview twice.

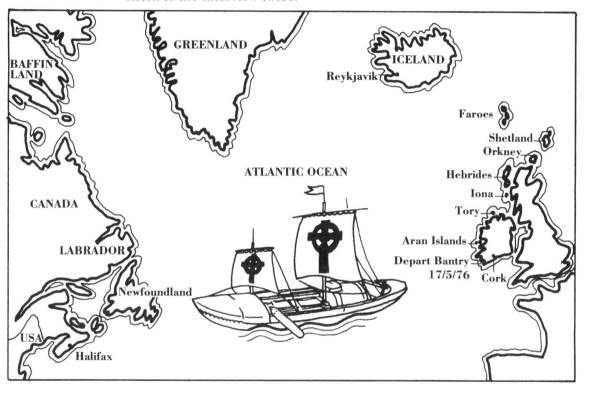

1. Draw the route followed by Tim and his crew from Ireland to Newfoundland on this map of the North Atlantic.

2. Mark the following places on the map using the letters indicated:

   A. the Dingle Peninsula
   B. where St Columba founded a monastery
   C. where another member of the crew was picked up
   D. where they broke their journey for several months
   E. ⎫
   F. ⎬ three places where they experienced difficult conditions
   G. ⎭

3. Which of these statements about the boat used by Tim and his crew is untrue?

A. Its name is Brendan.
B. Its leather covering saved them from probable death at one point.
C. There is no comparison between it and the curraghs used today.
D. In shape and structure it resembles a Great Whale.

4. Why does Tim describe their arrival on North American soil as an anti-climax?

A. The voyage hadn't proved anything.
B. There was no sense of surprise about reaching their destination.
C. They were too exhausted to care.
D. There was nobody their to welcome them.

SHAMROCK POWER

Now you know why the shamrock is a symbol of Ireland. Where have you seen it used? If you haven't, keep your eyes open!

Over a long time, when the native language and religion were suppressed, the shamrock took on a very powerful significance as a way for Irish people at home, and their compatriots exiled in other countries, to express their Irishness. Two lines of one of the many songs about the shamrock express this poignantly:

> Oh, Paddy dear, and did you hear the news that's going around?
> The shamrock is forbid by law to grow on Irish ground.

A sense of nationality can be expressed by symbols, flags, anthems, and even holidays.

1. With your partner or group, describe the form these symbols take in your own country, and discuss the importance they have. Do people respect them or are they largely indifferent to them?

2. Compare your views with the rest of the class. Can you draw any significant conclusions from your discussion?

A GREAT DAY FOR THE IRISH!

Sprigs of shamrock are worn on St Patrick's Day, 17th March, which is celebrated in every part of the world where there are Irish people. The biggest and most impressive parade—it takes over five hours to pass the reviewing stand—is held in New York. As one writer comments, 'you would be amazed how many black Irishmen there are in the United States of America!'

While great efforts have been made in recent years to mark the national holiday at home, largely by imitating the American style with specially imported high-school bands and majorettes, not to mention green beer, the following observation by an Irishwoman brought up in London is very apt: 'One of the great mysteries of our time is why, when the rest of the world is celebrating St Patrick's Day with almost manic fervour, the Irish at home, who normally have an infinite capacity for enjoying themselves, immediately sober up, and generally act as if it wasn't happening at all.'

1. The following are some samples of the press coverage of St Patrick's Day 1991. In each case two extracts are taken from the same article or report. Read them; then, with your partner or group,

    (*a*) match each pair of extracts, and decide the order they appeared in;

    (*b*) discuss what the writer's main purpose was (e.g. to inform, to express opinion, to entertain, to amuse), and then decide which are reports of actual events and which are articles written for the occasion;

    (*c*) compare your answers with the rest of the class and, having checked that you have correctly matched the pairs of extracts, read them again and answer the questions that follow.

A

They provided colourful and entertaining spectacles in many cities and towns, but none quite reached the tension and drama of the spectacular New York parade, where cans of beer were thrown at the mayor, Mr David Dinkins, as he led a 200-strong Irish gay and lesbian contingent.

B

We had a few lessons in the morning after assembly, where we belted out 'Hail, Glorious St Patrick', drowning out the piano accompaniment of a nun playing all the wrong notes, but in the afternoon, all stopped, and along with the enormous treat of ice-cream in school hours (we enjoyed simple pleasures then) we had the Match—a netball match between the Irish and the English.

C

But even if the place to be on the national day is New York instead of Dublin, Boston instead of Cork, it is nothing compared to the intensity which went into celebrating St Patrick's Day during my schooldays in London.

D

Dublin Tourism, which organised the parade, likes to stick to the tried-and-tested formula, but this year there was a difference. The fact that the GPO is swathed in scaffolding and hidden from view for cleaning purposes meant the parade went down the east side of O'Connell Street. It was as if we were driving on the right—very European for the cultural capital.

Many of our own native politicians will be over there, parading their nationality and having a good time, as will lesser patriots in Australia and Canada, for this is the day when patriot hucksters parade the green flag abroad and with palms outstretched, beg alms on behalf of the Poor Ould Country …

F

Such excitement on the way into the parade. Would the army be there? Last year a young one fell and everyone marching behind her fell over too, but they were only babies … you never catch a balloon because they go into the air too fast … are we going to McDonald's afterwards? What's a majorette?

G

There are slightly more than 41,000,000 Americans who are under the impression, according to the last US census, that they are of Irish, or predominantly Irish, ancestry, and almost all of whom will be adorning themselves today with coarse lumps of clover, flogged to them by unscrupulous hucksters under the denomination of shamrock.

H

The organisers of the parade, the Ancient Order of Hibernians, turned their backs on him as he passed the reviewing stand outside St Patrick's Cathedral. Afterwards he said, 'Those who booed had a right to boo, but some of the ugliest expressions reminded me very much of the Birmingham route that Dr Martin Luther King marched.'

I

The bus was packed on the way into town. There was a rush of noise through the double-doors when they opened at the stop and a smell of pink chewing-gum inside. Children simmered in this mobile pressure cooker, bubbling and bouncing, weighed down by firm adult hands.

J

Otherwise tradition was upheld. There was the interdenominational blessing of the shamrock … the Lord Mayor, Alderman Michael Donnelly, arrived in his horse-drawn coach and the Taoiseach, Mr Haughey, told a forest of microphones pushed under his nose that it was a day of joy for all Irish people.

QUESTIONS

1. Insert here which extracts belong together. The order in which you put the letters should indicate the order in which you think the extracts appeared.

1: .... and ....

2: .... and ....

3: .... and ....

4: .... and ....

5: .... and ....

2. Now say which of these extracts (1, 2, 3, 4, or 5)

(*a*) expresses a sense of nostalgia

(*b*) is most concerned with the atmosphere of the occasion

(*c*) conveys a rather cynical attitude

(*d*) is the straightest report

(*e*) intersperses a report of the facts with comment.

3. What were the dates of publication of the above extracts? Put a circle round what you think is the correct answer in each case; in other words, you should circle five answers:

13 March 1991:   1   2   3   4   5

17 March 1991:   1   2   3   4   5

18 March 1991:   1   2   3   4   5

WRITING

Describe a national or local festival celebrated in your own country.

1. What are the most striking features of the festival you are going to describe? For five to ten minutes make a random list of any ideas that come into your head, keeping in mind that small details (sights, sounds, smells, remarks) can do more to express atmosphere than facts of time and place.

2. Now compare notes with your partner. You may well find that this activity will give you further inspiration.

3. Work out a plan for your composition by organising your notes—i.e. deciding which ideas go logically together, which aspects of the festival you intend to deal with, and how many paragraphs you will need. When

66

you begin to write, it is possible that you will want to make changes or additions, but having a basic plan means you won't ramble on aimlessly.

4. Remember the importance of the opening sentence. How would you rate these possible beginnings? (Give A for the most interesting to E for the least interesting.)

- (*a*) In our country we have many national festivals, but the one I am going to describe …
- (*b*) Ever since I was a small child I have looked forward to the festival that takes place in our village every year …
- (*c*) A kaleidoscope of colour greeted us as we pushed our way to the front of the crowd …
- (*d*) A little girl screamed in terror as the pipe band suddenly erupted into a rousing march …
- (*e*) We do a lot of different things to celebrate our national festival.

TREASURES OF THE GOLDEN AGE

The cultural flowering of Ireland during the Early Christian period manifested itself in the magnificent art and artefacts now on display in museums and libraries and also in the sculpture and stone-work that have survived in many places throughout the country. Here are photographs of six of the most famous of these.

A

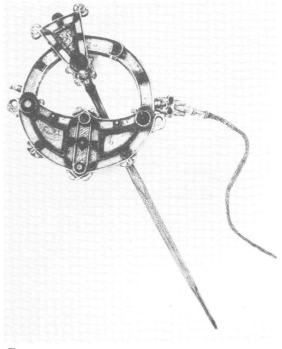

B

67

C

D

E

F

1. Working with a partner or group, describe what you see in each photograph. Say what you think it is, what it's made of, and how and why it was made.

2. Now read these extracts from descriptions of the treasures, and say which description should accompany each photograph.

i

One of the masterpieces of insular art and probably the finest example of non-ecclesiastical ornamentation. It has sunken panels that contain filigree designs on a gold-foil base, and circular and rectangular studs of amber and domed hemispheres of glass are set in silver-gilt depressions.

ii

The fantastic little animals which adorn the paper of this illuminated manuscript show that the monks who laboured long and hard to produce it did not lack a sense of humour.

iii

The oldest example of its type. Constructed without any mortar, in a development of the corbelled style used in the Newgrange burial chamber.

iv

Dates from the tenth century. The central area represents the Crucifixion, while the shaft shows Christ giving the keys to St Peter and the Law to St Paul, and, in descending order, Doubting Thomas and the arrest of Christ.

v

A wonderful illustration of the reluctance of the craftsmen of the time to leave any area undecorated. Even the stud at the bottom, which would never have been seen by anybody other than the celebrant of Mass, is completely covered with minute engravings.

vi

Like the harp and the shamrock, they have become a symbol of Ireland. This is one of the few undamaged ones that remain. Its original function was probably as a campanile, but it was later used for defensive purposes.

A: ....   B: ....   C: ....   D: ....   E: ....   F: ....

3. Below are the captions explaining what each photograph is of. Now that you have matched the descriptions with the photographs (or most of them, anyway!), put the correct letter and number beside each caption.

Photograph	Description	Caption
....	....	Gallarus Oratory, Dingle Peninsula, Co. Kerry
....	....	High cross at Monasterboice, Co. Louth
....	....	Round tower at Glendalough, Co. Wicklow
....	....	A detail from the Book of Kells (Trinity College Library)
....	....	The Ardagh Chalice, Ardagh, Co. Limerick (National Museum)
....	....	The Tara Brooch, Bettystown, Co. Meath (National Museum)

69

4. How many of these, or indeed other treasures of Ireland's Golden Age, have you seen? Where would you go to see them, and how would you get there?

5. What survives today of the same period (sixth to twelfth century) in your own country, and how does it compare with Ireland?

THE SAINT OF GLENDALOUGH

Ireland may be a religious country, but while the Irish are justly proud of their saints, they are not beyond poking a bit of irreverent fun at them!

Take this song about St Kevin, the seventh-century founder of the monastic settlement at Glendalough, Co. Wicklow. Apart from the interest of its early Christian ruins, Glendalough (meaning 'valley of the two lakes') is a place of great natural beauty.

Who Kitty was, history doesn't relate, except that she lived 'over the way', i.e. opposite him. The 'rockery' mentioned is probably 'St Kevin's Bed', a ledge cut into the rocks where he is reputed to have prayed and slept in true hermit style.

1. The seven verses are not given in their correct order. Can you reorganise them so that they make sense?

1: .... 2: .... 3: .... 4: .... 5: .... 6: .... 7: ....

2. According to the song, what secular pleasure was St Kevin quite definitely not interested in? And what one did he apparently enjoy?

3. It goes without saying that the song is not meant to be taken seriously. Does it, nevertheless, reveal anything interesting about the traditional concept of piety?

A

One day the saint landed a trout,
He landed a fine, fat trout, sir,
When Kitty from over the way
Came to see what the monk was
    about, sir.

B

He gave her a terrible shake,
And I wish a policeman had caught him,
For he threw her right into the lake,
And, be Jasus, she sank to the bottom.

C

In Glendalough lived an old saint
Renowned for his learning and piety.
His manners were curious and quaint,
And he looked on all girls with
    asperity.

D

And ever since then it's been said
Her ghost walks abroad on the river.
Poor St Kevin never lifted his head,
For she died of a cold-water shiver.

E

He was fond of reading a book,
If he could get one to his wishes;
He was fonder of casting a hook
In the lake among the young fishes.

F

But Kitty she wouldn't give in,
And when he got home to his
    rockery
He found she was seated therein,
A-polishing up his old crockery.

G

'Get out of my way,' said the saint.
'Can't you see I'm a man of great
    piety,
And my good manners I wouldn't
    taint
By mixing with female society.'

VOCABULARY PRACTICE

In each case choose the word that best completes the sentence, but keep in mind that the word you have come across earlier in this unit is not necessarily the right answer!

1. ...., the Government could do a lot more to help unemployed people.

      (*a*) From my view   (*b*) In my opinion
      (*c*) In my point of view   (*d*) According to me

2. He may not have done well academically but he was a ....
businessman and had made his first million by the time he was thirty.

    (*a*) shrewd   (*b*) cunning   (*c*) sly   (*d*) shifty

3. When they heard that a number of people were going to be made
redundant, the .... in the office was unbearable.

    (*a*) shock   (*b*) strain   (*c*) stress   (*d*) tension

4. Belt ....! You're making such a noise I can't hear myself talking on the phone.

(a) out   (b) up   (c) down   (d) away

5. If you want to take Irish smoked salmon home with you, the easiest thing to do is to buy it from the .... at the airport.

(a) dealer   (b) retailer   (c) hawker   (d) huckster

6. We object to the proposed changes in the law because we .... the principle that a person is innocent until proved guilty.

(a) keep up   (b) hold up   (c) hold on   (d) uphold

7. I can't possibly go out tonight; I have a .... of work to do for the morning.

(a) lump   (b) mass   (c) quantity   (d) profusion

8. You should always .... cabbage as fast as possible. There's nothing worse than soggy, overcooked green vegetables.

(a) simmer   (b) steam   (c) boil   (d) broil

9. Up to a year ago he was an unemployed layabout, but .... he's making a name for himself playing the lead guitar with a new rock group.

(a) actually   (b) in the moment   (c) in the meantime   (d) these days

10. There was one particular scene in the horror film that was so ghastly I all .... fainted!

(a) but   (b) except   (c) almost   (d) only

11. When St Patrick was brought to Ireland as a slave, he spent six years .... after sheep on a hill in Co. Antrim.

(a) looking   (b) tending   (c) seeing   (d) caring

12. The .... stories told about St Patrick show how much he was loved and admired.

(a) innumerable   (b) legion   (c) amount of (d) infinite

13. The best time for .... daffodil bulbs is late September or early October.

(*a*) sowing (*b*) sewing (*c*) cultivating (*d*) planting

14. She was a quiet, mousy little girl at school, but as soon as she went to university she .... into an attractive, self-confident young woman.

(*a*) bloomed (*b*) flowered (*c*) blossomed (*d*) grew up

15. If it'll help you to decide which curtain material you want, we can give you a book of .... to take home overnight.

(*a*) snippets (*b*) samples (*c*) examples (*d*) styles

CLOZE

In the listening comprehension test in this unit you heard Tim Severin talking about his journey across the Atlantic in a currach called *Brendan*. In the following extract from his book *The Brendan Voyage* he describes what it must have been like for the medieval monks who made long journeys in small open boats. Fill each of the numbered spaces with one suitable word.

What .... [1] of men, then, were these monks who deliberately launched out into .... [2] Atlantic in small open boats? Many must never have returned, but perished .... [3] sea. Aboard Brendan we had the advantages of being in .... [4] with the outside world .... [5] radio, and we knew that .... [6] they could .... [7] us fast enough, the Coast Guard or the deep-sea fishermen of the North Atlantic would have .... [8] to rescue us in an emergency.
But the Irish monks and their currachs had .... [9] of these advantages. A dozen or .... [10] men would have been packed into a boat the .... [11] of *Brendan* and would have endured .... [12] greater discomfort. They would have been colder, wetter, and—in one

sense—more isolated than we were .... [13] *Brendan*.
Such men must have been special people, even .... [14] the exacting
standards of their .... [15] day. They were directed by a sense of
dedication which .... [16] have been the single most important factor
in their success. .... [17] of this dedication came much of their
suitability as open-boat sailors on long northern voyages. .... [18]
monks they were .... [19] to hardship; life in a medieval monastery
was an ideal training for a long journey in an open boat. Equally, their
mental preparation must have matched their .... [20] readiness. The
outlook of their leaders was a bold combination of intellectual curiosity
and a fearless trust in God.

Unit
5

A SPORTING NATION

ARE YOU A SPORT?

Sport divides people into three categories: people who fanatically play it, people who fanatically follow it, and people who fanatically hate it! Which are you?

Working with a partner or group, discuss your answers to the following questions.

1. What are the most common sports played in your country? Can you divide them into different categories—e.g ball games, team sports, and so on?

2. Is there a particular sport that is played only in your own country? If so, explain how it is played and, if you know, what its origins are. Why has it not become popular in other countries?

3. Can you pick one game that might be said to be the national sport, i.e. one that the entire country follows keenly, even fanatically? Does its popularity manifest itself in both positive and negative ways?

4. What sports do you play yourself, and what benefits do you gain from doing so?

75

Read this description of a popular Irish sport. You may not be able to say what it is, but can you say what it is *not* by pointing out how it differs from other games you know?—e.g. it's not soccer/rugby/American football, because …

It consists of two teams of fifteen men each. They use sticks made of ash-plants with broad, flat ends and a small leather-covered ball. The goal is a set of posts like those in rugby or American football; a point is scored when the ball goes over the cross-bar between them, and a goal when the ball goes under the cross-bar past the goalkeeper into the net. One goal equals three points. The ball may be carried on the stick if a player can find a gap in the defence, and these swift solo runs are among the most exciting moves in the game.

IT'S A GOAL!

If you do not yet know what game was being described, the following passage will enlighten you! After reading the passage, work with your partner or small group to answer these questions.

QUESTIONS

1. What are the two traditional Irish games?

2. In what ways are an All-Ireland final and a World Cup match (*a*) similar and (*b*) different?

3. Why and how is the GAA more than a sports organisation?

4. What is the state of (*a*) rugby and (*b*) soccer in Ireland?

ti:ʃəx

a:r'deʃ
f'iənə fa:l'

The former Taoiseach* Garret FitzGerald once admitted that he would rather study a train timetable than watch a football match. He paid for the remark by losing several points in a subsequent popularity poll. On another occasion the ard-fheis* of Fianna Fáil* was adjourned to give
5   delegates a chance to watch the Grand National and the international rugby match between England and Ireland on television. Sport is not so much a pastime in Ireland as a way of life; if you don't play it, you watch it, talk about it, get into arguments and debt over it, and, of course, retire to the pub because of it. If your man, team, horse or dog wins, you have
10   just cause for celebration; if not, you have a very valid reason for drowning your sorrows.

And that's the way it's been for quite some time. The myths tell us that long before the Greeks worked out a blueprint for the Olympics, organised games were regular events in Ireland, with competitions in running, jumping, spear or javelin throwing and hurling. According to legend nobody could join the Fianna, that heroic band of fighting men led by Fionn mac Cumhaill*, without first proving himself an athlete par excellence; and the great Cú Chulainn, apart from being a keen huntsman, was a dab hand at hurling from the moment he could stand on his own two feet.

15
f'in mak kuːəl'

Speaking of hurling, if it isn't the oldest it must surely be the fastest (and when played badly, the most dangerous) field game in the world. Fifteen men wielding hurleys—sticks made of ash-plants—use every trick in the book to get the ball past their opponents' goal-keeper and over the cross-bar for a point, or into the net for a goal, the equivalent of three points. The speed of the game and the high scoring (the area round the goal-posts has been called 'Hell's Kitchen') make it a riveting spectator sport, but because it requires such a degree of physical and mental skill, only certain counties have a tradition for good hurling. More generally popular is the other traditional Irish game, Gaelic football, which seems to be a combination of soccer, rugby and American football and, in fact, was very likely the prototype for all three.

20

25

30

For followers of both sports the highlight of the year is the All-Ireland championships, when the best counties from each province play against each other to huge crowds in Dublin's Croke Park stadium. An All-Ireland final has all the atmosphere and trappings of a World Cup match; it is attended by the President, Taoiseach, Government ministers, and church hierarchy, and it is televised live to audiences as far away as Australia. The rival supporters get up to all the usual activities of soccer fans, from waving flags to blowing klaxons, but, unlike the latter, they are not segregated into two hostile and potentially violent factions. At a Dublin-Kerry football final, for example, a 'true-blue Dub' is as likely to find himself rubbing shoulders with a 'culchie' from Ballyferriter as with one of his own. Hooliganism has rarely raised its ugly head in Gaelic games, and rivalry tends to be expressed in terms of wits rather than fists. 'Have you heard the latest Kerry joke?' asks the nobody's-fool Kerryman, obligingly answering his own question: 'The Dublin football team!' The rear window of many a capital city car has sported stickers declaring: *Dublin for the Sam Maguire—Kerry for the holidays!*

35

40

45

The point is that Gaelic games have a unifying rather than a divisive influence. It all goes back to the late nineteenth century, when feelings of nationalism were running high. A certain Archbishop of Cashel noted that traditional Irish sports were being neglected in favour of 'such foreign and

50

fantastic field sports as lawn tennis, polo, croquet, cricket and the like,' as alien to the native culture as 'the men and women who first imported them.'

55　To rectify matters the Gaelic Athletic Association was set up. From the word go the GAA was more than an amateur sports organisation: it served as a powerful morale-booster for the ordinary rural population, who, through it, found a way of counteracting English cultural domination. More than that, it became closely associated with the struggle for independence, and

60　even today makes no secret of its nationalist leanings. In 1981, for example, it came under fire for placing notices of sympathy on the deaths of IRA hunger-strikers in the newspapers. And although the ban on members playing or attending foreign sports was dropped in 1971, twenty years later it was reaffirming its policy of barring members of the security forces in

65　Northern Ireland, to the righteous indignation of hard-line Unionist politicians. It begs the question, of course, how many police officers and British soldiers would be found queuing up for membership cards if they were given the significant green light!

Since the lifting of the 'ban' it is not uncommon to find good soccer or rugby

70　players who grew up on the hurling or Gaelic football field. Rugby is the one game that embraces all classes and creeds in Ireland. On certain winter Saturdays, anyway. On an international day in Lansdowne Road, Dublin hostelries burst at the seams with northern supporters, all amiably soaking their vocal chords. For a few brief hours northerner and southerner,

75　Protestant and Catholic, unionist and republican are united in the cry for 'Ireland,' and the day this fails to happen, the politicians might as well give up. Soccer, by contrast, is a victim of politics; hence the absurdity of one small country being represented internationally by two teams, Northern Ireland and the Republic. The home soccer scene is staged mainly on the

80　playing-fields of England or Scotland, where all the best Irish talent is to be found. Manchester United and Sheffield Wednesday have a faithful Irish following among the urban working class, who trace their fortunes on television or through the sports pages of the British tabloid press. Let Ireland be playing in the World Cup or European Cup, however, and soccer becomes

85　Cinderella on the night of the ball. For his role as fairy godmother the Leeds-born trainer Jackie Charlton has been hailed as the greatest Irishman in history. Well, since Cú Chulainn.

NOTES

ard-fheis: party conference.
culchie: a pejorative word used by town people (mainly Dubliners) to describe a country person.
Sam Maguire: the Sam Maguire Cup, awarded to the winning team in the All-Ireland football championship.

MORE QUESTIONS

Now read the passage again and answer these questions as precisely as you can. You may do this orally with a partner, and/or in writing as homework.

1. What is the connection, in paragraph 1, between Garret FitzGerald and the Fianna Fáil ard-fheis?

2. What does 'that' refer to in line 12?

3. How might 'for quite some time' (line 12) be more accurately expressed?

4. Explain in your own words why hurling is an interesting game to watch.

5. Why do you think the area round the goal-posts has been called 'Hell's Kitchen'?

6. Who or what does 'the latter' refer to in line 39?

7. Explain in your own words what is meant by the statement 'rivalry … fists' (line 44).

8. What does 'that' refer to in line 59?

9. What evidence is given of the GAA's nationalist leanings?

10. What is suggested about the answer to 'the question' in line 66?

11. Why is the 'green light' (line 68) described as 'significant'?

12. What does the writer imply when he says, 'the day … give up' (lines 76–77)?

13. In what way is the Irish soccer scene ironic both at national and international level?

14. Explain why Jackie Charlton has been 'hailed as the greatest Irishman in history' for 'his role as fairy godmother'.

SPORTING PICTURES

Six different sports are represented in these photographs. Work with a partner or group to answer the following questions.

1. Describe in detail what you see in each photograph. What has just happened? What is happening? What do you think is going to happen? What do people's (or animals'!) expressions tell you? What about the background?

2. Identify each of the six sports. There are seven photographs, so which is the odd one out? What aspect of sport does it represent?

3. Here are the captions that accompany the photographs. Can you match each caption with its photograph and say why it is appropriate?

(i)   I wish it would stop wriggling?

(ii) Beat me if you can, fellows!

(iii) Stop looking at me—you're putting me off my stroke!

(iv) Very funny, but you're not going to get it!

(v)   So that's why they've been going to ballet classes in their spare time!

(vi) Keep your feet up!

(vii) Serious business in progress.

A

B

C

D

E

F

G

81

WRITING

A dictionary definition of 'sport' is 'physical activity done, especially outdoors, for exercise and amusement, usually played in a special area and according to fixed rules.'

This being so, how true is it to say that in today's world

'The real meaning has been taken out of sport'?

Write a balanced composition on this topic. First of all, with a partner or group, discuss your answers to these questions.

1. As you will have discovered from reading the passage 'It's a goal!', criticism has been made of the GAA for allowing politics to interfere with sport. Can you think of any other instances in recent times when there has been political interference with sporting activities? To what extent do you agree with what happened or is happening?

2. There are, of course, other factors involved—positive as well as negative. Here are the notes one person has jotted down, but they need to be organised. Sort the ideas into two lists: those supporting the statement and those denying that it is true. Then discuss the relevance and validity of each point. Can you add to the lists you have made?

Television—sport more accessible to more people.
Drugs (athletes taking steroids).
Professionalism—only meaning is money.
People have more leisure time and money.
Increased awareness of health—interest in diet and physical activities.
But—fanatics! e.g. people who give themselves heart attacks by jogging.
Violence, e.g. rivalry between soccer fans.

3. By now you should have a number of ideas. As homework, (*a*) decide what your approach is going to be, and (*b*) organise your ideas, paragraph by paragraph, into a coherent argument that reaches a logical conclusion. Then write your composition, keeping in mind the advice you have been given in previous units.

HORSE TALK

Here are the names of some equestrian sports and the words connected with them. Check their meanings, then use them to fill in the numbered spaces.

race meeting	gymkhana	dressage
point-to-point	show-jumping	cross-country
eventing	clear round	fault (2)

i

.... [1] is an all-round equestrian sport. It involves (a) .... [2], i.e. the horse performs a number of controlled movements in response to the rider's commands, (b) .... [3], i.e. horse and rider are timed as they cover a course that includes fences, and (c) jumping in an arena.

ii

The children always look forward to the local .... [4]. Besides jumping, there are all kinds of competitions for them to take part in. Their ponies seem to love it too!

iii

The difference between a .... [5] and a .... [6] is that the former takes place on a permanent, specially designed course while the latter is run across open country.

iv

The aim in .... [7] is for horse and rider to complete a set course in which there are a number of different kinds of jumps. If a jump is knocked down, the penalty is four .... [8]. A .... [9] means that the course has been completed without any .... [10].

For many people Ireland is synonymous with horses. As one writer put it, 'some foreigners still seem to think an Irishman is a horse with red hair.' Knowledge about and respect for the noble animal cuts right through society, from the business magnate with his string of racehorses to the traveller who deals in ponies at country fairs. Quite apart from regular race meetings, point-to-points, and gymkhanas, not a month passes that doesn't feature an important equestrian event. For the show-jumping world the highlight of the year is the Dublin Horse Show, held each August in the grounds of the Royal Dublin Society in Ballsbridge.

83

Read the two passages and discuss with your partner or group what each tells you about (A) the horse show and (B) the writer.

A

Dublin Horse Show was a triumph. The Irish needed a good one, after last year's rain-drenched summer show. The weather was reasonably co-operative this time, but there was more to it than that: the Irish actually won their own Aga Khan Nations Cup, and better still, me boys, it was a great week for sellin' the horses.

For remember, the Dublin Horse Show is a sale just as much as a rosette-winning affair. And the great virtues of the Irish horse—equable temperament, versatility, and above all durability—were being sought by buyers from all over Europe, and further afield.

Some British show organisers should go on a refresher course to Dublin Horse Show, because, dare I say it, they still do things in style. And let us not forget they inherited that style from the bad old days of British rule.

On Aga Khan day they have no fewer than three splendid military bands to march in the national teams. They play everyone's national anthem, at great length. All the stewards and judges wear full morning dress and carry furled umbrellas.

And best of all, the crowd 'ooh' and 'aah' in a way we have almost forgotten in British outdoor show-jumping. Every round is a tense affair, closely scrutinised by a rapt crowd. They shush anyone who dares to clap during the round, but afterwards they give thunderous applause to friend and foe alike.

The exultation when the Irish team won on Friday afternoon had to be seen, and heard, to be believed. Even a burst water pipe in the main ring failed to dampen the occasion.

B

I always find the Spring Show absolutely delightful, but I cannot say the same for the Horse Show in August. This, it must be said, is a purely personal opinion and not at all shared by the rest of the world. The Horse Show attracts horses, which is good, and people who like horses, which is also good. But it brings with it its own brand of 'Hooray Henrys' and terrible shouting, affected people, which is bad. Or I think it brings them …

It's sort of burned into my brain—the stories about debs coming from other lands and attending Horse Show Balls and behaving badly and throwing bread rolls at each other and at the waiters and squirting syphons of soda water. It all seemed a really idiotic and offensive way to carry on, and I never saw a strand of humour in it at all. But as I say, I am in the minority about the Horse Show. Thousands of people who like horses and who like people have a marvellous time on green turf among white fences and bright flowers and lovely hats every August. My own sourness about the place is not echoed at all.

In fact I was once interviewed about the Horse Show on British television, and it's a bad memory. 'Do many people come to the Horse Show?' the smiling David Dimbleby asked me. 'No, it's only a few upper-class people,' I said confidently, and indeed wildly inaccurately, as it turned out. The camera cut to thousands of people streaming in the gates. 'Are the Irish people very interested in the results of the jumping?' he asked. 'No, no, only a few. The great mass of the people couldn't care less,' I said, with all the sureness possible. The camera cut to a shot of 10,000 Irish people screeching their support for the Irish horse and rider in the National Cup. My views on the Horse Show are obviously unsound.

NOTES

Hooray Henrys: a British idiom for young men of the upper classes whose only concern is to have a good time.

debs [an abbreviated form of 'debutantes']: upper-class young women who are making their first appearance in society.

MULTIPLE-CHOICE QUESTIONS

Now read the passages again and answer these multiple-choice questions. Choose the best answer in each case.

1. Which kind of publication do you think passage A was written for?
   (*a*) a women's weekly magazine
   (*b*) an international news magazine
   (*c*) a social gossip magazine
   (*d*) an equestrian magazine

2. The tone of passage A could best be described as—
   (*a*) generally admiring but slightly patronising
   (*b*) unreservedly approving
   (*c*) sarcastic and condescending
   (*d*) frivolous.

3. It seems most likely that passage B was written by
   (a) an exponent of Irish life and traditions
   (b) a sports commentator for Irish television
   (c) a well-known media personality
   (d) a freelance journalist commissioned to do an article on the Dublin Horse Show.

4. In expressing her opinions, the writer of passage B is
   (a) ignorant
   (b) indifferent
   (c) defensive
   (d) dishonest.

5. How do you think the writer of passage B felt after the television interview?
   (a) unsound
   (b) embarrassed
   (c) sour
   (d) annoyed.

TO HUNT OR NOT TO HUNT

Blood sports are alive and well in Ireland. Coursing—where trained greyhounds are sent after a hare—has an enthusiastic following in certain parts of the country. (This is not to be confused with greyhound racing, commonly known as 'the dogs', where the greyhounds chase a mechanical hare on a specially designed track.) The other most popular—or most notorious, as the case may be—blood sport is hunting to hounds. In fact Ireland probably has more hunt clubs per square kilometre than any other country, with over a hundred recognised packs, including 2 staghound, 32 foxhound and 41 harrier (hare-hunting) packs. Oscar Wilde described fox hunting as 'the unspeakable in pursuit of the uneatable.' In recent years the Irish Council Against Blood Sports has campaigned to have coursing and hunting made illegal. The fight goes on.

Here you have (A) a letter to a newspaper in support of fox hunting, and (B) excerpts from *Animal Watch*, the magazine of the Irish Council Against Blood Sports.

1. Working in groups of three, one student should read A and make a note of the points in favour of hunting, another should read B and list the points against it, while the third reads both A and B to see both sides of the story.

In the following role play, the As will be Roland Rountree, the Bs will be the editor of Animal Watch and the Cs will be the presenter of a radio programme.

2. Roland Rountree and the editor of *Animal Watch* (you should give him or her a name) have been asked to express their points of view on a radio programme presented by Gay Kenny. Gay's job is to introduce the debate, ask leading questions, intervene when necessary—in other words, guide and control the proceedings. You have five minutes on the air, after which Gay should decide who has won the argument.

3. The radio presenters should now compare their verdicts to see what the overall result is: 'to hunt or not to hunt.'

A

Sir,

The rantings of ignorant town folk against the ancient and noble sport of fox hunting provoke me to put pen to paper in its defence. May I remind those with apparently more refined sensibilities than mine that it was the poet Oisín* who told St Patrick, 'To the chiefs of the Fianna it is sweeter to hear the voice of the hounds than to seek salvation.'

oʃiːnˊ

Leaving aside the fact that hunting is a centuries-old tradition and an important part of our heritage that must be preserved at all costs, let me also remind people that foxes are pests that feed on valuable livestock. Any farmer will tell them that if it weren't for the much-appreciated work of the local hunt in controlling the fox population, he would have to use his own infinitely more cruel and less dignified method of ridding his land of the vermin: by shooting or gassing. Moreover, huntsmen and women are, by the very nature of their activities, confirmed conservationists, helping not only to preserve the ecological balance but to care for the countryside they ride through.

I cannot expect anybody who has not ridden to hounds to understand the thrill of the chase for both hunter and hunted. Yes, the fox is given a glorious chance to disport himself in his own environment in a manner that is totally natural to him. No fox worth his salt has made that final bid for freedom without taking pleasure in his physical prowess and the instinctive desire to 'out-fox' the hounds.

For those who remain unconvinced I might add that hunting people are not the blood-thirsty ghouls they believe us to be. It is the chase, not the kill, that we enjoy, and in fact it is relatively uncommon to catch a fox. The majority of Reynards live to run another day.

Yours faithfully,
Roland Rountree
The Den,
Ballyblazes, Co. Galway

B

'Hunting down a fox with sixty to eighty howling dogs is savage beyond all doubt. In some cases it is hunted from three to five hours until fear and exhaustion finally wear him down. The hounds close in and seize him. He is pulled from one to the other, and death comes slowly because he is tough.' (Letter from a Co. Galway farmer.)

'The killing of foxes in the interests of sheep farming cannot be justified. This is the clear message of a three-year scientific investigation conducted by Aberdeen University. The survey found that when left in peace, even when other food was scarce, foxes rarely took lambs, and that the fox population did not increase beyond a level consistent with the availability of rabbits, voles, and carrion. The fox's preference for rabbits, voles and carrion means that farmers may have more to gain from the presence of foxes.' (Report on new research.)

Reports from a recent issue of the *Irish Field*:
The Scarteen Hunt: hunting started the second week in August and hounds worked well in spite of the drought and too many foxes, a lot of them small and poor, maybe second litters. In all, 15 brace were accounted for, at least half of these above ground.
Tipperary Hunt: have had a successful season so far with 10½ brace having been killed above ground. In spite of very dry conditions, a healthy average of 1½ brace a day has been accounted for.

NOTE

brace: a pair of foxes

BLOOD SPORTS—WHERE DO YOU STAND?

Coursing and fox-, hare- and stag-hunting are legal in Ireland. Otter- and badger-hunting, cock-fighting and dog-fighting are not, although they are still pursued in certain areas.

What blood sports (apart from those mentioned) are pursued in your own country? Have any efforts been made to ban them? Do you think they should be banned? You can discuss this informally as a class, i.e. with each person expressing his or her opinion, or you can organise a formal debate, with half the class proposing and the other half opposing the motion:
'All blood sports should be banned by law.'

VOCABULARY PRACTICE

In each case choose the word that best completes the sentence, but keep in mind that the word you have come across earlier in this unit is not necessarily the right answer!

1. Because of the cramped, unsanitary conditions, feelings among the prisoners were .... high.

(*a*) rising   (*b*) running   (*c*) roused   (*d*) raised

2. After I failed my exams, being given this job as translator was just the morale .... I needed.

(*a*) raiser   (*b*) booster   (*c*) lifter   (*d*) rise

3. The reason I have a hangover is that my brother's girl-friend gave him the push and I had to spend the evening helping him to drown his ....

(*a*) disappointment   (*b*) depression   (*c*) grievances   (*d*) sorrows

4. What I need is a good long walk to work .... that huge dinner we've just eaten.

(*a*) off   (*b*) out   (*c*) away   (*d*) in

5. Quite honestly, getting away at this time of the year is so expensive and so difficult that it .... the question whether we should go on holiday at all.

(a) asks   (b) raises   (c) poses   (d) begs

6. What have you children been getting .... while we were out? Some devilment, judging by the look on your faces!

(a) on with   (b) off with   (c) around to   (d) up to

7. Such blood sports .... fox hunting and bull-fighting should be made illegal.

(a) for example   (b) as   (c) like   (d) such as

8. The protest march was very well attended. People came from all over the city and even further ....

(a) afield   (b) abroad   (c) afoot   (d) distant

9. I get great satisfaction out of doing the ironing and seeing a pile of neatly .... clothes afterwards.

(a) rolled   (b) furled   (c) folded   (d) bent

10. Don't let Patrick's criticisms .... your enthusiasm for the project. He's just envious because he can't take part.

(a) dampen   (b) moisten   (c) fade   (d) decline

11. How's Una .... on these days? I haven't seen her for months.

(a) carrying   (b) going   (c) getting   (d) doing

12. The way to make sure you've washed all the shampoo out of your hair is to run your fingers tightly down a few strands; it should make a .... sound.

(a) screeching   (b) squealing   (c) screaming   (d) squeaking

13. What you do is a matter of complete indifference to me. I really couldn't care ....

        (*a*) less   (*b*) least   (*c*) anything   (*d*) nothing

14. Our estimate of how much it would cost to build the conservatory was .... inaccurate. It cost us three times as much as we intended to spend!

        (*a*) wildly   (*b*) widely   (*c*) fairly   (*d*) quite

15. They packed their bags with sweaters, boots and anoraks for their holiday in Connemara. As it .... out, they didn't need them because the weather was exceptionally hot.

        (*a*) came   (*b*) happened   (*c*) turned   (*d*) transpired

CLOZE

The following report (by Séamus Martin) appeared in the *Irish Times* on 28 March 1991, the morning after Ireland played England in a qualifying match for the 1992 European Cup. Read it, then fill each numbered space with one suitable word.

'We beat them one-all again!' That was the general verdict among celebrating Dubliners .... [1] the Republic of Ireland's draw with England at Wembley. That 5–0 .... [2] against Turkey in the first game of the series now looks .... [3] being a major factor when it .... [4] to deciding the single qualifier from group 7 of the European championship.

A .... [5] at Wembley and an extremely favourable goal difference .... [6] the people of Dublin out on the street shortly before 10 o'clock .... [7] night as Dublin .... [8] alive again, ... [9] been a ghost town for almost three hours.

.... [10] early as 6.45 the traffic thinned; there were Christmas-like queues for taxis as citizens .... [11] a dash to watch the game on television in the comfort of .... [12]—a place for .... [13] most of the taximen had already opted.
In the Clock Bar .... [14] Thomas Street in the Liberties, the heart of Dublin's real working-class soccer support, the customers .... [15] on their seats to watch the game on the big screen.

This reporter walked from .... [16] to the city centre at half ....
[17]. A peek through the .... [18] of Dame Street's myriad
restaurants .... [19] empty tables all the way, ... [20] in the
expensive 'Les Frères Jacques', where the well-to-do filled the seats in
sublime and sedate isolation from the real world.

One of the most important events on the Irish sporting calendar is the
Galway races, held every August. Quite apart from racing enthusiasts, it
attracts huge crowds of people who are simply there for the social occasion.
This song will tell you who they are, where they come from . . . and even
why they're there!

NOTES

boozer: (informal) pub

ould one: while 'an ould one' simply means a woman, 'my/your/his etc.
              ould one' refers to the person's mother or wife

crubeen: an Anglicised form of the Irish word for a pig's trotter—
              popular fare in the pre-burger-and-chips days!

failte: the Irish word for 'welcome'.

Listen to the song on the cassette and then sing along with it.

The Galway Races

1.

As I roved out to Galway town to seek for recreation
On the seventeenth of August my mind was elevated,
There were multitudes assembled with their tickets at the station;
My eyes began to dazzle and I goin' to see the races.
With me Whack, fol the do, fol the did-de-ley, i-dle ay.

2.

There were multitudes from Aran and the cleaver lads from Clifden,
The boys from Connemara and the Clare unmarried maidens.
There were people from Cork city who were loyal, true and faithful
Who brought home Fenian prisoners from dying in foreign nations.
With me Whack, fol the do, fol the did-de-ley, i-dle ay.

3.

The tents are in rotation round the middle of the course,
With the best accommodation that the world can produce.
The landlady's ide with her bottle and her water
And she's multiplying the whiskey lest the boozer should run shorter.
With me Whack, fol the do, fol the did-de-ley, i-dle ay.

4.

It's there you'll see the pipers and the fiddlers competing
And the nimble-footed dancers and they tripping on the daisies.
And they call for whiskey freely and they pay before they go,
And they tickle the girls among the crowd and their ould ones never know.
With me Whack, fol the do, fol the did-de-ley, i-dle ay.

5.

It's there you'll see confectioners with sugarsticks and dainties,
The lozenges and oranges, the lemonade and raisins,
The gingerbread and spices to accommodate the ladies
And a big crubeen for threepence to be picking while you're able.
With me Whack, fol the do, fol the did-de-ley, i-dle ay.

6.

It's there you'll see the gamblers, the thimbles and the garters
And the sporting Wheel of Fortune with the four and twenty quarters.
There were others without scruple pelting wattles at poor Maggy
And her father well contented and he looking at his daughter.
With me Whack, fol the do, fol the did-de-ley, i-dle ay.

7.

It's there you'd see the jockeys and they mounted on most stately;
The pink and blue, the orange and green, the emblem of our nation.
When the bell was rung for starting all the horses seemed impatient;
I thought they never stood on ground, their speed was so amazing.
With me Whack, fol the do, fol the did-de-ley, i-dle ay.

8.

There was half a million people there of all denominations;
The Catholic, the Protestant, the Jew and Presbyterian.
There was yet no animosity, no matter what persuasion
But failte and hospitality inducing fresh acquaintance.
With me Whack, fol the do, fol the did-de-ley, i-dle ay.

Unit 6

MAKING HISTORY

WHAT DO WE LEARN FROM THE PAST?

Assuming that history is a subject you have studied at one time or another, discuss your answers to the following questions with a partner or group, and then compare them with the rest of the class.

1. How well was the history of your country taught at school? Did you, for example, learn local history? Are there gaps in your knowledge? If so, why? Did learning about the past help you to understand the present? Can you think of specific examples to support your view?

2. History is made by people. In general, do people learn from the mistakes made in the past? If not, why not?

3. John de Courcy Ireland, a well-known maritime historian and socialist, known especially for his dedicated work on behalf of the lifeboats, was educated at an English public school in the 1920s. His stepfather, he says, forbade him to learn history, because a knowledge of this subject would only be a hindrance in the career he had chosen for him: the British civil service. In fact the young man studied history on his own, and won a scholarship to Oxford. Can you suggest any possible reasons for his stepfather's attitude? Are any of them valid, in your opinion? Are there ever valid reasons for not being allowed to study the history of one's own country?

CONQUEST

Understanding Ireland today means understanding its troubled past: its long history of colonisation, the repeated attempts to subjugate its people, and their struggle for freedom. Read the following passage about the period when Ireland was first colonised by England; then, with a partner or group, answer these questions.

QUESTIONS

1. In what ways did Ireland benefit from the Viking settlers?

2. How did the country and the way of life change under the Normans?

3. What comparison can be drawn between the two waves of settlers?

4. What reasons are given for the bond established between the Normans and the Gaels? How and why was it strengthened, and what were the repercussions?

The round towers built by the monks were put to good use when the Norse invaders began arriving in their longboats. They first plundered the coastal settlements as early as 795, carrying away with them whatever loot they could find. The gold and bronze treasures of the monasteries were particularly at risk, hence the round towers with their high entrances, to which the monks would retreat by means of ladders when an attack was threatened. These Vikings came and went, and finally came and stayed. Their presence forced the Irish to unite under the high king, Brian Ború of Munster, and their military power was finally broken at the Battle of Clontarf in 1014. In one way the Danes were defeated, but their influence remained, as they intermarried with the Irish, and they are remembered now not as fierce plunderers but as traders, shipbuilders, the introducers of coinage, and the founders of towns in the modern sense. Howth, Wicklow, Wexford and Waterford are all Viking names, but when they established themselves on the site of the future capital city, they gave it the Irish name Dubh Linn ('black pool'). Baile Átha Cliath, the name used by the early native settlers on the mouth of the Liffey, is retained in Irish, and can be seen on signposts, buses, and postmarks.

Although the Battle of Clontarf was a victory for the Irish, the powerful uniting force behind it was decimated by the death of Brian Ború. So, while William the Conqueror was setting himself up as king of England, the Irish were quarrelling among themselves in a continual struggle for the high kingship. It was only a matter of time before William and his powerful Norman barons would turn their attention to the smaller island, and the opportunity was soon provided by the king of Leinster, Diarmaid Mac Murchú*. This gentleman can be said to have a lot to answer for; finding himself on the losing team regarding the high kingship, and embroiled in domestic problems (an indiscretion with another king's wife), he invited the Norman adventurer Strongbow to help him. Strongbow not only obliged but married Mac Murchú's daughter and became the next king of Leinster. Thus began the political struggle between England and Ireland that has dominated Irish history until the present day.

The Normans who followed Strongbow very quickly stamped their identity on the country. The bickering Irish chieftains could offer little resistance to their superior strength in arms, and soon the countryside featured the walled-in land, Norman castles and Romanesque abbeys and cathedrals that betokened the permanence of their occupation. Today's telephone directory proves how well they dug themselves in: its pages are liberally scattered with the names of their descendants, distinguished from those of the native Irish by the prefixes *de* and *Fitz* instead of *Mac* (meaning 'son of') and *Ó* (meaning

d'iərməd' mak morəxu:

'grandson of'). Yet while the Normans made great social and political changes, such as introducing the feudal system of government and inheritance through the first-born male, from the moment of their arrival the
45   same process of assimilation that had characterised all previous invasions began to take effect. To the consternation of the English crown, they became 'more Irish than the Irish themselves.' In an effort to control the wayward Norman barons, Edward III took stern measures in 1366. The Statutes of Kilkenny forbade the settlers to speak Irish, use Irish names, marry into
50   Irish families, dress like the Irish, adopt Irish laws, or play the Irish game of hurling. That it was felt necessary to pass these statutes speaks for itself; the settlers had done precisely what their name suggests, and done it so thoroughly that Edward's punitive measures were a total failure. On the part of both conquerors and conquered, it was a case of 'if you can't beat them,
55   join them.' By the end of the fifteenth century only a small area known as the Pale was effectively under the rule of the English crown, and whatever life existed outside it was considered uncivilised. From this derives the common idiom 'beyond the pale', used of any behaviour that is unacceptable or unreasonable.

60   The bond between the Normans and Gaels was further reinforced a century later by their common Catholicism. But while attempts to impose the new religion of Reformation England had little success, the English policy of bringing the Irish to heel throughout the following centuries was ruthless in its methods and far-reaching in its consequences. The country was
65   devastated by perpetual warfare, and those who survived, deprived of their homes, their lands, their possessions, their religion, and their dignity, were forced to grovel to alien overlords or go into exile in France and Spain.

MORE QUESTIONS

Now read the passage again and answer these questions as precisely as you can. You may do this orally with a partner, and/or in writing as homework.

1. Explain how the Norse invaders 'plundered the coastal settlements' (line 2–3).

2. Why did the round towers have high entrances?

3. What is suggested by the phrase 'in one way' (line 10)?

4. What does 'it' refer to in line 20?

5. Why is the death of BrianBorú of such significance?

6. What is the effect of referring to Diarmaid Mac Murchú as 'this gentleman' (line 26), and why can he be said 'to have a lot to answer for'?

7. In your own words, say why the Irish chieftains could offer little resistance to the Normans.

8. Give another word for 'betokened' in line 38.

9. What is the connection between *de* and *Fitz*, and *Mac* and *Ó*?

10. Why are the Norman barons described as 'wayward' (line 47), and what examples can you give of their waywardness?

11. What 'speaks for itself' (line 51), and what does the phrase mean?

12. What precisely had the settlers done (line 52)?

13. In your own words, describe the English policy in Ireland from the sixteenth century onwards and its effects on the people.

WRITING

Choose either question 1 or question 2 but don't make a decision until you have fully discussed both questions.

1. 'The only thing that history has taught us is that it teaches us nothing.' Think about this for a few minutes, then share your views with the rest of the class. The opinions expressed will, hopefully, help you to work out a good argument for your composition.

Remember: the more you can illustrate the points you make, the more convincing and interesting your writing will be.

2. If you had the opportunity to step into a time machine, which period in history would you choose to go back to (for a temporary visit only!), and why? Imagine that the machine breaks down; which period would you least like to be stranded in, and why?

Again, think about these questions for a few minutes before discussing them with the class. Then write your composition as homework.

LISTENING

You are going to hear a lecture from a series of radio broadcasts, 'Understanding Ireland'. Below are the notes made by a student who has already heard the lecture, but, because he wasn't concentrating at the time, he failed to get all of the important facts. Read his notes and be prepared to fill in the missing information. Then listen to the lecture twice.

<u>1601</u>   Defeat of the Irish and .... [1] armies at Battle of Kinsale.

____ [2] Flight of the Earls.

          Plantation of Ulster. Settlers from .... [3] brought over to colonise province.

____ [4] Catholic-Gaelic rebellion.

<u>1649</u>   Cromwell arrives in Ireland. Catholic landowners forced to west; hence expression 'To .... [5] or to Connacht.'

____ [6] Catholic James II deposed in England.

<u>1689</u>   Siege and relief of Derry.

____ [7] William of Orange defeats James II at Battle of the Boyne. (Commemorated annually by Orangemen on the .... [8] July.)

____ [9] Catholic defeat marked by Treaty of Limerick. Only .... [10] per cent of the land now owned by Catholic Irish.

<u>1695</u>   Flight of the Wild Geese—thousands of Irishmen flee to .... [11].

          First Penal laws enacted against Catholics.

          .... [12] per cent of land held by Catholics.

<u>1714</u>   7 per cent of land held by Catholics.

THE MAKING OF A CAPITAL CITY

If 'clothes maketh the man,' as the proverb says, then it is equally true to say that bricks and mortar and great slabs of grey granite made Dublin a capital city. The appearance of the city changed gradually from the time it was founded by the Vikings, each age of cultural and political domination stamping its own architectural identity. Then in the eighteenth century, despite the harsh Penal Laws, there was relative political stability and, for the privileged classes, peace and prosperity. Within the space of a hundred years Dublin underwent a thorough and very dramatic face-lift. The face has suffered from the ravages of time since then, but the character of the city today is essentially the creation of what became known as the Georgian Age.

To celebrate Dublin's millennium year in 1988, the *Irish Times* produced a supplement including an article by Thomas Pakenham on the 'long and turbulent history' of the capital. Here are six photographs of different parts of Dublin, and six extracts from Thomas Pakenham's article. Each extract describes one of the photographs. Working in pairs or groups—

1. Describe what you see in each photograph. You may immediately recognise some of the places or buildings, but what can you say about their function, their style of architecture, the kind of people they were designed for, etc.?

A

B

C

D

E

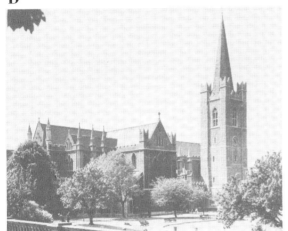

F

2. Now read the extracts from the article and match them with the appropriate photographs.

A: .... B: .... C: .... D: .... E: .... F: ....

i

The brutal wars of Elizabeth's reign propelled the city to a new prosperity. English mercenaries flooded over, complaining loudly of the price of Irish ale but dependent on Dublin merchants for their supplies. Though the city still clung to its medieval walls, castle, and narrow lanes, the wattle-and-daub houses were at last changing to stone and slate. Elizabeth's most lasting contribution to Dublin was to sanction a handsome new public building south-east of the walls on the site of an old abbey: Trinity College. It was designed to educate Protestant clergy for her Irish subjects and prevent their infection 'from Popery and other ill qualities.'

ii

The Restoration gave Dublin time and confidence at last to slough off its medieval skin, and a great viceroy determined to reshape the city. He was James Butler, first Duke of Ormonde, an urbane Irish grandee who had shared Charles II's exile in Paris … His first great splash was to buy up 1,500 acres of open fields west of the city. In Phoenix Park he gave the people a royal deer park, bigger and more splendid than any royal park in London. His second big splash complemented it. Just across the Liffey, at Kilmainham, he constructed the Royal Hospital, a home for old soldiers modelled on the Invalides in Paris. The first stone was laid by Ormonde in 1680, and the vast building was completed in 1684.

iii

When the Normans came in 1170, it was again the result of a local squabble. They were invited by a king of Leinster who had fled to England. Within a few years they had tidied up the confusion of centuries. Norman architecture and Norman institutions were imposed on Dublin and the Pale—the territory within about thirty miles. Two great stone cathedrals, Christ Church within the walls and St Patrick's just beyond, soon towered over the wooden houses of the city. Both were built in an uncompromising Anglo-Norman style, apt symbol that Dublin was and would be for the next seven hundred years a British garrison town in Ireland.

iv

Now followed the golden age of their enemies, the century of Protestant peace and Protestant triumph. No-one would now defend their political ideals, nor the methods they used to keep the Catholics out of power. But they had a style and a sense of pride that set them apart from a mere English garrison. It was this colonial pride that gave—and gives—the eighteenth-century streets of Dublin their special feel. The streets would be wider, the squares would be larger, the great monuments—Parliament, the Four Courts, the Custom House—would all be more splendid. It took a century, and in the process the city became a masterpiece: one of the wonders of the eighteenth-century world.

v

Meanwhile, inspired by Ormonde, Dublin Corporation began to pull up its socks. It enclosed the ancient commonage on the south-east, at St Stephen's Green, to create a public pleasure ground flanked by terraces. Their guiding principle was Ormonde's: the cult of splendour. As the corporation minutes put it, 'the whole design of all persons concerned … is chiefly the reputation, advantage and pleasure of the cittie.' Stephen's Green was to be the pattern for Dublin's broad eighteenth-century streets and leafy squares.

vi

The pioneer of the housing drive south-east was the young James Fitzgerald, Earl of Kildare and later first Earl of Leinster. He bought some cheap land east of Coot's Lane, which he renamed Kildare Street, and built himself a great mansion in 1745: Leinster House. It was designed by Richard Cassels, the leading Palladian architect and specialist in country houses, and even today as home of the Dáil and Seanad it still has the incongruous feel of a country house. When the Duke of Leinster was asked whether this site was not somewhat remote, he is supposed to have replied, 'They will follow me wherever I go.'

3. Can you now put the photographs in chronological order? To do this you will need to read the texts again to find clues about the date of each place.

(*a*) Now the Bank of Ireland, this was the first building in the world designed and built (1728) to house a parliament.
(*b*) Once a private house, now the seat of Dáil Éireann.
(*c*) Built in 1591, the Rubrics are the oldest part of Ireland's oldest university.
(*d*) The largest enclosed park in Europe.
(*e*) Eighteenth-century house in the heart of Dublin.
(*f*) Founded by Archbishop Comyn in 1191, it was named after Ireland's patron saint.

1: ……. 2: ……. 3: ……. 4: ……. 5: ……. 6: …….

THE MAKING OF A MAN

A city is made by people: people found it, plan it, change it, and, just by living and working there, give it its character. Is the opposite true—i.e. to what extent is a person 'made' by the city (town, village, neighbourhood) he or she lives in?

Dublin has had a profound influence on a long list of writers—not all of them Dubliners, or, for that matter, Irish. Here are extracts from two poems about Dublin.

1. To help you to appreciate them, first do this vocabulary exercise with a partner or group. Check the meaning of

(a) the nouns 'catcalls', 'squalor', 'bravado', 'lash',

(b) the adjectives 'seedy', 'arid', 'cute', 'dreary', and

(c) the verbs 'wallow', 'crouch', and 'disclaim'. Then use them to complete the following sentences:

i.

The poor dog! He knew I'd be angry with him for digging a hole in the flower-bed, so he tried to hide; I found him .... behind the garden shed.

ii.

The students rented a cheap flat in a rather .... part of the city. When I went to see them I found them living in .... Nobody had bothered to do any washing-up for weeks, and the place smelt of stale beer and cigarette smoke.

iii.

You won't impress me by going in for a swim in the middle of January. I know you're only doing it for ....!

iv.

The jockey gave the horse a .... of his whip to make it gallop harder.

v.

When the department store approached him about the unpaid account, he said, 'My wife bought those things. I .... all responsibility for her debts.'

vi.

On the first day of my holidays I just lay on the beach and .... in the sunshine, thinking about all my poor colleagues working in the office!

vii.

Another .... winter day. I'm so fed up with grey skies and rain.

viii.

The Minister for Health's decision to close down the hospital was met with .... and other noises of protest.

ix.

Despite the jokes made about them, Kerry people are very .... You won't find one you can outwit.

x.

The preacher gave a long, ... sermon on the evils of money. Well, I think that's what it was about, but frankly it was so boring that I stopped listening after the first five minutes.

2. Now read each poem—or better, listen to it being read aloud—several times. Don't try to 'understand' it immediately. Read or listen to it first for the rhythm, then with your senses for the sights, sounds, smells, etc., before you begin to respond to what the poet is saying. At each stage compare your reactions with your partner or group. Then discuss your answers to the questions that follow.

DUBLIN MADE ME

Dublin made me, not the secret poteen still,
The raw and hungry hills of the West,
The lean road flung over profitless bog
Where only a snipe could nest,

Where the sea takes its tithe of every boat.
Bawneen and currach have no allegiance of
    mine.
Nor the cute, self-deceiving talkers of the
    South
Who look to the East for a sign.

The soft and dreary midlands with their tame
    canals
Wallow between sea and sea, remote from
    adventure,
And Northward a far and fortified province
Crouches under the lash of arid censure.

I disclaim all fertile meadows, all tilled land,
The evil that grows from it and the good,
But the Dublin of old statutes, this arrogant
    city,
Stirs proudly and secretly in my blood …

Donagh MacDonagh (1912–1968)

DUBLIN

Grey brick upon brick,
Declamatory bronze
On sombre pedestals—
O'Connell, Grattan, Moore—
And the brewery tugs and the swans
On the balustraded stream
And the bare bones of a fanlight
Over a hungry door
And the air soft on the cheek
And porter running from the taps
With a head of yellow cream
And Nelson on his pillar
Watching his world collapse.

This was never my town,
I was not born nor bred
Nor schooled here and she will not
Have me alive or dead
But yet she holds my mind
With her seedy elegance,
With her gentle veils of rain
And all her ghosts that walk
And all that hide behind
Her Georgian façades—
The catcalls and the pain,
The glamour of her squalor,
The bravado of her talk.

Louis MacNeice (1907–1963)

(For notes on each poem, see page 106)

NOTES (DUBLIN MADE ME)

poteen [an Anglicised spelling of the Irish word 'poitín']: a form of illicit alcohol made from barley or potatoes in various parts of the country, especially the west.

bog: area of wet, peaty land typical of many parts of Ireland, particularly the west.

snipe: a species of water-bird.

tithe: literally a tenth part, traditionally the contribution people had to make to the church.

bawneen [an Anglicised spelling of the Irish word 'báinín']: home-spun tweed cloth traditionally woven in the west.

NOTES (DUBLIN)

declamatory bronze: The statues, cast in bronze, look as though they were declaiming because of their oratorical poses.

brewery tugs: the small boats belonging to Guinness's brewery that travelled up and down the Liffey.

balustraded stream: The bridges over the river, e.g. O'Connell Bridge, have balustrades (like the banisters of a staircase).

fanlight: the small semi-circular window over a typical Georgian door, shaped rather like an opened fan.

Nelson: Until it was blown up in 1966, Nelson's Pillar, with a statue of the British admiral Lord Nelson on top, dominated O'Connell Street.

QUESTIONS

1. Donagh MacDonagh was a native Dubliner, while Louis MacNeice was born in Belfast. How is this difference shown in their poems?

2. Ironically, MacNeice's poem tells you more about Dublin. What picture does he present of the city, and what is his relationship with it? Pick out and discuss what you think are key words, phrases, or lines.

3. MacDonagh defines his relationship with Dublin by taking you on a journey through provincial Ireland. Why? What image does he give of the places he mentions? How important are the last two lines?

4. Compare the feelings of the two poets for Dublin. Are they totally different or can you see some similarity between them?

5. Has any city, town or village—not necessarily the one you were brought up in—had a profound influence on you?

AN IRISH SOLUTION TO AN IRISH PROBLEM

Poverty, injustice and corruption were rife in the eighteenth century. Absentee landlords, so called because they rarely visited their properties, employed bailiffs to collect extortionate rents from their peasant tenants—an open invitation for them to line their own pockets. In the meantime Georgian Dublin was taking shape, with its elegant town-houses and magnificent Palladian public buildings. As Dean of St Patrick's Cathedral, Jonathan Swift (1667–1745), author of *Gulliver's*

Travels, was very much aware of the squalor and misery of the poor in Dublin. He reckoned that 120,000 children were born every year to people who had no means of looking after them. In 1729 he made a suggestion about how the situation might be alleviated, which he called *A Modest Proposal for Preventing the Children of the Poor in Ireland from being Burdensome, and for Making them Beneficial*. Read this extract from it, and answer the questions that follow.

I have been assured by a very knowing American of my acquaintance in London, that a young healthy child well nursed is at a year old a most delicious, nourishing and wholesome food, whether stewed, roasted, baked, or boiled, and I make no doubt that it will equally serve in a
5   *fricassee* or a *ragout*.

I do therefore humbly offer it to public consideration, that of the hundred and twenty thousand children, already computed, twenty thousand may be reserved for breed, whereof only one-fourth part to be males, which is more than we allow to sheep, black cattle, or swine, and my reason is that these
10   children are seldom the fruits of marriage, a circumstances not much regarded by our savages, therefore one male will be sufficient to serve four females. That the remaining hundred thousand may at a year old be offered in sale to the persons of quality, and fortune, through the kingdom, always advising the mother to let them suck plentifully in the last month, so as to
15   render them plump and fat for a good table. A child will make two dishes at an entertainment for friends, and when the family dines alone, the fore or hind quarter will make a reasonable dish, and seasoned with a little pepper or salt will be very good boiled on the fourth day, especially in winter …

I grant this food will be somewhat dear, and therefore very proper for
20   landlords, who as they have already devoured most of the parents, seem to have the best title to the children.

Infant's flesh will be in season throughout the year, but more plentiful in March … Fish being a prolific diet, there are more children born in Roman Catholic countries about nine months after Lent, than at any other
25   season: therefore reckoning a year after Lent, the markets will be more glutted than usual, because the number of popish infants is at least three to one in this kingdom, and therefore it will have one other collateral advantage by lessening the number of papists among us.

I have already computed the charge of nursing a beggar's child (in which
30   list I reckon all cottagers, labourers and four-fifths of the farmers) to be about two shillings *per annum*, rags included, and I believe no gentleman would repine to give ten shillings for the carcass of a good fat child,

which, as I have said will make four dishes of excellent nutritive meat,
when he hath only some particular friend, or his own family to dine with
35 him. Thus the squire will learn to be a good landlord, and grow popular
among his tenants, the mother will have eight shillings net profit, and be
fit for work until she produces another child.

Those who are more thrifty (as I must confess the times require) may flay
the carcass; the skin of which, artificially dressed, will make admirable
40 gloves for ladies, and summer boots for fine gentlemen.

As to our City of Dublin, shambles may be appointed for this purpose, in
the most convenient parts of it, and butchers we may be assured will not
be wanting, although I rather recommend buying the children alive, and
dressing them hot from the knife, as we do roasting pigs.

QUESTIONS

1. Which of the following statements are true and which are false,
according to the passage?
   (a) Swift recommends that only a quarter of the poor should be allowed
       to reproduce.
   (b) He proposes that, like livestock, there should be only one male to
       service several females.
   (c) The majority of babies born to the poor should be fattened for the
       market, slaughtered at a year old, and eaten by the wealthy.
   (d) Since cannibalism was common among the landlords of the time,
       he feels that baby meat would be extremely suitable for them.
   (e) The main benefit of his proposal is that it would reduce the
       Catholic population.
   (f) For the sake of economy, he suggests that accessories could be
       made from baby skin.
   (g) In Swift's opinion, the fresher the baby meat the better.

2. The manner in which the proposal is made could best be described as
   (a) angry and accusing
   (b) humble and apologetic
   (c) arrogant and contemptuous
   (d) polite and reasonable.

3. It is most likely that Swift was motivated to make such a proposal by
   (a) a sincere desire to improve the economy of the country
   (b) a sadistic impulse to offend his readers
   (c) a deep sense of outrage at man's inhumanity to man
   (d) a conviction that the number of Catholics should be controlled.

4. Swift calls the poor people 'savages' (line 11)
   (*a*) to distinguish them from people of his own class
   (*b*) to be deliberately provocative
   (*c*) to stress how uncivilised they were
   (*d*) to show how callous he was.

5. The implication of the phrase 'rags included' (line 31) is that
   (*a*) beggars cannot afford to buy their children decent clothes
   (*b*) beggars' children don't need decent clothes
   (*c*) two shillings a year covers all the needs of a beggar's child
   (*d*) rags are not very expensive.

VOCABULARY PRACTICE

In each case choose the word that best completes the sentence, but keep in mind that the word you have come across earlier in this unit is not necessarily the right answer!

1. I don't need to tell you how unreliable she is. The fact that she didn't turn up for the meeting yesterday .... for itself.

   (*a*) shows   (*b*) speaks   (*c*) signs   (*d*) is indicative

2. He'd certainly be doing me a great favour if he lent me his car. I'll ask him nicely, but I'm not going to .... to him for it.

   (*a*) grovel   (*b*) plead   (*c*) ingratiate   (*d*) beg

3. The effects on agriculture of two extremely wet summers were ....

   (a) far-fetched   (*b*) far-gone   (*c*) far-flung   (*d*) far-reaching

4. The colonisers used extreme force to bring the country under ....

   (*a*) power   (*b*) control   (*c*) hand   (*d*) heel

5. That's the last time I'll go on holiday with Maureen and her sister. Their constant .... got on my nerves.

   (*a*) incompatibility   (*b*) argument   (*c*) disputing   (*d*) bickering

6. Many of the shops near the soccer stadium had to close down because they were being repeatedly .... by football hooligans.

(a) looted   (b) plundered   (c) pillaged   (d) burgled

7. You're crazy to put your job at .... just because of a silly misunderstanding with the boss.

(a) hazard   (b) danger   (c) risk   (d) peril

8. It's a post office regulation that recipients have to pay double the charge for letters that aren't ....

(a) sealed   (b) stamped   (c) addressed   (d) franked

9. Could you all .... yourselves out a bit to make room for the three new students.

(a) spread   (b) scatter   (c) disperse   (d) widen

10. I was going to leave the party early but they implored me to stay, so I've decided if you can't .... them, join them.

(a) conquer   (b) win   (c) persuade   (d) beat

11. He was to have been married next Saturday, but to his .... he got a letter from the bride-to-be calling the wedding off.

(a) consternation   (b) shock   (c) wonder   (d) irritation

12. I got home to find he'd drunk a bottle of my best whiskey and broken my Waterford glass jug. I consider such behaviour quite .... the pale.

(a) outside   (b) over   (c) against   (d) beyond

13. Thank you very much for the coffee percolator you gave me for Christmas. It's already been put .... good use.

(a) at   (b) in   (c) to   (d) into

14. That singer made quite a .... on her first public performance by appearing with all her hair shaved off.

(a) scene   (b) show   (c) splash   (d) dash

15. It's about time he .... his socks. He hasn't done a stroke of work all term and he's got exams in three weeks.

    (*a*) pulled up   (*b*) puts up   (*c*) put on   (*d*) pulls up

CLOZE

Read this passage by the architect Patrick Shaffrey on the development of Dublin through the centuries, and fill each numbered space with one suitable word.

Dublin is now, of .... [1], one of Europe's capital cities, and has always benefited .... [2] the many famous literary figures associated with it. Its real international significance, ... [3], rests on the physical beauty of its central area, the foundations of .... [4] were .... [5] in the eighteenth century, when Dublin was the second city in the empire.

Dublin, however, is more than .... [6] a Georgian city. Its foundations go .... [7] over a thousand years. It was .... [8] by the Vikings in the ninth century, and the street patterns laid down then formed the basis .... [9] the later medieval city. Much of the material from Viking Dublin .... [10] now be seen in the National Museum. .... [11] are few tangible remains of medieval Dublin .... [12] scattered fragments of the city walls. The two cathedrals, St Patrick's and Christ Church, have been .... [13] altered through the centuries, and were extensively rebuilt in the nineteenth century.

In the sixteenth century the city spread .... [14] beyond its medieval core with the establishment of Trinity College. .... [15] the troubles of the seventeenth century came the development of Georgian Dublin .... [16] we know it today, beginning on the north side of the city and eventually culminating .... [17] the fine squares and streets of the south side. These fine streets and individual buildings have been in a continual state of decline for .... [18] a hundred years.

The .... [19] of development slackened off after the Act of Union in 1801, but the Georgian influence remained. Many suburban streets have a distinctive Georgian character .... [20] in some instances they were built towards the end of the nineteenth century.

Unit 7

A ROOT PROBLEM

Have you any idea what the following have in common?
- records
- Kerr pinks
- golden wonders
- Arran banners

Or what their connection is with
- spuds
- murphies
- praties?

If you don't know, go through the following clues with a partner and see how quickly you can find the answer.

a. They originally came from America.

b. They live underground.

c. Although they have eyes, they can't see.

d. They come with their jackets on.

e. For hundreds of years many Irish people were totally dependent on them.

f. In spring, new ones arrive from warmer places such as Egypt and Cyprus.

g. Without them, McDonald's would go out of business!

h. And your freshly laundered table napkin would be as limp as a stale lettuce leaf!

i. They are the most versatile of all tubers.

j. They are to the Irish what rice is to the Chinese.

And if you're still in the dark, you'll find the answer at the end of the unit (page 127)!

THE STORY OF THE SPUD

Read the passage below, then, with a partner, find answers to the questions that follow.

QUESTIONS

1. What influence had the potato on the course of Irish history since its introduction in 1587?

2. What were the advantages and disadvantages of having potatoes as a staple diet?

3. What were the immediate effects of the Great Famine?

4. What further repercussions were there?

112

Since its introduction to Ireland in 1587, the potato has played a key role in the history and culture of the Irish. Until that time the diet of the ordinary people was reasonably varied, if humble; and indeed Captain de Cuellar, a survivor of the Spanish Armada in 1588, was able to remark that the food of the people in the wildest parts of the west of Ireland consisted of 'butter with oaten bread … and some flesh half-cooked.' While this may not sound very appetising by modern standards, it should be noted that this civilised Spanish gentleman, who looked upon the native population as savages living 'as the brute beasts among the mountains,' conceded that 'the men are all large-bodied, of handsome features and as active as the roe-deer.' And as for the women, 'most of them are very beautiful, but badly dressed'! Faint praise, perhaps, but it does suggest that the people were healthy, well built, and well fed.

However, the fact that potatoes were easy to grow in the poorest soil and conditions and that enough to support a whole family could be produced in a very small area had a depressing effect on both diet and culture. As the population expanded, the tiny plots of land that the peasants rented from the landlords were divided and subdivided among larger and larger families until eventually, by the middle of the eighteenth century, people were literally subsisting on potatoes. The poorest, unable to pay their rents otherwise, had to hire out their labour in return not for a wage, but for a small plot on which to grow them.

Potatoes, with the addition of milk or buttermilk, form a scientifically balanced diet. So as long as the crop thrived, there was hardship—those who did not have enough to eat undercooked their potatoes, because that way they stayed in the stomach for a longer time and cut down the number of hunger pangs felt—but no cause for alarm. When the supply was plentiful, it was not uncommon for a labourer to sit down to a meal of 6 or 7 kilograms of potatoes, while an average consumption of 4 kilograms a day for each member of the family is well authenticated. All kinds of tricks were used to supplement the diet and vary the monotony. Those living near the sea boiled their potatoes (in their 'jackets', of course) in sea-water, which prevented the skin from cracking and thus preserved the mineral content; and the craving for relish or 'kitchen' would be satisfied by anything from seaweed to congealed sheep or pig's blood.

In 1800 the population of Ireland was about five million. By 1841 it had risen to over eight million. With a substantial part of that population depending on the potato crop for survival, it is not hard to imagine the disastrous consequences of its failure. In fact failures occurred repeatedly during the first half of the nineteenth century, causing famine and thousands of deaths, but despite the forewarnings, nothing was done to

prevent or provide for eventual calamity. Potato blight (*Phytophthora infestans*), caused by warm, wet weather conditions, struck the crops of 1845, resulting in what came to be known as the 'great hunger', the
45   famine years of 1846–49, causing starvation, fever, death, and emigration. Suffice it to say that, despite an increase of over three-quarters of a million during the 1960s and 1970s, the population of Ireland today is just over five million. And, as if the destruction of the vital food supply were not enough, throughout those years corn, which
50   could have alleviated the suffering of the destitute, continued to be exported from the country, and those who could no longer pay their exorbitant rents were forcibly evicted from the hovels they occupied. The dreaded Victorian workhouses were unable to accommodate the thousands of homeless and starving people who clamoured for shelter,
55   and the relief schemes, whereby those in want had to work on building roads—often going nowhere—to earn a few miserable pence, were totally ineffectual: people died because they were too weak to work or their wages were not paid in time.

The crisis of the Great Famine was a major turning-point in Irish history,
60   such was the magnitude of the disaster and its political and social repercussions. But alongside the well-documented story of bitterness towards the British (the establishment indifference and downright callousness at the suffering of the Irish stretches credulity to the limit), the rise of nationalism, and the struggle for independence, there was a
65   general reaction against everything associated with the famine. Paradoxically, while people were being exhorted to take pride in their nationality, another nail was driven into the coffin of the Irish language: what point was there in speaking Irish if you had to cross the Atlantic or the Irish Sea in the effort to keep body and soul together? And those who
70   were 'fortunate' enough to survive the dreadful conditions on the emigration boats invariably settled in large towns and cities, where life was as far removed as possible from their rural background. For the survivors who remained in Ireland and succeeding generations, anything associated with famine became a symbol of poverty; even in the 1950s a
75   Donegal small farmer kept a horse, which he could ill afford, for fear of being unable to marry off his daughters if he only had a donkey.

To a great extent, and understandably enough, the fabric of traditional life was threatened by the notion that what was old was bad and what was new was good. Apart from the abandoned villages, in the west of Ireland you
80   will find 'smart' new bungalows standing beside the ruins of thatched cottages; for decades traditional music was looked down on until it began to become fashionable in the 1960s. Even today, when there is so much talk of high-fibre and low-cholesterol diet, many households prefer shop-

bought, refined white bread to the typical home-made brown soda, and
85 recent statistics show that the Irish eat more meat per capita than any
other European country.

But speaking of paradoxes, what might whimsically be referred to as the
root of the problem, the humble potato, never lost its popularity, and for a
very large majority of Irish people a meal will simply never be a meal
90 without spuds.

MORE QUESTIONS

Now read the passage again and answer these questions as precisely as
you can. You may do this orally with a partner, and/or in writing as
homework.

1. In your own words, say what Captain de Cuellar's opinion of the people
he met in the west of Ireland was.

2. Explain what the 'depressing effect' (line 16) was.

3. Suggest a suitable phrase that could replace the word 'otherwise' in
line 21.

4. 'There was hardship … but no cause for alarm' (lines 24–27); what
example is given of the hardship, and why was there no cause for alarm?

5. What is 'kitchen' (line 34), why is the word in quotation marks in the
passage, and why do you think there was a craving for it?

6. What does 'it' refer to in line 38?

7. Give an alternative phrase for 'suffice it to say' in line 46.

8. How was the situation of those affected by the failure of the potato crop
exacerbated?

9. Explain in your own words why the Great Famine is considered a
'turning-point in Irish history' (line 59).

10. Why is the word 'fortunate' (line 70) in quotation marks?

11. How did those who emigrated demonstrate their reaction to poverty?

12. In what ways is it possible to see the effects of the Great Famine on
life in more recent times?

13. Why is it whimsical to refer to the potato as 'the root of the problem' (lines 87–88)?

14. Can you comment on the general tone of the passage? To do this, pick out any words and phrases that you think indicate the writer's attitude to the subject, and say what that attitude is.

PICTURES OF DISASTER

These four pictures illustrate different aspects of the Great Famine.

A

B

C

D

Working with a partner or group—

1. Describe each picture in detail, and say which aspect of the famine it illustrates.

2. Here are the captions that accompany the pictures. Now match the caption with the picture.

(i) 'The most appalling sight I ever witnessed … unable to pay their rents, families were made homeless.'
(ii) Soup kitchens and a government decision at last to distribute free food … but the soup was often such a 'vile compound' that people refused to eat it because it gave them 'bowel complaints'.
(iii) For many, escape was the only hope. But conditions on board were so bad that many died before they reached their destination.
(iv) Aftermath.
A: ....
B: ....
C: ....
D: ....

3. Do you find the pictures distressing? Can drawings or paintings of disasters be as effective as the visual media of today? Compare the impact of particular paintings with photographs or television reports you remember.

4. How do written reports, or even fictional descriptions, compare with visual images? Read this account by a British government official of what he saw in Skibbereen in Co. Cork in 1846.

On Sunday last, 20 December, a young woman begging in the streets of Cork collapsed and was at first unable to move or speak. After being given 'restorations' and taken home to her cabin she told those helping her that both her mother and father had died in the last fortnight. At the same time she directed their attention to a heap of dirty straw that lay in the corner and apparently concealed some object under it. On removing the covering of straw, the spectators were horrified on beholding the mangled corpses of two grown boys, a large proportion of which had been removed by the rats while the remainder lay festering in its rottenness. They had remained there for perhaps a week or maybe a fortnight …

The officer wrote this in response to a statement in *The Times* maintaining that the situation in Ireland was grossly exaggerated. How effective do you think it was?

Can you think of anything you have read about human suffering, whether fact or fiction, that has affected you more profoundly than any picture? If so, can you say why?

WRITING

Work in pairs to answer the following questions.

1. Catastrophes can be categorised into three types:

(a) Natural catastrophes, like perennial famine (usually caused by severe drought) in certain African countries. What others can you think of?
(b) Man-made catastrophes, like wars and plane crashes. Can you add more to these?
(c) Ones that can be considered a mixture of the two, like the Great Famine in Ireland, which had natural causes but would not have reached the awful proportions it did if the authorities had intervened. What else could be put into this category?

Now compare your answers with the rest of the class, adding to your lists any catastrophes you didn't think of.

2. Divide the class into three groups, each taking one of the above categories, and discuss the various catastrophes on your list, using these questions as guidelines:

(a) Was the disaster foreseen, and could anything have been done to prevent it?
(b) When it did happen, what action was taken to minimise it, and how effective was this?
(c) What were the immediate effects of the disaster, and what further repercussions were there?
(d) Can anything be done, and if so has anything been done, to prevent something like this from happening again?

3. For homework, write about one of the catastrophes you have discussed, taking into account its causes and effects; say whether, in your opinion, it could have been prevented and if it could possibly happen again.

Failure of the potato crop was by no means confined to the nineteenth century, as this extract from the book *Children of the Dead End* all too clearly shows. The Co. Donegal author Patrick MacGill (1891–1963) left school when he was only twelve, emigrated to Scotland, and became a navvy there at the age of fourteen. (The word 'navvy', meaning an unskilled labourer, derives from the 'navigators' or canal-diggers who opened the waterways of industrial England and later built the first railways of North America; many of them were Irish.) MacGill had this, his first of many works, published in 1914, when he was twenty-three.

Read the passage and discuss the picture the writer conveys of the poor people, the merchant, and the priest. Then answer the multiple-choice questions that follow.

For supper we had potatoes and buttermilk. The potatoes were emptied into a large wicker basket round which we children sat with a large bowl of buttermilk between us, and out of this bowl we drank in turn. Usually the milk was consumed quickly and afterwards we ate the potatoes dry.

Nearly every second year the potatoes went bad; then we were always hungry, although Farley McKeown, a rich merchant in the neighbouring village, let my father have a great many bags of Indian meal on credit. A bag contained sixteen stone of meal and cost a shilling a stone. On the bag of meal Farley McKeown charged sixpence a month interest, and fourpence a month on a sack of flour which cost twelve shillings. All the people round about were very honest and paid up their debts whenever they were able. Usually when the young went off to Scotland or England, they sent home money to their fathers and mothers and with this money the parents paid Farley McKeown.

'What doesn't go to the landlord, goes to Farley McKeown,' was a Glenmornan saying.

The merchant was a great friend of the parish priest, who always told the people if they did not pay their debts, they would burn for ever in Hell. 'The fires of eternity will make you sorry for the debts that you did not pay,' said the priest. 'What is eternity?' he would ask from the altar steps. 'If a man tried to count the grains of sand on the seashore and took a million years to count every grain, how long would it take him to count them all? Just think of it! Burning in hell while a man, taking a million years to count a grain of sand, counts all the sands on the seashore. And this because you did not pay Farley McKeown his lawful debts, his lawful debts within the letter of the law.' That concluding phrase, 'within the letter of the law,' struck terror into all who listened and no one, maybe not even the priest himself, knew what it meant.

Farley McKeown would give no meal to those who had no children. 'That kind of people who have no children to earn for them never pay their debts,' he said. 'If *they* get meal and don't pay for it, they'll go down—down,' said the priest. ''Tis God himself that would be angry with Farley McKeown if he gave meal to people like that.'

The merchant established a great knitting industry in west Donegal. My mother used to knit socks for him and he paid her at the rate of one and threepence a dozen pairs, and it was said that he made a shilling of profit on a pair of these in England. My mother usually made a pair of socks daily, but to do this she had to work sixteen hours at the task. Along with this she had her household duties to look after. 'A penny farthing a day is not much to make,' I once said to her. 'No, indeed, if you look at it in that way,' she answered. 'But it is nearly two pounds a year and that is half the rent of our farm of land.'

Every Christmas Farley McKeown paid £250 to the church. When the priest announced this from the altar he would say, 'That's the man for you!' and all the members of the congregation would bow their heads, feeling very much ashamed of themselves because none of them could give more than a sixpence or a shilling to the silver collection which always took place at the chapel of Greenanore on Christmas Day.

NOTES

Indian meal: maize flour, yellow in colour; considered a poor substitute for white flour.

a shilling a stone: In the British system of weights, still used in Ireland side by side with the international system, a stone is 14 pounds; a pound is 0.45 kg. In the old currency system (before 1971) a pound was divided into 20 shillings, and a shilling was divided into 12 pence (pennies). A shilling therefore was the equivalent of the present-day 5p (five pence). The value of money has changed dramatically since the days MacGill wrote about, of course. The point is that all the sums mentioned are relative.

one and threepence: one shilling and three old pence, or 6¼p.

a penny farthing: A farthing was a special name for a quarter of an old penny; 'a penny farthing' meant a penny and a farthing, i.e. 1¼ old pence or about ½p.

the silver collection: a collection in which only silver-coloured coins—those from six old pence (2½p) upwards—were acceptable.

MULTIPLE-CHOICE QUESTIONS

Choose the phrase that best completes the sentence.

1. At suppertime the children usually drank the milk first because
   (a) they were bored with the monotonous diet of potatoes
   (b) they were determined not to miss their fair share of the milk
   (c) it was easier to eat the potatoes after drinking the milk
   (d) buttermilk was a special treat.

2. The Indian meal the writer's father got from Farley McKeown would
   (a) prevent them from feeling hungry
   (b) do little to alleviate their plight
   (c) be given out of the merchant's sense of duty
   (d) contain sixteen stones.

3. The purpose of the priest's homily on eternity was to
   (a) explain the concept in simple terms
   (b) frighten the people into paying their debts
   (c) inculcate a sense of morality in them
   (d) threaten them with the law.

4. Farley McKeown wouldn't give meal to those with no children, because
   (a) they were untrustworthy
   (b) they were a bad risk
   (c) they didn't need it
   (d) God would be angry.

5. Patrick implies that the sock knitting industry
   (a) was a great help to his family
   (b) was of no help whatsoever
   (c) was shameless exploitation of the poor people
   (d) kept his mother from doing the housework.

SPADE WORK

The best homage that can be paid to those whose lives were governed by the spade is a poem by Séamus Heaney. Heaney, who was brought up on a small farm in Co. Derry, is looked upon as one of the greatest poets writing in English. The poem that appears below is taken from his earliest collection, *Death of a Naturalist*.

First work in pairs or groups to do this preparation exercise. Check the meaning of the words given at the top of each section, and complete the sentences using each word once.

1. squat sloppy snug rasping gravelly soggy curt

   (a) Don't be put off by his .... manner. He doesn't mean to be rude or anything; he's just very shy.
   (b) The wheels of my bicycle sank into the .... surface of the driveway, so I had to get off and walk.
   (c) My old maths teacher used to torment us by scraping his nail against the blackboard. The .... sound would always make me wince.
   (d) Oh, hell, I've gone and spilt coffee on my toast. I'm not going to eat that .... mess!
   (e) The baby looked so .... all wrapped up and fast asleep in her carry-cot, it seemed a pity to disturb her.
   (f) I've never seen such .... work in my life! Apart from being quite illegible, it must have been written in McDonald's—there's grease and tomato sauce all over it!
   (g) He may be a good rider but he'll never look well on a horse. He's too short and thickset—in a word, ...

2. squelch turf bog rump shaft lug

   (a) Large areas of the west of Ireland are covered with ...., which is wet, spongy land unsuitable for cultivation.
   (b) Most people in those parts burn ...., or peat, in their fires. It gives off a beautiful fragrant smell.
   (c) The .... of a spade is the long wooden handle, while the .... is the part you put your foot on when you're digging.
   (d) The farmer gave the cow a slap on the .... to get it to move out of his way.
   (e) The little boy ran round the field delighting in the .... his wellington boots made in the mud.

3. stoop nestle nick heave (use a suitable form of these verbs)

   (a) After being fed, the little baby .... contentedly in its mother's arms.
   (b) I .... down to pick a needle off the floor, and as soon as I tried to straighten up I did something awful to my back.
   (c) He was exhausted after he had .... the huge rocks into the corner of the garden so that he could clear a space for a new rose bed.
   (d) Before he started sawing he always .... the edge of the plank. That way the saw didn't jump all over the place.

DIGGING

Between my finger and my thumb
The squat pen rests; snug as a gun.

Under the window, a clean rasping sound
When the spade sinks into gravelly ground:
My father, digging. I look down

Till his straining rump among the flowerbeds
Bends low, comes up twenty years away
Stooping in rhythm through potato drills
Where he was digging.

The coarse boot nestled on the lug, the shaft
Against the inside knee was levered firmly,
He rooted out tall tops, buried the bright edge deep
To scatter new potatoes that we picked
Loving their cool hardness in our hands.

By God, the old man could handle a spade.
Just like his old man.

My grandfather cut more turf in a day
Than any other man on Toner's bog.
Once I carried him milk in a bottle
Corked sloppily with paper. He straightened up
To drink it, then fell to right away
Nicking and slicing neatly, heaving sods
Over his shoulder, going down and down
For the good turf. Digging.

The cold smell of potato mould, the squelch and slap
Of soggy peat, the curt cuts of an edge
Through living roots awaken in my head.
But I've no spade to follow men like them.

Between my finger and my thumb
The squat pen rests.
I'll dig with it.

Séamus Heaney

Remember that *understanding* poetry is only one way of appreciating it. The best idea is to listen to it being read to you several times—once simply for the rhythm and movement, once with your senses, for the sights, sounds, smells, etc., and once for the 'meaning'.

When you have done this, work with your partner or group to answer the questions that follow, then pick out any lines or phrases you particularly like and say why you like them. Finally, discuss your answers with the rest of the class.

QUESTIONS

1. How many different types of digging does the poet describe?

2. The poet uses the flashback technique in the poem. Where does it occur, and how does it work?

3. Which lines most directly convey his admiration for his father and grandfather?

4. How does he see himself similar to yet different from his father and grandfather?

5. Is the poet satisfied or dissatisfied with his role? Give reasons for your answer.

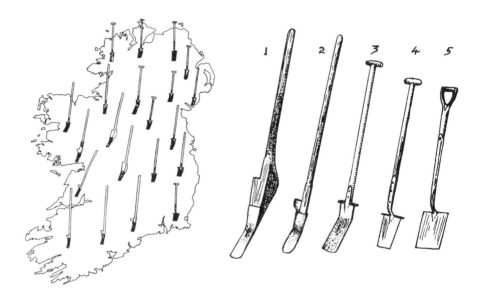

Spade types: left Nos. 1–4: Evolution of Irish spade; No. 5: English spade

VOCABULARY PRACTICE

In each case choose the word that best completes the sentence, but keep in mind that the word you have come across earlier in this unit is not necessarily the right answer!

1. She .... a cottage in Connemara while she was researching her book on the Famine.

       (*a*) lent   (*b*) let   (*c*) hired   (*d*) rented

2. He pretended he was sick and took the day off work to go to the races; but he suffered from such .... of guilt that he didn't enjoy himself!

       (*a*) pains   (*b*) pangs   (*c*) aches   (*d*) stabs

3. The death toll in last night's train crash has now .... to forty-five.

       (*a*) risen   (*b*) arisen   (*c*) raised   (*d*) reached

4. The problems caused by unemployment in Ireland are innumerable. .... that every year thousands of young people have to emigrate to find work.

    (*a*) Suffice to say   (*b*) Sufficient to say
    (*c*) Suffice it to say   (*d*) Is enough to say

5. I love reading his zany stories. It's probably because we share the same .... sense of humour.

       (*a*) imaginative   (*b*) whimsical   (*c*) amusing   (*d*) comic

6. The poor peasants, starving for lack of food and evicted from their homes because they couldn't pay their rents, were in a dreadful ....

       (*a*) calamity   (*b*) tragedy   (*c*) disaster   (*d*) plight

7. If you eat sensibly, you really don't need to take all sorts of vitamins to .... your diet.

       (*a*) add   (*b*) augment   (*c*) supplement   (*d*) complete

8. In recent years, schemes have been set up in Co. Donegal for the
.... of Aran jumpers, to a great extent replacing the traditional
cottage industry.

    (a) fabrics   (b) factories   (c) manufacture   (d) fabrication

9. I really enjoyed my holiday in the south of France, but their ....
beaches are nothing in comparison with our lovely sandy strands.

    (a) gravelly   (b) pebbly   (c) stoned   (d) rubbly

10. My brother and his wife set up a small restaurant in a remote part of
Co. Donegal last year, and, despite the family's discouragement, it's now a
.... business.

    (a) blooming   (b) blossoming   (c) thriving   (d) profiting

11. The wind was so strong that the sheets I had hung out to dry made a
loud ....

    (a) suck   (b) squelch   (c) flap   (d) flutter

12. By the time income tax and social insurance has been deducted, my
monthly .... cheque is little more than half of what I actually earn.

    (a) pay   (b) salary   (c) wage   (d) income

13. The dress she wore was the most expensive one she had ever bought,
but he damned it with .... by telling her it was 'all right'!

    (a) a weak compliment   (b) faint praise
      (c) false modesty   (d) damp enthusiasm

14. You weren't just tactless—you were .... rude!

    (a) outright   (b) downright   (c) somewhat   (d) insolently

15. By comparison with the tall, slender round towers built in the Early
Christian period, Martello towers, like Joyce's tower in Sandycove, are
....

    (a) fat   (b) thick   (c) low   (d) squat

CLOZE

This passage tells you a little about the importance of the spade in Ireland and some of the customs connected with it. (The diagram on page 124 should give you a better understanding of the descriptions.) Fill each space with one suitable word.

When a person in Ireland, particularly in the north, wonders 'what foot' another .... [1] 'digs with' he is euphemistically asking .... [2] his religious persuasion is. If the .... [3] is 'he digs with the other (or wrong) foot,' .... [4] means that the speaker is a Catholic and the person in question a Protestant, or vice versa.

Why? you may .... [5] ask! The answer can be traced .... [6] to the not too distant past when .... [7] people in this country depended .... [8] the spade for their livelihood. It is estimated that at one time there were .... [9] a hundred types of spades in Ireland; .... [10] from the fact that the .... [11] they were made varied from place .... [12] place, since spades .... [13] to be made locally, there were different types specially designed for different functions. The 'loy', for example, a one-eared spade used as a kind of plough, was totally different .... [14] the 'slane', a tool with a double-edged blade, which is still widely popular in turf cutting.

The now common two-eared spade did not appear .... [15] the early nineteenth century, and even to .... [16] day it differs from its English counterpart by having iron foot-plates to prevent the digger, whose light shoes would offer .... [17] protection, from cutting his feet.

The one-eared spade, however, continued to be popular well .... [18] the twentieth century, with the majority of people using the right foot for digging and a .... [19], mainly in the Protestant districts of the north-east, digging with the .... [20], or 'other' or even 'wrong', foot!

[The answer to the quiz on page 112 is, of course, potatoes.]

There are countless Irish songs associated with the sorrows of emigration. While many of them go back to famine times, some have been written quite recently. The sad truth is that, because so many young people are leaving the country today, contemporary song-writers have good reason to exploit an already well developed theme. In this song an old man laments the fact that he ever left his home, Galway Bay. Why do you think he left, where did he go and what does he miss about his native land?
Listen to the song on the cassette and then sing along with it.

GALWAY BAY

1.

'Tis far away I am today from scenes I roamed a boy,
And long ago, the hour I know, I first saw Illinois.
Not time nor tide nor waters wide can steel my heart away,
Forever true it flies to you, my own dear Galway Bay.

2.

Oh grey and bleak by shore and creek, the rugged rocks abound,
But sweet and green the grass between that grows on Irish ground.
There friendship fond, all wealth beyond, and love that lives always
Bless every home beside your foam, my own dear Galway Bay.

3.

Had I youth's blood and thoughtful mood and hear of joy once more,
For all the gold the world can hold, I'd never leave your shore.
I'd stay content with whate'er God sent, with neighbours old and grey
And I'd lay my bones 'neath churchyard stones above you, Galway Bay.

4.

The blessings of a poor old man be with you night and day;
The blessings of a lonely man whose heart will soon be clay.
'Tis all the heaven I ask of God upon my dying day,
My soul to soar forever more above you, Galway Bay.

Unit 8

SAYING IT WITH MUSIC

The following is an experiment in the use of your imagination!

Before you begin, elect a student to do the blackboard work. He or she should divide the board into two sections, heading one *Losses* and the other *Gains*. Now, shut your eyes for a minute or so and try to imagine— LIFE WITHOUT MUSIC!

As soon as you're ready, contribute your thoughts, indicating which heading they should be written under. When everybody has finished, analyse the contributions and see what general conclusions you can draw about the place music has in our lives.

Now work with a partner or group to answer and discuss these questions.

1. What kind(s) of music do you like?

2. What pleasure do you get out of being able to sing or play a musical instrument? If you can't, would you like to be able to do so? Why, or why not?

3. Is there a strong tradition of folk music in your country? If so, how popular is it and where and when can you hear it?

4. Have you ever heard Irish music in your own country? If so, say as much as you can about it. Where and when did you hear it? Was it instrumental or singing? Do you know what the name of the singer, musician or group was? What impact, if any, did it make on you?

5. Here are pictures and the names of six instruments used in traditional Irish music, two from each of the following categories:

wind   percussion   string

Indicate the name of each instrument by putting the correct number with each letter.

il'ən

baura:n

(i) the uilleann* pipes   (iv) the fiddle
(ii) the harp   (v) the tin whistle
(iii) the bodhrán*   (vi) the spoons

A: .... B: .... C: .... D: .... E: .... F: ....
Now say which categories they belong to:
Wind: .... and ....
Percussion: .... and ....
String: .... and ....

A

B

C

D

E

F

6. How many more musical instruments can you name? What categories do they belong to? (Besides the ones mentioned above, there are brass and woodwind.) Is there any instrument that is played only in your country?

LETTING THE MUSIC SPEAK FOR ITSELF

Read this passage on Irish music, then with your partner or group discuss your answers to the questions.

QUESTIONS

1. Why was Irish music not popular until the 1960s, and what were people's attitudes towards it?

2. In what way did traditional music manage to survive?

3. The revival of Irish music went through three (or perhaps four) stages. What were they?

You can't make—or rather, push—your way down Grafton Street these days without passing at least a couple of fiddlers, a tin-whistle player, possibly an uilleann piper, and definitely an amplified guitar group. In fact, you may have noticed that wherever you go in Ireland, it's very hard

5 to avoid Irish music in all its myriad forms, from sean-nós singing (the old-style singing, which is very like desert Arab music) to the synthesised compositions of contemporaries like Enya. But it wasn't always like this. Up to and well into the 1960s, Irish music was to a large extent looked down on, in much the same way that city children disparage their country

10 cousins for being rather behind the times. Like the Irish language, it belonged to a cultural tradition that was associated with oppression and poverty, a past that many people in the middle of the twentieth century

wanted to forget. While herculean efforts were made to revive Irish, however, little or nothing was done to promote what is now accepted as an equally important aspect of the nation's culture: its music.

Up to the 1960s, popular attitudes ranged from indifference to downright hostility. Traditional music was considered, at worst, a form of low-life entertainment indulged in by 'tinkers', that distinctive and controversial breed of travelling people whose life and culture is another story. At best it was barely tolerated céilí* band music played on accordions with the inappropriate backing of a piano. In an era innocent of discos, every neighbourhood had its dance hall, where the young (and often not so young!) would gather on Saturday or Sunday nights, the women standing in self-conscious groups against one wall, and the men, waiting for dutch courage to move them, against the opposite wall. The speculation about who was going to dance with whom and the dancing itself was executed to the strains of a show band playing the popular music of the day: jazz, jive, rock, and that distinctive Irish export to America re-imported under the name of 'country and western'. The transatlantic influence would be reinforced for romantically minded couples with sentimental renderings of such pseudo-Irish songs as 'The Forty Shades of Green'. In those days dancing was banned during Lent, but the church made an exception for dancing to traditional music on St Patrick's night. As Fintan O'Toole says, 'If ever there was a formula for making Irish music penitential, the artistic equivalent of salted herring on a Friday, this was it. The result, not surprisingly, was that the more exotic the music, the better it must be.' And the writer Flann O'Brien once caustically commented, 'A dance is regarded as successful according to the distance the band has to travel. For the best possible dance, the band would have to come from India.'

This is not to say that traditional music had no following. It had an extremely active and devoted one that kept it very much alive. From the suburbs of Dublin to the most isolated corners of Co. Kerry, those who had the ability played for the sheer love of it, usually gathering in somebody's house and often playing till dawn. The skill and techniques were passed on from one generation to another, which explains why many of the top fiddle and pipe players today come from long lines of musicians. But while the following was fervent, it was not popular, and it lacked organisation. It was not until 1951 that a concerted effort was made to promote the tradition, with the setting up of Comhaltas Ceoltóirí Éireann* by the Dublin Pipers' Club. By the end of the decade this organisation, run by musicians for musicians, had branches all over the country and was holding an annual fleá cheoil*—a music festival in which people play together as well as competing against one another.

15

ˈkˈeːlˈiː   20

25

30

35

40

45

ˈkoːltəs ˈkˈoltoːrˈiː
ˈeːrˈən -   50

fˈlˈaː ˈxˈoːlˈ

Then, with the burgeoning international interest in folk music in the 1960s, came the ballad groups, which finally tipped the balance. If you ask anybody old enough to be out of nappies when the Beatles were hitting the big time, 'What first got you on to Irish music?' the answer will invariably be the Dubliners or the Clancy Brothers—or both. These were not only competent performers but also good entertainers, appealing to ever-increasing audiences with the help of such gimmicks as Aran jumpers, shaggy beards, and on-stage clowning. They opened the eyes of the unenlightened to the realisation that their musical heritage was not something to be despised as unsophisticated and old-fashioned but an inherent part of their culture that they could both enjoy and be proud of. Instead of being ignored, the country cousin was all of a sudden the centre of attention! Singing pubs, folk groups and clubs began to spring up everywhere; and, indeed, so infectious was the movement that for a few glorious years it even crossed the political divide, with northern unionists belting out republican songs with as much ease as their nationalist neighbours.

Once the breakthrough had been made with the ballad groups, the way was paved for the traditional musicians since people, having acquired a taste, were now ready to sample more. The classical musician and composer Seán Ó Riada had a profound influence on the future shape and form of Irish music at this time; in fact it has been said that he did for Irish music what Joyce did for literature. Among the many things he achieved before he died at the age of forty were the revival of interest in the works of the eighteenth-century blind harper O'Carolan, orchestral arrangements of traditional airs for films, a Mass in Irish, and the forming of an ensemble, Ceoltóirí Cualann, which consisted of the top musicians of the day. One of these, Paddy Moloney, went on to found the Chieftains, which must be the most celebrated folk group of all time. They were the first band to play in the Capitol building of the United States, the first musicians in history to perform on the Great Wall of China, and the first Irish group to win an Oscar. They look so unconventionally conventional on stage that a writer once likened them to 'a cluster of civil servants', and they perform without gimmicks, yet they have built a massive following for what was once considered a non-commercial art form. When asked to explain the phenomenon, Paddy Moloney says, 'We let the music speak for itself.'

MORE QUESTIONS

Now answer these questions as precisely as you can. You may do this orally with your partner, and/or in writing as homework.

1. What is implied by the phrase 'or rather, push' in line 1?

2. What is the connection between sean-nós singing and the synthesised compositions of Enya (line 5–7)?

3. In what way are the language and music of Ireland compared, and in what way are they contrasted?

4. How is the phrase 'from indifference to downright hostility' (line 16–17) illustrated?

5. Explain what is meant by 'an era innocent of discos' in line 21.

6. Why do you think the women in the dance-hall were self-conscious; and why, according to the passage, were the men waiting?

7. What information does the passage give about country and western music?

8. What does 'This' refer to in line 40?

9. In your own words, say what was positive and what was negative about the way Irish music was kept alive.

10. What do the phrases 'tipped the balance' (line 55) and 'hitting the big time' (line 57) have in common, and what does each mean in context?

11. Why did groups like the Dubliners and the Clancy Brothers gain such popularity?

12. Which sentence in paragraph 4 both sums up the situation and forms a link with the opening paragraph?

13. In what sense did the ballad groups pave the way (lines 71–72) for the traditional musicians?

14. Explain more fully what is mean by the description of the Chieftains as 'unconventionally conventional' (line 85). What other description illustrates this?

15. What does 'what' refer to in line 88?

16. What is the phenomenon Paddy Moloney was asked to explain?

LISTENING A.

An international group of students are attending a two-week summer course on Irish culture in Dublin. They are being accommodated in the college where the course takes place. This is Monday, their first day, and at their morning coffee break they are being addressed by the organiser of the social programme.

One of the students, Antoinette, has made a plan of how she intends to spend her time during the first week but she didn't get all of the details. Fill in the missing information in question 1 and answer 2. Listen to the piece twice.

1. Fill in the missing information in the lettered spaces provided below.

Night	Entertainment	Place	Time	Cost	
Monday	Reception	Great Hall	(A)	(B)	
Tuesday	Friel's play	(C)	8 pm	(D)	
Wednesday	Dolores Keane	Harcourt Hotel	(E)	(F)	
Thursday	Traditional music		Brazen Head	(G)	(H)
Friday	Weekend Trip	(I)	(J)	(K)	
Saturday	"	"	"	"	
Sunday	(L)	Bad Bob's	10.30	(M)	

A. ——— B. ——— C. ——— D. ——— E. ———

F. ——— G. ——— H. ——— I. ——— J. ———

K. ——— L. ——— M. ———

135

2. Say whether the following statements are true or false.
  A. The college where the course is being held is in a south-side suburb of Dublin.
  B. This will be the first time a Friel play has been performed in the States.
  C. The organiser advises against discos and night clubs because you won't hear traditional Irish music there.
  D. It is important to take your invitation card to the Reception because it will be attended by the President.
  E. The speaker mentions four activities which she has organised for the group.

LISTENING B.

Seamus Glackin is a traditional fiddle player from a well-known musical family. You are going to hear him talking to a young American student. Look at the questions below and then listen to the conversation twice.

Choose the correct answer in each case.

1. From the way Seamus talks to Susie it is clear that he

a. wishes she'd stop annoying him

b. is genuinely pleased by her interest

c. hopes to get more intimately involved with her

d. is expecting her to buy him a drink

2. The bit of music he plays for her

a. illustrates the influence of Irish music in America

b. was composed by a professional musician

c. cannot be considered traditional

d. is not as old as the dance music he plays

3. Susie says he must have music in his blood because

a. he comes from a musical family

b. he started learning the fiddle when he was seven

c. his father is from a county renowned for fiddle music

d. he plays and talks with obvious enthusiasm

4. Which of the following statements about Donegal music is *not* true?

a. it has been influenced by Scottish music

b. It has influenced Scottish music

c. it is exclusively fiddle music

d. it has influenced music in the United States

WRITING

Choose either question 1 or question 2.

1. Write about a concert you have been to (whether classical, rock, etc.).
Try to convey the atmosphere, the mood of the audience, and the impact
the music made, as well as what you saw and heard. Follow the advice
given in previous units by comparing and discussing your experiences
before you begin to plan your composition.

2. How important is music to your life? Your answers to the discussion
questions at the beginning of the unit should already have provided you
with some interesting ideas, but a brief summary of the conclusions your
group reached will help to clarify your thoughts.

**BREAKING
NEW GROUND**
Once traditional music had regained popularity it began to develop in
different directions. Read the following extracts from *Bringing It All Back
Home*, the book based on a BBC television series shown in 1991, and
answer the multiple-choice questions that follow.

A

Horslips was to become the most influential and popular Irish rock band of the seventies, and gave birth to a new phenomenon. The psychedelia-powered hippy culture of the time spawned an interest in the ancient myths and legends of Celtic Ireland. This was an important visual and conceptual element in the band's presentation. Horslips knew that many young people in Ireland could not identify with the official view of Irish culture as presented by the Irish tourist board, Irish radio, Irish schools, and so on. On the other hand they included members whose knowledge of Irish ranged from fluent to fair, and who were interested in and players of Irish traditional music. Their mixture of acoustic and rock interpretations of Irish instrumental music was instantly attractive. Their clothes and appearance reinforced the Celtic hippy theme. Their stage show incorporated coloured back-projections and Celtic set designs.

B

In March 1973 an Irish single went into the English charts and reached number six. The singer was Phil Lynott, an Irishman born in England of an Irish mother and Brazilian father. The band was Thin Lizzy. The single was a well-known Irish ballad, 'Whiskey in the Jar', a hearty song of a highwayman betrayed by his sweetheart. Phil Lynott was a singer and song writer heavily influenced by Jimi Hendrix and progressive rock music of the day. He had also spent time with the folkies and blues players around Dublin and was attracted by the lyrical element in the folk repertoire. His songs were set in contemporary Ireland, particularly in the Dublin of his childhood. Lyrically he was a romantic, and his fans approved. Early in the seventies Thin Lizzy adopted a heavy rock format to harness their loud and energetic output. They gained admission to the American and British progressive rock circuit and achieved the status of superstars in the mid-seventies.

C

From the beginning, the jazz, blues and gospel influences were mixed in a brew that was inimitably Van Morrison's. He is on record as saying that Celtic music is 'soul music'. Ireland and the Belfast of his youth are at the centre of his creative source. The mystical, soul quality of his song writing arises from his belief in a Celtic consciousness. Van's nasal tonality and the extended decorative melody line produced a result which was both contemporary and true to the spirit of the folk song. In 1980 he devoted much time to studying Celtic culture, in its philosophical and mystical dimensions, [but] he admitted in 1982 that he hadn't really 'rated' Irish music in Belfast when he was young. Now he was returning to the roots. 'I think,' he said, 'it can be dangerous to not validate the music of where you're from, for anybody … For me it's traditional. I believe in tracing things back to the source and finding out what the real thing was, and how it changed.'

D

Undoubtedly the most important rock band to come out of Ireland and feature on a world stage is U2. The distinctive U2 style, developed over the years, is loud and raw, characterised by Bono's huge voice and impassioned lyrics, which range from political and social issues like American imperialism, heroin addiction, human rights violations and war to more personal songs of love and relationships. U2 differs from other aspiring rock bands in that it set its sights on America rather than Britain. Bono drew from American musical and lyrical inspiration. It was after all 'the birthplace of rock and roll'. It came as a revelation to him that Irish music had contributed to rock and roll. Bono had rejected all aspects of Irish music and culture at school: 'I rebelled against being Irish, I rebelled against speaking the Irish language … Batman, Robin, Superman—that was more part of my experience than Fionn mac Cumhaill and the legends and mythology of Ireland.' Something of Irish culture did manage to penetrate this attitude. One of his teachers introduced him to the music of Seán Ó Riada, which, despite himself, he liked. Then in 1973 Thin Lizzy had a hit with 'Whiskey in the Jar'. Since then he has been on 'a voyage of self-discovery' through Irish music. He now finds himself drawn to 'the pure … poetic spirit of an instrument like the uilleann pipes.'

MULTIPLE-CHOICE QUESTIONS

Choose the extract or extracts to which the following five statements are applicable.

1. Specific mention is made of the group's or singer's conversion to Irish music.
   A. A & B
   B. B & C
   C. C & D
   D. B & D

2. The group or singer is said to have set a trend.
   A   B   C   D

3. The group's or singer's vocalisation is described as having the character of traditional singing.
   A   B   C   D

4. Reference is made to the group's or singer's non-musical appeal to the audience.
   A   B   C   D

5. We are told that the group or singer made a conscious decision to pursue the Irish dimension of their or his music.
   A   B   C   D

WHOSE KIND OF MUSIC?

These five photographs show Irish music in its myriad forms.

A

B

C

D

E

1. Discuss your answers to these questions with your partner or group.
   (a) What kind of music is being played/sung? Do the instruments give you a clue?
   (b) Where was the photograph taken? What does this tell you about the audience?
   (c) What can you tell from the appearance of the singers/musicians?

2. Out of these eight captions choose the five that match the five photographs.
   (i)   At one time show bands were all the rage. Their repertoire included everything from jazz to country and western.
   (ii)   'A cluster of civil servants' — The Chieftains play traditional music without gimmicks.
   (iii) Wherever you go, it's hard to avoid Irish music — free entertainment on the boat to the Aran Islands!
   (iv)   For a long time Irish music meant the much despised céilí band.
   (v)   Sean nos (or old-style singing). Not everybody's taste, but still live and well.
   (vi)   The Clancy Brothers and Tommy Makem — they did much to popularise Irish ballads.
   (vii) Traditional meets punk in the performance of Shane McGowan of The Pogues.
   (viii) The tradition never died out. People would gather in somebody's house and play all night for the sheer love of it.

   A: .... B: .... C: .... D: .... E: .... F: ....

3. Of the kinds of music represented by the above captions, which would you prefer to listen to? Compare and discuss your choice with the rest of the class.

THE BALLROOM OF ROMANCE

William Trevor, from Cork, is a contemporary novelist and short-story writer with an international reputation. His prize-winning story 'The Ballroom of Romance' (which, incidentally, was made into an excellent television play) is a superb evocation of a past era. It is set at a time when—despite the gradual spread of discos—dance halls and show-bands were still holding their own in country areas. The following extract will give you some further idea of the dance-hall scene mentioned earlier in the unit. Read it and discuss your answers to the questions with the rest of the class.

Although her father still called her a girl, Bridie was thirty-six. She was tall and strong: the skin of her fingers and her palms were stained, and harsh to touch. The labour they'd experienced had found its way into them, as though juices had come out of vegetation and pigment out of soil: since childhood she'd torn away the rough scotch grass that grew each spring among her father's mangolds and sugar beet; since childhood she'd harvested potatoes in August, her hands daily rooting in the ground she loosened and turned. Wind had toughened the flesh of her face, sun had browned it; her neck and nose were lean, her lips touched with early wrinkles.

But on Saturday nights Bridie forgot the scotch grass and soil. In different dresses she cycled to the dance-hall, encouraged to make the journey by her father. 'Doesn't it do you good, girl?' he'd say, as though he imagined she begrudged herself the pleasure …

The dance-hall, owned by Mr Justin Dwyer, was miles from anywhere, a lone building by the roadside with treeless boglands all around and a gravel expanse in front of it. On pink pebbled cement its title was painted in an azure blue that matched the depth of the background shade yet stood out well, unfussily proclaiming *The Ballroom of Romance*. Above these letters four coloured bulbs—in red, green, orange and mauve— were lit at appropriate times, an indication that the evening rendezvous was open for business …

People came on bicycles or in old motor-cars, country people like Bridie from remote hill farms and villages. People who did not often see other people met there, girls and boys, men and women. They paid Mr Dwyer and passed into his dance-hall, where shadows were cast on pale blue walls and light from a crystal bowl was dim. The band, known as the Romantic Jazz Band, was composed of clarinet, drums and piano. The drummer sometimes sang.

Bridie had been going to the dance-hall since first she left the Presentation Nuns, before her mother's death. She didn't mind the journey, which was seven miles there and seven miles back: she'd travelled as far every day to the Presentation Nuns on the same bicycle, which had once been the property of her mother …

She paid her entrance fee and passed through the pink swing-doors. The Romantic Jazz Band was playing a familiar melody of the past, the 'Destiny Waltz'. In spite of the band's title, jazz was not ever played in the ballroom: Mr Dwyer did not personally care for that kind of music, nor had he cared for various dance movements that had come and gone over the years. Jiving, rock and roll, twisting, and other such variations had all been resisted by Mr Dwyer, who believed that a ballroom should be, as much as possible, a dignified place. The Romantic Jazz Band consisted of … three middle-aged men … amateur performers who were employed otherwise by the tinned-meat factory, the Electricity Supply Board, and the County Council …

At ten o'clock there was a stir, occasioned by the arrival of three middle-aged bachelors who'd cycled over from Carey's public house. They shouted and whistled, greeting other people across the dancing area. They smelt of stout and sweat and whiskey. Every Saturday at just this time they arrived, and, having sold them their tickets, Mr Dwyer folded up his card-table and locked the tin box that held the evening's takings; his ballroom was complete … The bachelors would never marry, the girls of the dance-hall considered: they were wedded already, to stout and whiskey and laziness, to three old mothers somewhere up in the hills.

QUESTIONS

1. What picture of rural Irish life does it give you?

2. How familiar are you with the rural way of life in your own country? Is it totally different from the scene William Trevor presents, or can you see certain similarities?

3. Rural life, even in the remotest areas, has changed significantly in the past few decades. Do you agree? If so, why? Have the changes all been for the better, or has anything of value been lost?

IN PRAISE OF THE HARP

This poem by the nineteenth-century poet Thomas Moore is one of the many sentimental lyrics he wrote and set to old Irish airs. Moore's *Melodies*, as they were called, were highly popular in the Anglo-Irish and English drawing-rooms of the Victorian age—about the same time as Irish peasants were suffering from the effects of the Great Famine.

These rhyme words are missing from the poem:
   tells   more   walls   days   lives   breaks
Now read it and with your partner or group decide where the missing words belong. Then answer the questions which follow.

The Harp that once through Tara's Halls

The harp that once through Tara's halls
The soul of music shed,
Now hangs as mute on Tara's .... [1]
As if that soul were fled.
So sleeps the pride of former .... [2],
So glory's thrill is o'er,
And hearts, that once beat high for praise,
Now feel that pulse no .... [3].

No more to chiefs and ladies bright
The harp of Tara swells;
The chord alone, that breaks at night,
Its tale of ruin .... [4].
Thus freedom now so seldom wakes,
The only throb she gives,
Is when some heart indignant .... [5],
To show that still she .... [6].

NOTES

Tara: once the seat of the High Kings of Ireland; it is situated in Co. Meath, about 50 km from Dublin.
o'er: poetic abbreviation for 'over'.

QUESTIONS

1. Discuss the significance of the harp in the poem; what does it represent?

2. What kind of music do you imagine the poem is sung to—fast, slow, loud, gentle? And what does your answer tell you about the mood of the poem?

VOCABULARY PRACTICE

In each case choose the word that best completes the sentence, but keep in mind that the word you have come across earlier in this unit is not necessarily the correct answer!

1. Oh, I do wish you'd belt ....! You haven't stopped complaining all morning. Can't you see I'm trying to work?

    (*a*) up   (*b*) out   (*c*) away   (*d*) off

2. For ages we couldn't decide whether to buy the house or not. It was hearing that another couple were interested in it that finally .... the balance.

    (*a*) turned   (*b*) tipped   (*c*) topped   (*d*) outweighed

3. I wouldn't touch that washing powder. It only sells well because of all the advertising .... they use, like winning a free holiday in the Bahamas for two!

    (*a*) gadgets   (*b*) trickery   (*c*) gimmicks   (*d*) fiddles

4. Because of the heavy snowfall, all trains are running ....

(a) behind schedule (b) behind the times (c) lately (d) overdue

5. He is now a well-known fiddle player, but at one time it was his mother's .... desire that he should join the priesthood, like his uncle the bishop.

(a) fervent (b) zealous (c) eager (d) enthusiastic

6. She's an insufferable snob. She looks down .... the rest of us just because she went to a private school.

(a) on (b) at (c) to (d) over

7. At one time .... hairstyles were all the fashion. You had to look as if you hadn't combed your hair for months.

(a) tossed (b) unkempt (c) curly (d) shaggy

8. Although the scientist did not actually find the cure for the disease, her discoveries .... the way for future research.

(a) paved (b) prepared (c) made (d) laid

9. With the money she inherited from her father, she .... up an organisation to subsidise talented young musicians.

(a) put (b) set (c) founded (d) initiated

10. Twenty Years a-Growing by Maurice O'Sullivan is a delightful book about life on the Blaskets, a small .... of islands off the coast of Co. Kerry.

(a) clan (b) crowd (c) cluster (d) clique

11. My mother devoted eleven years of her life to .... my invalid father.

(a) look after (b) tend to (c) caring for (d) taking care

12. After a .... breakfast of bacon and eggs we were ready for a long hike over the hills.

(a) strong (b) hearty (c) heavy (d) greedy

13. Considering that he set his .... on becoming an explorer when he was only six, it's hardly surprising that his teenage daughter has gone with him on his latest expedition to Peru.

    (*a*) sights   (*b*) ambitions   (*c*) mind   (*d*) vision

14. Just imagine how cheap electricity would be if we could find a feasible way of .... the wind's energy!

    (*a*) haltering   (*b*) harnessing   (*c*) taking control   (*d*) curbing

15. I won't be coming in to the office tomorrow, but if anything important ...., give me a ring.

    (*a*) raises   (*b*) rises   (*c*) arises   (*d*) rouses

CLOZE

Read the following passage about the changing fortunes of the Irish harp, and then fill each numbered space with one suitable word.

.... [1] the shamrock, the harp has become a distinctive symbol of Ireland. It turns .... [2] everywhere: on coins, emblazoned against the azure background of certain beer cans, printed on Government stationery, and .... [3] from the president's flagstaff. Harp playing is by no .... [4] peculiar to Ireland, as many of you reading this will .... [5] doubt know. So why, you .... [6] well ask, has the instrument taken on .... [7] a degree of significance that it stands .... [8] the very soul of the nation?

The harp made its debut .... [9] a symbol for Ireland in the thirteenth century, but it had been around as a musical instrument .... [10] a considerable time before that. Among the instruments in use in ancient Ireland .... [11] was given pride of place; it features in the earliest myths and legends, and in historical times the chief performer on .... [12] was accorded the rank of nobleman. The oldest surviving Irish harp .... [13] be seen in Trinity College Library, Dublin. It was once known as the Brian Ború Harp, but it is not quite as .... [14] as that name alleges: Brian Ború died in 1014, whereas this harp .... [15] back only to the fifteenth or sixteenth century.

The bardic tradition of the seventeenth and eighteenth centuries, when harpers (many of .... [16] were blind, ... [17] the famous O'Carolan) .... [18] travel round the country entertaining the 'quality', sadly died out. For a long time the harp was used only ....
[19] a suitably dulcet accompaniment for silver-toned sopranos. It was Seán Ó Riada .... [20] reinstated it to its former glory by including it in his arrangements of traditional music.

Unit 9

THE WEE NORTH

With a partner or group, look at these photographs. Describe what you see, and say what the scenes suggest to you. (You might make a list of key words that come up, like 'beauty', 'enjoyment', etc.)

Do the places photographed appeal to you? Would you like to visit them—perhaps spend a holiday there? Compare your responses with the rest of the class.

These photographs were all taken from a brochure published by the Tourist Board for Northern Ireland. Does knowing this now change your answer to the earlier questions in any way? Say why (or, indeed, why not).

As a class, make a brainstorm on the board of all you associate with Northern Ireland: facts, impressions, opinions, etc. Summarise these by picking out the predominating ideas.

For most people, Northern Ireland means violence; like other trouble-spots in the world, it is a place they would rather avoid. A joke is told about the competition that offered as first prize 'A week in Belfast'. Second prize was 'Two weeks in Belfast'.

Since many of the people who live there have a limited understanding of the situation they live in, it's forgivable for outsiders to be more than a little confused! The previous activity, however, may have helped to clarify for you what you know and what you don't know.

WHAT'S IN A NAME?

Of the thirty-two counties making up Ireland, six (Antrim, Armagh, Derry, Down, Fermanagh, and Tyrone) form Northern Ireland, the part that belongs to the United Kingdom. The name a person uses to refer to that place can tell you something about the person and his or her attitudes.

1. Look at how these six people describe themselves, and then read the explanations of the different names used.

2. With your partner, decide which name each person is most likely to use. (Keep in mind that no answer is actually wrong in each case, but one is more appropriate than the others.)

A

I come from Co. Antrim, and my ancestors were planters from Scotland. To me, being Irish means being Roman Catholic and republican. Sometimes, when I think the boys in Westminster are going to abandon us to the Dublin government, I wonder why I bother to call myself British. Well, I'll fight to the bitter end to hold on to the place I live in: ....

B

I'm a journalist with the BBC. I frequently have to report on events in ....

C

I've been living in Dublin for years now, but I still get homesick. At Christmas and Easter and any other time of the year I can manage it, I just love going home to my family and friends in ....

D

British-occupied Ireland, that's how I see it. The British have no right to be there; they should go home and leave .... to us Irish.

E

I've never been to Ireland, and I don't know much about it except that in part of it—............. I think it's called—there's a lot of trouble.

F

I was born and brought up in ....—a town called Enniskillen in Co. Fermanagh, to be precise. That makes me a British subject and entitles me to a British passport. I'm sick of all the violence and wish we could learn to live together in peace, no matter what our religion or political views are.

THE NAMES

Northern Ireland—to those who recognise it as part of the United Kingdom, the other part being Great Britain.
The North—(and sometimes affectionately 'the wee North') a common way of distinguishing it from that part of Ireland known as the South.
The Six Counties—to those who do not recognise it as a separate political entity belonging to Britain. Some Northerners retaliate by calling the South 'Éire' (which really means Ireland, i.e. the whole island and its thirty-two counties) or 'the Free State' (this title was dropped when Ireland became a Republic in 1949).
Ulster—a misnomer commonly used by (a) the media, because it is shorter than the other names, (b) those who deny that they are Irish and for whom the name provides a sense of identity, and (c) people who don't know any better. Ulster is, in fact, one of the four ancient provinces of

Ireland (the others being Munster, Leinster, and Connacht); it consists of the six counties of Northern Ireland and three counties of the Republic: Monaghan, Cavan, and Donegal.

SIMPLIFICATION

The two traditions in the North of the planter and the Gael (i.e. the Scottish Presbyterians who arrived in the seventeenth century and the native Catholic Irish) today express themselves politically in terms of unionism and republicanism. Like most generalisations, that is an oversimplification. But then there is a tendency to oversimplify things in the North.

Take the man, for instance, who was called for interview for a job. As he entered the room where the interview was to take place, the personnel manager was studying his application form. 'I see you've put down atheist as your religion,' he said. 'That's right,' replied the man. 'Fine,' said the manager, looking somewhat confused, 'but are you a Protestant atheist or a Catholic atheist?'

FACES OF THE NORTH

What aspects of the North do these pictures present? Below is a brief outline of events in the history of Northern Ireland. With your partner, decide which picture each text relates to.

A.

B.

C.

RESULT OF LOCAL ELECTIONS IN DERRY CITY 1967

NORTH WARD
39% Catholic Voters
61% Protestant Voters
8 Unionist Councillors elected

Total Protestant
Population: 8,781
Represented by
12 Unionist Councillors
Total Catholic
Population: 14,429
Represented by
8 Nationalist Councillors

CREGGAN
ESTATE

BOGSIDE

WALLED CITY

SOUTH WARD
90% Catholic Voters
10% Protestant Voters
8 Nationalist Councillors elected

RIVER FOYLE

WATERSIDE WARD
33% Catholic Voters
67% Protestant Voters
4 Unionist Councillors elected

D.

ULSTER'S SOLEMN COVENANT

SIR EDWARD CARSON

HEROES OF THE UNION

E.

F.

'Home Rule is Rome Rule!' Under the leadership of Edward Carson, the mainly Protestant Ulster is prepared to fight to maintain the union with Britain. This leads to the creation of Northern Ireland in 1921.

(ii)

Government established at Belfast—'a Protestant parliament for a Protestant people' (approximately one-third are Roman Catholic). Unionists win every election until the suspension of Stormont in 1972.

(iii)

Gerrymandering (rigging of electoral boundaries) keeps Nationalists out of power in predominantly Catholic areas. Vote in local elections confined to 'resident occupier', which means some that adults (mainly Catholics) have no vote and others (mainly Protestants) have up to six votes each. Result: preferential treatment in housing etc. given to Protestants.

(iv)

High unemployment a perennial problem—up to 25 per cent of insured population on the dole. Hardest-hit areas west Belfast and border towns such as Derry and Strabane. 'I recommend those people who are Loyalists not to employ Roman Catholics, ninety-nine per cent of whom are disloyal,' said Lord Brookeborough (Prime Minister 1943–1963).

(v)

'One man, one vote'—peaceful demonstrations organised by the Northern Ireland Civil Rights Association (founded 1967). Hard-line unionists opposed to reform. Marchers brutally attacked by militant Protestants and police in 1968 and 1969, quickly followed by full-scale rioting. British troops called in. IRA begins vigorous campaign. Stormont suspended in 1972; direct rule from Westminster.

(vi)

Repeated attempts to restore peace by political means brought down by extremists championed by hard-line unionist leader Ian Paisley. Vehement opposition to power-sharing with nationalists and involvement of Dublin government in Northern Ireland affairs.

A: .... B: .... C: .... D: .... E: .... F: ....

In his book *Holidays in Hell*, the American journalist P. J. O'Rourke wrote about his experiences in various trouble-spots in the world, including Northern Ireland. Here is an extract from the chapter he calls 'The piece of Ireland that passeth all understanding'. Read it, then answer the questions that follow.

The best thing about the violence in Northern Ireland is that it's all so ancient and honourable. And I'm proud to say it began in the household of my own relative Tighernan O'Rourke, Prince of Breffni. In 1152 Tighernan's comely wife Dervogilla ran off with Diarmuid MacMurrough, King of Leinster. Cousin O'Rourke raised such a stink (and army) that MacMurrough had to call King Henry II of England for help. The Brits arrived, somewhat tardily, in 1169 and proceeded to commit the unforgivable sin of having long bows and chain mail. For the next 819 years (and counting) the English stole land, crushed rebellions, exploited the populace, persecuted Catholics, dragged a bunch of Scottish settlers into Ulster, crushed more rebellions, held potato famines, hanged patriots, stamped out the language, taxed everybody's pig, crushed more rebellions yet and generally behaved in a manner much different than the Irish would have if it had been the Irish who invaded England and the shoe was on the other foot (assuming the Irish could afford shoes).

At any rate, the Irish are in the same terrific position as the Shiites in Lebanon, the peasants in El Salvador, the blacks in America, the Jews in Palestine, the Palestinians in Israel (and everybody everywhere, if you read your history)—enough barbarianism has been visited on the Irish to excuse all barbarities by the Irish barbarians.

MULTIPLE-CHOICE QUESTIONS

Choose the best answer in each case.

1. The passage is
   (a) a tongue-in-cheek justification for the violence in Northern Ireland
   (b) blatant anti-British propaganda
   (c) an attempt to identify the problems of the Irish with those of other persecuted people
   (d) a completely fictitious account of the situation by an Irish-American.

2. Which seems to be the most apt description of the writer?
   (a) He is a cynical observer of life.
   (b) He is totally prejudiced in his opinions.
   (c) He is passionately involved with the problems of the Irish.
   (d) He is unreliable because he is ill-informed.

3. According to the writer, the position the Irish are in is 'terrific', because
   (a) they are in good company
   (b) they can be totally exonerated for their actions
   (c) like their counterparts in other trouble-spots, they are the focus of world attention
   (d) he is proud of his Irish roots.

4. The phrase that most clearly indicates the writer's tone when describing the English in Ireland is
   (a) crushed rebellions
   (b) persecuted Catholics
   (c) held potato famines
   (d) stole land.

5. He suggests that if 'the shoe was on the other foot'
   (a) the Irish would have invaded England
   (b) the English would not have invaded Ireland
   (c) the English would not have suffered what the Irish did
   (d) the Irish would have been just as bad as the English.

THE COLOUR ORANGE

The Irish national flag is a symbolic attempt to embrace the two traditions: green, the colour long associated with Ireland; orange, the natural choice for the loyal followers of the Dutch Prince William of Orange, the Protestant champion who defeated the Catholic King James at the Battle of the Boyne in 1690 (hence the Orange Order and Orangemen); and, in the middle, white, the peace reconciling the two.

In 1843, long before the Tricolour was flown, a song of reconciliation was written about the orange lily, a flower worn on 12th July to commemorate William's victory. This is the middle verse with the rhyme—words missing. The missing words appear at the side but they are not in order.

Behold how green the gallant .... [1]
On which the flower is .... [2];
How in one heavenly breeze and .... [3]
Both flower and stem are .... [4].
The same good soil, sustaining .... [5],
Makes both united .... [6];
But cannot give the Orange .... [7],
And cease the Green to .... [8].

flourish
glowing
stem
growth
nourish
blowing
beam
both

With a partner or group
(a) decide where the words should go;
(b) discuss how the writer uses the flower as a symbol of reconcilation.

ORANGE TALK Willie had been a staunch Orangeman all his life. As he lay on his death-bed, he called for the local Catholic priest. The priest came, had a private tête-à-tête with Willie, and left. Then the shocked family gathered round Willie and demanded to know what he'd done. 'I turned,' he said with a satisfied smile. Horror-struck, they chorused, 'Why?' 'Sure isn't it better for one of *them* to die than one of *us*,' he replied, and, as they say, passed away peacefully!

QUESTION

What do you think the verb 'to turn' means in this context?

GOODBYE TO INNOCENCE In the following passage the writer remembers her Protestant upbringing in a predominantly Catholic Northern town. The passage has been divided into three sections. Look at the pre-reading questions, and discuss your answers after you have read each section.

Do not attempt the detailed questions following each section until you have read the whole passage. These, as in previous units, may be done orally with your partner, and/or in writing as homework.

(A) What do you learn about (*a*) the writer, (*b*) her background, and (*c*) the town she grew up in?

If middle age begins at 45, then I am what I can no longer deny—middle-aged. And, I suppose, as mature as I'm ever going to be—whatever that means. Set in my ways and settled in my opinions, more likely. I have found on reaching this status that those who have yet to achieve it,
5   including those I consider to have more sagacity in their little toe than I am ever likely to be blessed with, tend to look to me for pearls of wisdom. As if age alone is the great revealer, and the voice of experience is by definition the voice of authority. I was born and reared in 'the North', another fact it is impossible to deny. And so it would seem, especially to
10 people who are neither middle-aged nor from the North, that I am eminently qualified to account for that part of the world I grew up in. I am not. That is perhaps the one thing I can be certain about, the part of the world I grew up in being unaccountable for. But people, particularly the young and inquiring, are persistent.

15 I was born in Strabane, Co. Tyrone; to be more precise, in the spare bedroom in the Main Street. Our house was called the 'Main Street' to distinguish it from the other houses occupied by relations of the same name. The less important people on either side of us lived in numbers: to

156

the right was what the Post Office called Lower Main Street, the humbler
end where the Catholics lived, and to the left was the Upper-in-every-way
end with its largely Protestant-owned businesses and banks. Being
Protestant and important, we needed neither number nor definer. My
father once boasted he received a letter with 'Northern Ireland' as the
only address. That's how important we were.

Strabane is a market town just over 20 kilometres south of Derry and
about as far away from Belfast as you can get without leaving Northern
Ireland. What could without much difficulty win an Ugly Town
competition is surrounded by rural loveliness. A five-minute walk from
the end of the Main Street takes you across the Border and into the most
beautiful county in Ireland, Donegal. Like other towns just inside the
Border, the majority of its population (about 60%) is Catholic. Another
prize Strabane could win without really trying is in the Who's Got the
Highest Unemployment contest. With an all-time record of 49% on the
dole to its credit, it has (or had) a reputation for corner boys equalled by
none—and claim to another gold medal.

Corner boys are men of indeterminate age who, having nothing better to
do and nowhere else to go, survey the world from a street corner. The only
qualification needed is to be unemployed; the only potential possessed, to
be unemployable. Corner boys were invariably Catholic and, like red hair,
ran in families. They were the ones not lucky enough to be usefully
employed in places like my father's egg store at the back of our house,
cleaning, testing and packing eggs. Since one of their favourite stamping-
grounds was just opposite my bedroom window, their muted conversation
used to be my lullaby at bedtime when I was a child. They were there
long after I had brushed my teeth and said my prayers, and there they
would be in the morning when I dragged my feet schoolwards.

School was not something I enjoyed much; it was, rather, a quite forgettable
process of ingesting irrelevant information in the company of other
Protestant boys and girls—'mixed' education, it was called. Apart from a
nodding acquaintance with the corner boys, the Catholics I knew were the
lucky-to-have-jobs-at-all egg packers. I spent a lot of time helping them, or
playing football with a parcel of old newspapers and learning jokes I didn't
understand (and wisely didn't repeat). 'Will you talk to us when you grow
up?' one of the lucky ones once asked me. I also marched behind the pipe
band on the Twelfth of July and played Royal Families with my cousins.
When I grew up, I decided, I'd be a piper in an Orange band and marry a
prince and become a princess. I'd do my hair in ringlets, too, and wear
patent shoes with silver buckles like the little girls down the street who did
Irish dancing, all pleasures which were mysteriously forbidden to me.

1. What do people think the writer should be able to do and why? Why does she disagree with them?

2. Explain what she means and implies by the phrase 'lived in numbers' (line 18).

3. What are the town's distinctive features, and what tone does the writer use in describing them?

4. The word 'usefully' (line 40) could be omitted. Why does the writer use it?

5. What are 'stamping-grounds' (line 42–43), and why is the term particularly suitable in the context?

6. How does the writer prepare you for the opening sentence of paragraph 4?

7. Why is the word 'mixed' in quotation marks in line 49?

8. In the description of her childhood activities and ambitions, what does the author suggest?

*   *   *   *   *   *   *   *   *

(B) Why was the writer's childhood 'comfortable and secure'? What note of doubt is introduced?

The world of my childhood was comfortable and secure. There was no room for doubts and no need for questions. 'Why is Esso the best petrol?' a younger cousin asked. 'Because it says so,' I answered, reading the ad. Life was that simple and that certain. It was the gospel truth that Catholics were poor and feckless, lived in squalor and bred like rabbits. You could tell a Mick by his dirty fingernails; you didn't have to wait to see if he crossed himself when he passed the chapel. Taigs worshipped statues, smelt of Guinness and played games on Sunday (all sins), priests drank whiskey (another sin), and nuns had gruesome bald heads to scare little children with. Protestants were neat and tidy; they worked hard, lived in nice houses, wore hats to church and went to heaven when God called them. (This unrelenting virtuousness made them vaguely boring.) King Billy was a handsome man with long hair and a white horse, and the national anthem was a song called 'God Save the Queen', which you stood up to sing even if you were only practising it with your cousins in the back yard.

158

My repertoire of known facts expanded by dint of sitting in the classroom. The War of Independence was an unfortunate affair conducted on American soil some time after the redoubtable Oliver Cromwell won the Civil War. History, in effect, was a series of wars mainly caused by the French and the Spanish, who were forever picking quarrels with the English (I didn't get as far as the twentieth century, so the Germans didn't figure). Why did they bother, I wondered. Since Britannia ruled the waves and God was on our side, we invariably won. Literature was something written by Englishmen like Shakespeare. We read a poem by Robbie Burns, so it could even include the odd Scot. England and Scotland and even Wales were all the same thing, anyway; put together, they made Great Britain. And if you added Northern Ireland you had the United Kingdom, which we were honoured to be part of, slightly detached from the mainland though we might be. As for Joyce, that was the name of the woman who worked in my father's office; and Wilde and Synge, like Pearse and Tone, were words you could find in the dictionary. The Border was there when I was born, so why wouldn't it be there when I died and went to heaven? It was there to separate the Irish in the Free State, where nothing was free and nobody knew the meaning of work, from us British in the North, where we had the welfare state with free education and medicine and everybody worked very hard—except the ones who had no work and therefore didn't count. Indelibly stamped on my memory is the tight-lipped remark of my maiden aunt. We were going through the wild and very wonderful Barnesmore Gap in the heart of Donegal on a sedate Sunday afternoon drive. 'Such a pity it doesn't belong to us,' she said.

I didn't see why. It seemed to me that since we had everything else, it was more than a little greedy to want what was rightfully theirs. Purple mountains with waterfalls, golden beaches and blue seas, red fuchsia and yellow whins, the acrid smell of turf, soft voices and a pace of life that would soothe a snail. Somewhere in my subconscious a thought conceived itself and began to grow. It wouldn't be a bad swop—having all that instead of the boring and decidedly un-beautiful benefits of life in the Main Street. The Free State was infinitely more attractive and, in my book, very aptly named. It may not have had the advantages enjoyed by us, but—it somehow made you feel free.

Which of the following statements are true, and which are false?
1. The child took everything she heard and read at face value.
2. Familiar as it was, the Protestant way of life seemed rather staid to her.
3. Her schooling helped to develop her enquiring mind.
4. The advantages of living in Northern Ireland outweighed the attractions of the Free State.

(C) What pattern did the writer's questions take and where did they lead her?

What happened when she returned to Strabane, and how did it change her?

 The thought grew with me. Like a loose tooth you worry with your tongue, it niggled me. It developed into disturbing questions. Why, considering all the advantages it implied, did I not feel 'British and proud of it'? Why, if it was such an inferior-in-every way place, did the South appeal more? Why did living in Strabane feel ever so slightly uncomfortable? The vibes the ugly little town gave out were ones of wariness and defensiveness—as if it was eternally on its guard. The air was full of unspoken words, the motto for living, 'Whatever you say, say nothing.' But every now and again the tight-lipped silence was broken and things were said that would bring the niggling thoughts and questions to the surface of my consciousness. A clergyman, new to the town, wanted to know which shops in the street were 'ours' so that he could avoid giving his custom to the wrong side. A Protestant draper was openly abused for attending the funeral of a Catholic neighbour. Another reverend gentleman directed me to be polite but not 'too friendly' towards any Catholics I chanced to meet, lest I should let the side down and marry one. There was a huge outcry from offended parents when the headmaster of our school (himself, rumour had it, a Protestant atheist) appointed a highly qualified young woman as the new science teacher. When the hapless foot she dug with was revealed, they had her removed forthwith before she could contaminate the two hundred innocents in her clutches. Where was the Christian value of charity and the British sense of fair play I had been brought up to believe in? The questions niggled and grew and, because there were no straight answers, continued to niggle and grow.

I began to look at all the things I had previously taken for granted, all those certainties I had blindly accepted. Being young, idealistic and oh-so-naïve, I found an inexhaustible fuel supply for my romantic imagination. Rebel, it said. And rebel I did. Replacing one set of certainties with another, I flung myself whole-heartedly into the role of black sheep. I toyed with the idea of joining the IRA and talked loudly about changing my faith. I bought an expensive volume of Yeats and a book of rebel songs; I changed my favourite colour from royal blue to emerald green, pinned the 1916 Proclamation to my bedroom door, and self-importantly flaunted an Irish passport. Then I went to university in Dublin, where I learnt to be apologetic about my background and defensive about my ignorance—and not much else.

Years later, when I returned to Strabane just after the outbreak of the 'present troubles', I was no better equipped to cope with the violence and suffering confronting me daily than I had been to deal with the disturbing questions of my youth. The ugly little town grew uglier still, until it began to look like a bad mouth with as many gaps as teeth. Then one November night the hotel next door was blown to kingdom come by an IRA bomb. I saw the 'Main Street', like the victim of a heart attack, lying dead before my disbelieving eyes. With it, pathetically scattered among the rubble and the debris, lay the twenty-seven years of my innocence. I said goodbye to certainties then—and to that part of the world where I grew up.

MULTIPLE-CHOICE QUESTIONS

In each of the following questions more than one answer may be correct.

1. Living in Strabane felt 'ever so slightly uncomfortable' because
    (a) it was so ugly
    (b) people didn't trust one another
    (c) there was an undercurrent of fear and suspicion
    (d) people were always careful what they said.

2. The questions that disturbed the young girl
    (a) had no satisfactory answers
    (b) made her think about things she had never thought about before
    (c) exposed her to bigotry and injustice
    (d) made her reject the principles she had been taught to believe in.

3. As a result of all the questions, she
    (a) gained an insight into the situation
    (b) set out to redress the injustices
    (c) adopted a pose
    (d) went from one extreme to another.

4. What happened 'one November night'?
    (a) The house she grew up in was bombed by the IRA.
    (b) Her illusions were shattered.
    (c) She was confronted with her own vulnerability.
    (d) She realised how naïve she had been.

VICTIM

Before you read the poem below by the Belfast-born poet Pádraic Fiacc—

1. Check on the meaning of these words, and use each one in the following sentences.

culvert   perched   bland   grin   side-whiskers

(a) When you .... like that I can see all the fillings in your teeth!
(b) Her .... remark showed that she didn't want to get involved in the argument.
(c) The little dog got stuck down a .... and had to be rescued by the fire brigade.

161

(*d*) The teacher .... on the edge of her desk where all the children could see her.

(*e*) He shaved his .... off because they were so uncomfortable in the hot weather.

2. If a 'teeny-bopper' is a young teenager who eagerly follows the current fashions, and 'weeny' or 'weenie' means tiny, what do you think a 'weenie-bopper' is?

3. Say what the title suggests to you and what you expect the poem to be about.

Now read (or listen to) the poem two or three times, and then discuss the questions that follow.

ENEMY ENCOUNTER

>   Dumping [left over from the autumn]
> Dead leaves, near a culvert
> I come on
>
>   a British Army soldier
> With a rifle and a radio
> Perched hiding. He has red hair.
>
> He is young enough to be my weenie
> -bopper daughter's boy-friend.
> He is like a lonely little winter robin.
>
> We are that close to each other, I
> Can nearly hear his heart beating.
>
> I say something bland to make him grin,
> But his glass eyes look past my side
> -whiskers down
>   the Shore Road street.
>
> I am an Irish man
>   and he is afraid
> That I have come to kill him.

Padraig Fiacc

QUESTIONS

1. Did thinking and/or talking about the title prepare you for the poem? If not, why not?

2. What image is created of the soldier, and what feelings does he arouse in the poet? Pick out the words and phrases that support your answers.

3. What do you imagine the poet might have said to the soldier? How did he react?

4. Do you think the heading of this section ('Victim') is appropriate?

WRITING

The troubles in the North have claimed many lives over the years; the death toll includes innocent civilians as well as members of the security forces and paramilitary organisations on both sides. Whatever the cause of their deaths and whoever was responsible for them, they are all victims of violence. Moreover, the families and friends they leave behind them are victims of sorrow and suffering, not to mention bitterness and hatred.

Choose one of the two suggested topics to write on:

1. Political violence may produce immediate results, but in the long run it is self-defeating. Do you agree? Discuss this briefly as a class before working out your own approach and argument.

2. Write a story entitled 'Victim'. Think again about the soldier in 'Enemy Encounter'—a victim is not necessarily an innocent person who dies as the result of violence or an accident. Checking your dictionary might be helpful here.

VOCABULARY PRACTICE

In each case choose the word that best completes the sentence, but keep in mind that the word you have come across earlier in this unit is not necessarily the correct answer!

1. We've got thirty invitations to write and post. The family and the neighbours don't ...., because we can just ask them when we see them.

    (*a*) figure   (*b*) count   (*c*) include   (*d*) import

2. She kicked up such a .... when he said he was going out to the pub to meet the lads that he had to stay at home and mow the lawn!

    (*a*) trouble   (*b*) noise   (*c*) hell   (*d*) stink

3. We liked each other's sweaters better than our own, so we decided to do a ....

    (*a*) swap   (*b*) swoop   (*c*) swipe   (*d*) swat

4. Going by his curriculum vitae he seems to be .... suitable for the job, but we'd still need to interview him.

    (*a*) completely   (*b*) eminently   (*c*) rather   (*d*) well

5. She was like a child with a new toy the way she was .... off her latest boy-friend at the party last night. It was sickening!

    (*a*) boasting   (*b*) bragging   (*c*) flaunting   (*d*) showing

6. His understanding of the political situation in Ireland is .... no one's.

    (*a*) equal to   (*b*) equalled by   (*c*) the equal of   (*d*) the equality of

7. The rebellion was ruthlessly .... down.

    (*a*) put   (*b*) pushed   (*c*) crushed   (*d*) suppressed

8. My boss made me the .... for everything that went wrong at the conference, even though I was just acting on her instructions.

    (*a*) black sheep   (*b*) stupid cow   (*c*) scapegoat   (*d*) Irish bull

9. If you keep .... that tooth, it's going to come out before the dentist has a chance to do something with it.

    (*a*) niggling   (*b*) wiggling   (*c*) waggling   (*d*) losing

10. I wish you'd stop .... your feet and tell me whether you're going to come on holiday with me or not.

    (*a*) stamping   (*b*) shuffling   (*c*) trailing   (*d*) dragging

11. The .... of victims killed in yesterday's train crash has now risen to fifty-six.

    (*a*) figure   (*b*) number   (*c*) amount   (*d*) toll

12. After galloping our horses over the hills all morning, we rode them back at a more .... pace.

    (*a*) sedate   (*b*) slow   (*c*) tardy   (*d*) leisured

13. She tried to get over her disappointment by .... herself into her studies.

    (*a*) immersing   (*b*) diving   (*c*) flinging   (*d*) burying

14. Such a .... the youngsters left after they'd had their picnic! They should have been made to clean it up.

    (*a*) debris   (*b*) rubble   (*c*) litter   (*d*) mess

15. I always find Chopin's music .... me when I've had a tough day at the office.

    (*a*) tranquillises   (*b*) sedates   (*c*) pacifies   (*d*) soothes

CLOZE

Nell McCafferty is a journalist who was brought up as a Catholic in Derry in the 1950s and 1960s. Here she writes about when she was a secondary school student attending Thornhill College. Fill each space with one suitable word.

We were taken to a free educational .... [1] in a city cinema. The Protestant schoolgirls sat in one block of .... [2] and we sat across the aisle in .... [3]. The boys were to come next day, sexual integration .... [4] considered the marginally greater danger. The cinema darkened, a drum roll began, the curtains parted, and onto the .... [5] flashed a picture of Queen Elizabeth the Second, Monarch of England, Scotland, Wales and Northern Ireland. The Protestants .... [6] smartly on their feet. Our escort, Miss McDevitt, an elderly aristocratic lady in tweeds, remained firmly .... [7]. We took our cue .... [8] her and sat stolidly through the national .... [9].

Miss McDevitt never afterwards alluded .... [10] the incident, and we knew better .... [11] to ask her why she did it. They followed the Queen; we .... [12] the Pope. The division was as simple as .... [13], ... [14] British nor Irish prime ministers having heard of us .... [15] the time. In .... [16] a small society the lines had occasionally been crossed, of course, but always discreetly. The matter was .... [17] painful and confusing to be dwelt on at length. My father's brother, Joe, for .... [18], had fought in the British Army in the First World War and his .... [19] was inscribed on the War Memorial ... But we never attended the annual commemoration ceremony, an occasion .... [20] underlining British citizenship.

The sight of children playing games in the street is no longer as familiar as it used to be. Sadly, hoops and skipping ropes, marbles and balls have largely given way to television and computer games. The dangers presented by modern traffic conditions are, no doubt, a contributing factor. In the days when the streets of Belfast were reasonably safe—from 'the troubles' as much as from fast vehicles—this was a song children sang while they were skipping.

Note: In standard English, 'me ma' is, of course, 'my mother' and a 'fella' is a 'fellow'.

Listen to the song on the cassette and then sing along with it.

I'LL TELL ME MA

1.

I'll tell me ma when I go home
The boys won't leave the girls alone,
They tossed my hair, they broke my comb,
But that's all right till I get home.

Chorus

She is handsome, she is pretty,
She is the belle of Belfast city;
She is courting, one, two, three,
Please can you tell me who is she?

2.

Albert Mooney says he loves her,
All the boys are fighting for her,
They knock at the door and they ring at the bell,
Saying, 'Oh, my true love, are you well?'

Chorus

3.

Out she comes as white as snow,
With rings on her fingers and bells on her toes,
Oul' Jenny Murray says she'll die
If she doesn't get the fella with the roving eye.

Chorus

4.

Let the rain and the wind and the breeze blow high,
The snow comes falling from the sky,
Jenny Murray says she'll die
If she doesn't get the fella with the roving eye.

Chorus

5.

One young man is fighting for her,
All the rest they swear they'll have her,
Let them all say as they will,
Albert Mooney loves her still.

Chorus

Unit 10

INFLUENCES

1. To what extent have the following influenced your outlook on life and your political views? Give each one 0 to 5 points, depending on how important you think they have been.

Parents, family   Social background   Studies
Politicians   Teachers   The media
Peers   Travel   Other

(*a*) Now compare and discuss your answers with the rest of the class. If you have rated 'other' highly, explain what you mean by it. Does any one of the above appear to have had a significant influence, in general, or to have had no influence at all?

(*b*) How important is the written word? Are there any writers whose works have had a formative influence on (i) your personal development and (ii) the development of your country?

2. Here is the first verse of 'Dark Rosaleen' by the nineteenth-century poet James Clarence Mangan.

(*a*) Read it, say who you think Rosaleen is, and discuss the image the poet presents of her and his feelings towards her.

> O my Dark Rosaleen,
> Do not sigh, do not weep!
> The priests are on the ocean green,
> They march along the Deep.
> There's wine from the royal Pope,
> Upon the ocean green;
> And Spanish ale shall give you hope,
> My Dark Rosaleen!
> My own Rosaleen!
> Shall glad your heart, shall give you hope,
> Shall give you health, and help, and hope,
> My Dark Rosaleen!

(*b*) In literature, Ireland has often been represented as a woman; Mangan 'Dark Rosaleen' is, in fact, Ireland. Now that you know this, read the verse again. What does it say to you?

Mangan's poem, which is a translation from an older Irish poem, first appeared in the *Nation*, a newspaper founded in 1842 by Thomas Davis and others. This served as a mouthpiece for the growing feelings of nationalism at that time. Davis himself was a rather mediocre poet, but his song 'A Nation Once Again' is still so popular that it is, in effect, an unofficial national anthem. The rousing chorus goes:

> A nation once again,
> A nation once again,
> And Ireland, long a province, be
> A nation once again.

POETS, PATRIOTS, AND POLITICIANS

Instrumental in the development of events in Ireland in the nineteenth century was the revival of interest in the country's Gaelic past and the wealth of literature this produced. The following passage is a brief account of the events that led to the eventual making of 'a nation once again'. Read it, then, with a partner or group, discuss your answers to these questions.

QUESTIONS

1. How much do you learn about the 1916 Rising, people's attitudes towards it at the time, and what happened afterwards?

2. What four causes of unrest in Ireland in the nineteenth century are mentioned, and how successful were the politicians in dealing with it?

3. What is the connection between poets, patriots, and politicians?

'Now, Pat, above all, don't do anything rash,' said Patrick Pearse's mother to him one April morning in 1916. 'No, Mother,' replied her dutiful son on his way out to lead a rebellion, proclaim the independence of his country from the steps of the General Post Office, hold out for a week against the
5 British forces, and, on surrendering, get himself executed by firing squad. There is hardly a more appropriate word than 'rash' to describe what Pearse, the poet and idealist, and all the other men and women who took part in the 1916 Easter Rising did. 'A hare-brained romantic adventure,' George Bernard Shaw called it. 'A more unlikely crowd to spark a nation
10 to freedom would be hard to imagine … poor writers and intellectuals' is how the writer John McGahern has more recently described them. The leaders themselves were not unaware of the likely outcome of their actions: 'We're going out to be slaughtered,' James Connolly confessed. And for many of them, that's exactly what happened.

15   It wasn't by any means the first time arms had been taken up against the
        British. Beginning with the United Irishmen in 1798 and all the way
        through the nineteenth century there had been a series of abortive
        rebellions. Abortive because they failed but, looked at from another
        perspective, successful in that they fanned the flames of nationalism and
20   made heroes of the men who led them; along with Pearse and Connolly,
        the names of Theobald Wolfe Tone, Robert Emmet and Thomas Davis are
        all written in capital letters on the Irish consciousness. In 1801 the Act of
        Union had placed Ireland under direct rule from Westminster. That,
        together with the inequalities suffered by a largely Catholic population
25   and the plight of peasants at the mercy of their landlords, made for a
        deeply and bitterly disturbed country. Add recurring famine and all its
        concomitants and you have an excellent recipe for trouble. Constitutional
        politics had achieved a measure of success through the efforts of two
        outstanding political figures: Daniel O'Connell, known as the Liberator
30   because he won emancipation for Catholics in 1829, and Charles Stewart
        Parnell, Ireland's 'uncrowned king', who successfully championed the
        cause of land reform. But Parnell's political career was brought to a tragic
        end before he achieved his real goal of re-establishing an independent
        Dublin parliament. His long-standing love affair with Katherine O'Shea
35   became public when her husband named him in a divorce petition,
        scandalising straight-laced Victorian England and ultra-Catholic Ireland.
        He died a broken man at the early age of forty-five, leaving behind him an
        irreparable rift in the Irish parliamentary party and, indeed, the whole
        country. People were either Parnellites or anti-Parnellites; and with what
40   frightening passion they held their positions is shown in the famous
        Christmas dinner episode in Joyce's *Portrait of the Artist as a Young Man*.
        A violent quarrel ends with Mr Casey, a grown man, breaking down and
        sobbing, 'Poor Parnell! My dead king!'

        Home rule was as far away as it had ever been, but the nationalist cause
45   was by no means dead. Exeunt the politicians and enter the poets. The
        artificers of words, who in Celtic times had enjoyed an exalted position
        second only to the king, were now the ones who fired the imagination of a
        politically fragmented country. A revival of interest in Gaelic culture,
        including the old sagas and folk-tales, the language and traditional
50   games, inspired a literary renaissance in which writers used English as
        the medium for essentially Irish themes and concerns. Top of the list was
        the poet and playwright William Butler Yeats, who, with Lady Gregory,
        founded the Abbey as the National Theatre in 1904. Two years prior to
        that, his overtly patriotic play, *Cathleen ni Houlihan*, had caused a
55   considerable disturbance. In it Ireland, symbolised by an old woman who
        suddenly changes into a beautiful young woman, calls her young men to
        rise up against her oppressors. Much later Yeats was to wonder:

> Did that play of mine send out
> Certain men the English shot?

60 Whether Yeats can be held personally responsible for the deaths of the
1916 leaders is, of course, debatable; but there is no doubt that the men
of words were men of no mean influence. Pearse the poet made his
position clear when he wrote:

> And I say to my people's masters: Beware,
65 > Beware of the thing that is coming, beware of the risen people,
> Who shall take what ye would not give.

And yet, when the Easter Rising did take place it was so unpopular that
the insurrectionists were spat on as they were led away to jail. The great
majority, assured of home rule as soon as the war with Germany was over,
70 and mindful of the thousands of Irish soldiers who had rallied to
England's side, were not sympathetic to the notion that 'England's
difficulty is Ireland's opportunity.' Yeats himself was scornful of
acquaintances he knew to be involved in preparations for an armed
struggle. It was the ritual execution of sixteen of the leaders in the
75 aftermath of the Rising—what McGahern calls 'British bungling'—that
turned the tide of opinion and caused Yeats to write the famous lines:

> All changed, changed utterly:
> A terrible beauty is born.

As Shaw said, 'those who were executed accordingly became not only
80 national heroes, but the martyrs whose blood was the seed of the Irish
Free State.' The beauty grew more terrible as the brutal struggle for
independence, ending in a treaty that partitioned the country and divided
the people, turned into an even more brutal civil war. The freedom that
eventually came was dearly bought and, as the continuing story shows, is
85 still being paid for.

Now, if Pat had listened to his mother that April morning …

MORE QUESTIONS

Now read the passage again and answer these questions as precisely as
you can. You may do this orally with a partner, and/or in writing as
homework.

1. What does the word 'dutiful' (line 2) tell you about the writer's tone?

2. How could 'get himself executed' (line 5) be more literally expressed?
What is suggested by the use of this construction?

3. Why were the actions of those who took part in the Easter Rising rash?

4. Were previous risings complete failures? Give reasons for your answer.

5. What does 'that' refer to in line 23?

6. What brought about Parnell's downfall, and what disastrous consequences did it have?

7. What phrase used earlier is illustrated by the Christmas dinner episode in Joyce's book?

8. In what way can writers be said to have succeeded where the politicians failed?

9. What does 'that' refer to in line 54?

10. What do the lines written by Pearse make clear about his position?

11. Why was the 1916 Rising not generally popular?

12. What is the connection between the quotations from McGahern (line 75), Yeats (lines 77–78), and Shaw (line79–81)?

13. Why can the 'freedom that eventually came' be described as 'dearly bought' (line 84), and what do you think the writer means by saying it 'is still being paid for'?

14. What does the writer mean to convey by the unfinished sentence that ends the passage?

WRITING

In 1991 there was some controversy about how the seventy-fifth anniversary of the Easter Rising should be commemorated—if at all. This was mainly because of continued IRA activity in Northern Ireland and the fact that a sizable portion of the Northern population would find any recognition of the event offensive. Since the majority of Northerners wish to maintain the union with Britain, any celebration of freedom from British rule is anathema.

1. Read this letter, which appeared in the *Irish Times* on 8 April 1991— just after Easter—and discuss your answers to the questions that follow.

A chara,

Having attempted to slither out of any public celebration of the events of Easter 1916 the Government was eventually shamed into doing something. And considering that their stated problem was any possible legitimising of the IRA, through Government stance in this matter, they unbelievably chose to put on a military ceremony. Was this just gauche, or simply an avoidance of the essential issues involved?

More than ten years ago you published a letter from me regarding the glorification of militarism, with reference to celebrations, commemorations, and particularly to the welcoming at airports of dignitaries, foreign and domestic, with the firing of massive guns and the obscene inspection of guns topped with wicked bayonets. I repeat that it would be at least as beautiful, and considerably less dangerous, should the particular dignitary inspect a row of bare bums.

> Le meas, mise,
> Flann Ó Riain.

NOTE

The opening and closing of a letter to the editor in English would usually be the rather formal 'Sir' and 'Yours faithfully'.

QUESTIONS

1. What is the letter-writer's complaint? And what is his tone? Pick out words and phrases that support your answers. Does he think the Easter Rising of 1916 should be commemorated? If so, how?

2. How are important historic events celebrated in your own and other countries? Do you agree with the form such celebrations take? If not, can you suggest any other way they might be recognised?

3. If such celebrations are going to cause negative feelings (bitterness, distress, anger, etc.) among certain people, should they be ignored altogether?

4. Now write a letter to the editor in reply to Flann Ó Riain's. In other words, agree or disagree with his point of view, making full use of your own experience and knowledge and placing the situation he refers to in an international context. Note that you are not writing directly to the letter-writer but, in a formal way, replying to his letter via the editor of the newspaper. Note also the way, mentioned above, such a letter should start and end. (The best guide is to read the letters page in one of the daily newspapers.)

WHERE THE WOMEN COME IN

1. What influence have women had on your country's past? Discuss this with the rest of the class by answering these questions.

(*a*) 'A woman's place is in the home' (or, even worse, 'at the kitchen sink'). Do you agree that this used to be the traditional view of the female role in society? If so, why? Did it mean that women in general had no influence on matters of importance?

(*b*) Can you think of any women before the second half of the twentieth century who were rulers, politicians, military leaders, religious leaders, philosophers, writers, artists, or composers? Were these women the exception rather than the rule? If so, why?

(*c*) What about the 'women behind the men'? Do you know of any women who made a significant contribution to history because of their influence as wives, mothers, daughters, sisters, or even lovers? What form did the influence take, and what effect did it have?

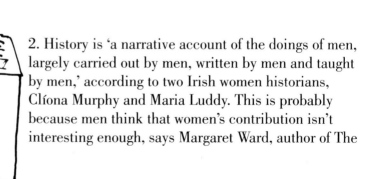

2. History is 'a narrative account of the doings of men, largely carried out by men, written by men and taught by men,' according to two Irish women historians, Clíona Murphy and Maria Luddy. This is probably because men think that women's contribution isn't interesting enough, says Margaret Ward, author of The

Missing Sex: Putting Women into Irish History. 'There is an unconscious, elitist sexism', she claims, 'which comes from the male academic idea of what is proper history and therefore worthy of research.'

What do you think? What is 'proper history', and who were the people who had the greatest influence on it? Debate this by dividing into two teams, one defending the men's claim and the other the women's. (Since the class is unlikely to be equally divided between males and females, some of you will have to do a quick sex change!)

(*a*) Each member of the team should have a role to play. It could be one of the following, but you may have your own ideas:
(i) a historian
(ii) a famous person in history (e.g. a monarch, explorer, thinker, politician, writer)
(iii) an ordinary person who lived in the past (e.g. a parent, spouse, servant)
(iv) a famous contemporary person
(v) an ordinary person living in the present

(*b*) With your team, discuss the points you might make that show the importance of your own sex, its contribution to and influence on history. Also decide the order you are going to speak in.

(*c*) Now the members of both teams should alternately make their case (women first, of course!). Make notes of the opposing team's opinions, but don't interrupt until everybody has finished speaking. You may then have an open debate.

(*d*) Which is the winning team—the 'men' or the 'women'? Take a vote on it—but remember, you are voting not for your own sex nor for your own personal views but for the team that made the best case.

Before you read the following passage on the role of women in Ireland, check on these idiomatic expressions and use them to fill in the spaces in the sentences below. Then read the passage and answer the questions that follow.

on the grapevine   draw a blank
on the dole   take by storm
take the biscuit   lie low
meet one's Waterloo   rock the boat

1. Well, that really ....! I spent ages making a special dinner for the dog with lovely beef gravy, and he's gone and eaten the cat food!

2. I tried everything I could to find the name of that book I want, but I've ....

3. After what you said to the boss this morning, I think you'd better .... for a few days till he calms down.

4. He's been .... ever since he was made redundant six months ago. He says he simply can't find a job.

5. I believe poor Pat's gone bankrupt. He was doing fine till he started having an affair with that gold-digging night-club singer; that's where he ....

6. I heard .... that Brian's given up his job and gone off to Australia. Is that true?

7. When they went on tour there a few years ago the Chieftains .... America .... They were even invited to play in the White House!

8. Look, we're all very happy with the way things are at work, so don't .... by making a fuss about a couple of hours' overtime.

Go back far enough and you find a woman who wasn't prepared to take nonsense from any man, 'better half' included. Maeve of Connacht was the daughter of a king and therefore a queen in her own right, as she liked to remind her spouse, Ailill*. It was high time he realised she could match him any day in terms of warriors and other valuables and that it was for his lack of jealousy that she had picked him, she would scold. Variety being the spice of Maeve's life, she was used to taking as a lover any fellow she fancied, so a jealous husband was not to be tolerated. The same lady can be held responsible for wiping out most of Connacht and

Ulster in her determination not to be outdone by her husband. The bold Cú Chulainn himself met his Waterloo in that particular squabble.

Move on a few centuries and you find the west coast of Ireland demented by a ferocious pirate, a female by the name of Grace O'Malley. The Gaelic chieftains at this stage were being forced to submit to Elizabeth I in order to hold on to their lands. It's about time, Grace thought, Lizzie was put in her place. So she sailed up the Thames in 1593 to confront the queen and demand her sailing rights, or carte blanche to carry on pirating. Elizabeth not only agreed but offered to make a lady of the wild Irishwoman. She needn't have bothered; such an honour, it was graciously explained to her, was an irrelevance to a female of equal rank.

And then we draw a bit of a blank for another three hundred years or so till we come to an Amazonian beauty who took the men of Ireland, and in particular W. B. Yeats, by storm. Maud Gonne, however, was more interested in freeing her country than marrying a poet. Her contemporary Constance Gore-Booth had similar priorities. In her role as the Rebel Countess she simply lost interest in her husband, the Polish Count Markievicz, finding better ways to occupy her time. These included teaching youngsters how to use a gun, featuring prominently in the 1916 Rising, getting locked up in a variety of prisons, and generally being a nuisance to the British, who really never knew what to do with her. On account of her sex they couldn't quite bring themselves to shoot her. Meanwhile, somewhere else, Constance's sister Eva was chaining herself to railings and doing all the other dreadful things women did to get the right to vote.

Given independence and the franchise, however, and the women of Ireland lay low for another few decades. The hand that rocks the cradle rules the world, they were told, and so they got on with playing the 'woman's role', rocking the cradle and not the boat. In essence this meant getting married as soon as you were asked; being grateful that you could now give up your job since, in your exalted status as a missus, you didn't need to earn and therefore no longer needed to work; and making babies (a new one every year, himself permitting) and bringing up as many budding little priests and nuns as the Church demanded and your savings (after the drink money) afforded. Each and every mother was a replica of Mary, the mother of Christ, and a housewife was, by definition, a woman who 'did nothing'. In return for such honours accorded them by God and their menfolk, it was hardly unreasonable to expect a modicum of obedience—whether it was putting the right amount of sugar in the tea or voting for the right political party.

For a while Mother Ireland struggled along quite nicely, thank you, filling the emigrant ships, lengthening the dole queues, and swelling the ranks of the ecclesiastical hierarchy. Of course the odd female, unappreciative of her affectionate husband or unsuited to the joys of perennial childbirth, let the side down. The even odder one, rejecting a life of decency, comfort, and conjugal bliss, disgraced herself and her sex by abandoning the call of duty and pursuing her own selfish interests. Edna O'Brien, for example, took herself off to London, where she was indoctrinated by the godless ways of the English and kept herself in sinful luxury by writing nasty books about the Irish.

Until one day the grapevine began to give out alarming news about women in foreign parts burning their bras and saying they wanted to be men, which was the height of nonsense and immodesty. These women wanted to do what everybody knew was men's work, like being doctors and engineers and bus drivers instead of teachers and nurses and secretaries. They were demanding to be paid the same as men even though, as everybody knew, it was less expensive to be a member of the weaker sex. Even worse, they were planning to abandon their babies and their husbands and their cosy homes to go out and wreak havoc on the nice stable working world men had never had cause to complain about. What really took the biscuit, however, was the rumour that some women were threatening to make babies only if or when it pleased them to do so. Wanting to wear the trousers was a simple violation of the natural order, but trying to usurp the role of divine authority was sacrilege beyond redemption.

Irish women were not amused—at first, anyway. The small handful who took up the war-cry of their sisters abroad, studenty types with more time on their hands than common sense, were more of an embarrassment than anything else. Their pranks, like brandishing packets of illegally imported unmentionables in front of red-faced customs men on what became known as the Belfast 'condom train', were condemned both by the grand old men of church and state and by the decent cradle-rockers of the country.

And yet ... while the outward struggle was being fought in the colleges and in the pages of the press by women like Mary Robinson and Nell McCafferty, an inward struggle was going on in the minds of women all over the country. As economic growth and membership of the Common Market was being translated into television and holidays abroad, glimpses of 'what might be if ...' were making room for doubt. Is what we have all we want? Could it be that there's a life beyond the kitchen sink? The possibilities that presented themselves were awesome; they were also awfully attractive. Gradually at first, and then with increasing momentum, Yeats's 'terrible beauty' took on a new significance, and liberation, which had always meant flying the Tricolour instead of the Union Jack, began to mean separate bank accounts and hen parties in pubs.

Habits don't change overnight, they say, so it stands to reason that a mentality conditioned over centuries will take a little longer. In the meantime, Mother Ireland is producing generations of intelligent, educated young women who find it much more interesting to rock the boat than the cradle and who, like Maeve of Connacht, are not prepared to take nonsense from any man.

MORE QUESTIONS

1. Which of the women mentioned—Maeve, Grace, Maud, Constance, and Eva—does each statement most obviously apply to?
    (*a*) She was devastatingly beautiful.
    (*b*) She fought for equal rights with men.
    (*c*) Her country came before her husband.
    (*d*) She wore the trousers.
    (*e*) She was extremely proud.

2. Say whether, *according to the writer*, these statements about Irish women in the past are true or false.
    (*a*) Married women didn't want to go out to work.
    (*b*) They didn't need money.
    (*c*) They were expected to produce as many children as they could.
    (*d*) Attitudes towards them were ambivalent.
    (*e*) They supported the traditional views of their role in society.
    (*f*) Women who failed in their role were weak, ungrateful, selfish, or immoral.

3. How many of these were what women in the liberation movement *really* wanted?
    (*a*) To be treated as men.
    (*b*) To take over men's jobs.
    (*c*) To have equal pay.
    (*d*) To abandon their families.
    (*e*) To wear trousers.
    (*f*) To plan their families.

4. According to the passage, which of these finally influenced Irish women to change their attitudes to women's liberation?
- (*a*) Having more money to spend on themselves.
- (*b*) The availability of contraceptives.
- (*c*) Articles in the newspapers.
- (*d*) Seeing other life-styles.
- (*e*) The success of the country's struggle for political independence.

5. Which of the following are true and which are false about Irish women today?
- (*a*) Some are still conservative in their attitudes.
- (*b*) They are playing an important part in the affairs of the country.
- (*c*) They are not interested in having children.
- (*d*) They are prepared to stand up for themselves.
- (*e*) They refuse to take advice from men.

LISTENING

You are going to hear different people talking about the lives of four women who have each played an important part in Irish affairs in the twentieth century.

Look at the questions on each woman separately and then listen twice to the description of her life.

A: MAUD GONNE MACBRIDE

1. Fill in the missing dates (year):
- (*a*) Born: ....
- (*b*) Married: ....
- (*c*) Widowed: ....
- (*d*) Died: ....

2. Tick any of the following that Maud Gonne did during her life. She—
- (*a*) had an illegitimate child
- (*b*) acted on stage
- (*c*) took part in the Easter Rising
- (*d*) married a Frenchman
- (*e*) was imprisoned by the Irish government
- (*f*) died on hunger strike
- (*g*) had many poems written about her

B: CONSTANCE MARKIEVICZ

Fill in the missing information in the following notes on her life:

Born in .... [1] at Lissadell in Co. Sligo. Studied .... [2] in Paris. Married a .... [3] count and set up home in .... [4]. Converted to the cause of independence by a .... [5] she read. After taking part in armed uprising in .... [6] was either in .... [7] or in hiding. Was first woman to be made a .... [8]. Also became first Minister for .... [9] in Irish government formed in 1919, just .... [10] years before her death.

C: BERNADETTE DEVLIN

1. Which of the following is not a reason for the poverty Bernadette grew up in?
   (a) Discrimination against Catholics.
   (b) Her father's early death.
   (c) Learning that she had to fight for anything she wanted.
   (d) Being part of a large family.

2. Which one of these is not true of her involvement in politics?
   (a) As a student she joined an illegal organisation.
   (b) She was assaulted by members of the constabulary.
   (c) Constitutional politics exasperated her.
   (d) She hit a British government minister.

D: MARY ROBINSON

1. How many of the following were distinctive features of the 1990 presidential election?
   (a) A woman won.
   (b) Brian Lenihan lost the election.
   (c) Many people chose not to vote for the conservative candidate.
   (d) Many women made independent decisions.
   (e) Traditional attitudes to the presidency were questioned.
   (f) A person who had not served the country was elected.

2. How many of these are true about traditional attitudes to the the presidency?
   (a) It meant a lot of diplomatic hand-shaking.
   (b) It was a suitable position for a distinguished and experienced politician.
   (c) It was a totally meaningless title.

3. How many of the following would have taken courage from Mary Robinson's election campaign?

(a) homosexuals
(b) people on the dole
(c) visiting dignitaries
(d) conservative Catholic housewives
(e) unmarried mothers
(f) young graduates working abroad

WHO WILL THEY REMEMBER?

The year is 2500, and a number of distinguished academics (writers, philosophers, historians, anthropologists, etc.) have been asked to take part in a television programme, 'Great Men and Women of the Late Twentieth Century'.

The preparation for this will best be done outside class. But first appoint a television presenter to chair the programme. The other members of the class are the distinguished academics!

1. Each of you should be prepared to talk about a person who, in your opinion, will be remembered for the influence he or she has had, and be able to give reasons for your choice. This is not a competition, and there are no winners. You are simply part of a discussion panel.

2. The presenter should find out who the participants in the programme are and who they are going to talk about. He or she should then introduce the programme and the panel, ask each person in turn to talk about his or her choice, invite questions and comments from the other members of the panel, and generally control the proceedings.

3. In the final stages of the programme it is the presenter's job to summarise the discussion. Were there any similarities between the people talked about? (It could be, for example, that the same person was chosen by more than one member of the panel.) Or were they all very different? And, as a matter of interest, how well were women represented?

VOCABULARY PRACTICE

In each case choose the word that best completes the sentence, but keep in mind that the word you have come across earlier in this unit is not necessarily the right answer!

1. I know you're in a rush, but just hold .... a minute and I'll see if I can get those figures for you.

      (*a*) out   (*b*) on   (*c*) off   (*d*) up

2. I'm afraid Sunday doesn't suit me. I have a .... arrangement to take my mother out to lunch on Sundays.

  (*a*) long-standing   (*b*) long-lasting   (*c*) long-lived   (*d*) long-drawn-out

3. When they woke up the next morning they found the sky overcast and a wind getting up. But nothing ...., they went ahead with their plan to spend the day on the beach.

    (*a*) discouraged   (*b*) put off   (*c*) daunted   (*d*) mattered

4. We just managed to get a .... of the President before she was driven away in a state car.

    (*a*) glimpse   (*b*) glance   (*c*) look   (*d*) sight

5. Judging by the stories he writes for school, your son is a .... young novelist, Mr Joyce.

    (*a*) flowering   (*b*) booming   (*c*) blooming   (*d*) budding

6. She was young and impressionable, so when she went to university she got .... with the wrong crowd and ended up on drugs.

    (*a*) in   (*b*) on   (*c*) off   (*d*) away

7. I wish you children would stop fighting. It's been one .... after the other all day.

    (*a*) tiff   (*b*) feud   (*c*) squabble   (*d*) skirmish

8. And then we went to see the Grand Canyon, which is truly a(n) .... sight.

(a) awesome   (b) awful   (c) fearsome   (d) gruesome

9. Well, since we've all known each other for so long, I think we can .... with the formalities and get on with the meeting.

(a) dispose   (b) discard   (c) dismiss   (d) dispense

10. Her husband's a well-known writer, but since she's just had a book of short stories published she's an author in her .... right.

(a) own   (b) proper   (c) personal   (d) particular

11. The hurricane swept through the town, wreaking .... everywhere.

(a) damage   (b) mayhem   (c) destruction   (d) havoc

12. If there was a serious leak from the nuclear power station, the neighbouring village would be totally wiped ....

(a) away   (b) up   (c) out   (d) off

13. It was your .... that lost us the deal. Everything was going fine until you started flirting with the director's secretary—who also happens to be his girl-friend!

(a) botching   (b) bungling   (c) boobing   (d) blundering

14. He left school at sixteen and had made his first million by the time he was twenty, which was no .... achievement.

(a) normal   (b) average   (c) mean   (d) little

15. My wife is the financial controller in our house, so it's up to her where we go for our holidays. I'm completely at her ....!

(a) power   (b) control   (c) mercy   (d) pleasure

CLOZE

Shortly after Mary Robinson won the presidential election, the *Irish Times* published a series of articles on 'Irish Women, 1990'. This is an extract from one by Kathy Sheridan, entitled 'Why Can't a Woman Be More Like a Man?' Fill each of the spaces with one suitable word.

People in power learn to shut .... [1] off from how their actions affect people. Margaret Thatcher .... [2] the lesson well and as a result did .... [3] for women either .... [4] a prime minister or as a role model. Any woman dedicated only to work, ... [5] three hours a night and specialising .... [6] public humiliations of one-time loyal friends and colleagues, doesn't demolish traditional stereotypes; she refashions them.

She .... [7] only provides further material to feed traditional chauvinism .... [8] also creates a monstrous new mythology about the female gender: that only .... [9] ruthless, ... [10] insensitive and the despotic can lead and survive. This has been the paradox about .... [11] in power: they are expected to behave like men to earn their place (no nonsense about taking .... [12] off to watch a child in the school play, ... [13] sign of emotional or physical weakness permitted).

But the omens are improving. We have a President .... [14] self-belief and achievements enabled her to reach out, amid the joy of the election, ... [15] the women who .... [16] for her, and say that at that point she needed to be surrounded by her family; a President and a woman in .... [17] the country has clearly recognised the supreme balance of .... [18] power and humanity.

Can it .... [19] that we are finally reaching the point .... [20] the women's agenda becomes *the* agenda: egalitarian, democratic, concerned with all of human life, rather than with bonuses and car allowances?

UNIT 11

ASSESS-MENTS

A NICE PLACE FOR A HOLIDAY—OR FOR GOOD?

Do you remember the quotation from the historian Brian Inglis in unit 1? 'It may happen that the visitor is so delighted with what he finds in Ireland that he decides to make his home here.' Check back to see what else he had to say.

1. Now that you have seen and learnt something about the country and its people, how would you feel about actually living here? Spend five minutes making two lists of what you think would be the pros and cons of staying in Ireland for good.

2. Compare and discuss each list with the rest of the class. What general conclusions can you draw?

3. Summarise the ideas expressed in your discussion by writing three short paragraphs: what advantages and what disadvantages might a visitor who decides to make his or her home in Ireland experience, and what are your conclusions?

LISTENING

'As long as Ireland produces men with sense enough to leave her, she does not exist in vain.'—George Bernard Shaw.

A. TO GO OR TO STAY

In more recent times the emigration problem has been described as the 'brain drain'. It is the bright young educated people who are opting for a life outside the country because they feel Ireland cannot offer them the lifestyle they deserve.

You are going to hear three teenagers discussing their views on whether to go or to stay. The feelings of the two girls, sisters Sarah and Frankie, are clearly different from those of their friend Alan.

Look at the following statements and, when you have listened to their conversation twice, decide which are true and which are false.

1. The girls maintain that it would be easier to get a job abroad because Irish people are considered to be well educated.

2. The number of people applying for a teaching position is given as an example of the job situation at home.

3. Alan has no interest whatever in going abroad.

4. The girls would like to support themselves while travelling by getting temporary jobs.

5. Alan thinks that people who have no choice but to emigrate should try to make the most of the experience.

6. The girls are very critical of emigrants who return to Ireland with a negative attitude towards the country they have left.

7. According to Alan, it is unlikely that people who emigrate out of economic necessity will think of it as a valuable cultural experience.

8. Alan changes his mind in the end.

B. A SELF-MADE MAN

Not all of the stories about people forced to emigrate in the past, however, are hard-luck ones. You are going to hear a highly successful businessman talking about his life. Read the questions and, in particular, check the meanings of the adjectives in number 1. Then listen to the conversation twice.

1. Three of these ten adjectives could be used to describe Paddy's character. Which are they?

A. affable   B. diffident   C. snobbish   D. good-natured

E. unpretentious   F. smug   G. boastful   H. ostentatious

I. overbearing   J. over-modest

In the following questions, choose the correct answer in each case.

2. What is Paddy's attitude to young people today?

A. He is unreservedly sympathetic towards them.
B. He feels they want things too easily.
C. He is sarcastic about their educational qualifications.
D. He thinks they should follow his example.

3. The way Paddy talks about his life in England shows that he

A. resents his parents having had such a large family.
B. is self-pitying about the hardships he had to endure.
C. regrets that he had to leave Ireland.
D. has a philosophical attitude towards his past.

4. One of the reasons why Paddy and Breege decided to come home was that

A. they wanted their children to respect their Irishness.
B. he wasn't making a success of things in England.
C. they were treated badly by the English.
D. Ireland was a less expensive place to bring up their family.

NEVER MIND THE WEATHER

It's a fairly safe bet that if the weather featured in your discussion about living in Ireland, it was in the 'con' list (if it didn't, you must be experiencing an uncommonly good spell!).

Nowhere is the paradox that underlies the Irish character more apparent than in attitudes towards the weather. 'Mild', 'equable', 'not subject to extremes' are ways the climate has been described: sub-zero temperatures are uncommon enough to be freakish, and if the thermometer hits 30°C it's record-breaking time. Yet for the people who live here, it's always too something: too hot, too cold, too dry, too wet, too windy, or too wind-less to dry the washing or sail a boat. At the same time, the weather can produce

conditions the foreigner finds frankly inhospitable but that the native will minimise with a philosophical pronouncement.

Match these common understatements about the weather with their more accurately expressed counterparts:

A. There's a bit of a breeze today.
B. It's a soft day, thank God.
C. Ah, sure a drop of rain'll make the grass grow.
D. There's a nip in the air this morning.
(i) It's lashing out of the heavens.
(ii) It's blowing a gale.
(iii) It's freezing cold.
(iv) The sky is grey and it's drizzling rain.
A: ......
B: ......
C: ......
D: ......

CLOZE

Read the following passage and fill each space with one suitable word.

.... [1] was the height of summer and the poet Oliver St John Gogarty was .... [2] by bus to his country house in Connemara in torrential .... [3]. Attempting to strike .... [4] a conversation with the old farmer sitting .... [5] him, he remarked, 'It is most extraordinary weather for this .... [6] of year.' 'Ah, sure,' replied the old man shaking his .... [7], 'it isn't this time of year at all.'

The vagaries of the Irish .... [8] are infamous. The fluctuations of the temperature alone have caused native and .... [9] alike to talk of the passing of four .... [10] in a morning. A clear blue sky .... [11] change in an instant to grey, moisture-laden .... [12], and then, just .... [13] suddenly, to the wonder of simultaneous sunshine and .... [14] with promises of pots of gold at the end of fairy rainbows. If you can see the mountains, they say, it's going to rain; if you can't, it's raining .... [15]!

Observers .... [16] believe that we are creatures of our environment maintain that the .... [17] temperament reflects the volatility of the .... [18]. The Spanish writer Salvador de Madariaga proved to

.... [19] own satisfaction that the Irish were really Spaniards who strayed too far north. When they left their moist and windy island for a warm climate, he said, they .... [20] drinking whiskey and turned to wine like civilised people.

PIT YOUR WEATHER WITS

See how much you really know about weather conditions in Ireland by answering the following questions.

1. The temperature in the coldest months ranges from
(*a*) −3 to 1°C (*b*) 1 to 4°C (*c*) 4 to 7°C (*d*) 7 to 10°C

2. The warmest months are
(*a*) May and June (*b*) June and July (*c*) July and August (*d*) June and August

3. The sunniest months are
(*a*) May and June (*b*) June and July (*c*) July and August (*d*) May and September

4. Which is most likely to be the driest month?
(*a*) April (*b*) May (*c*) July (*d*) September

5. In which county does it tend to rain most?
(*a*) Kerry (*b*) Wexford (*c*) Dublin (*d*) Donegal

A GUIDED TOUR

Three friends of yours are coming to Ireland by car next week. They arrive on the Rosslare ferry at 10 a.m. on Thursday and depart the following Wednesday at 6 p.m. They want to spend some time in Dublin and a few days seeing a bit of the country. They will be staying in guesthouses, which provide bed and breakfast only. You have agreed to act as their guide.

To make the best use of their time you have decided to plan a detailed itinerary, including interesting places to visit, how to spend your evenings, where to eat, etc. On your maps of Dublin and Ireland you have marked the places you think worth seeing, and you have drawn in a number of possible itineraries for your tour of the country. You have also made some notes in your diary about what each day should include.

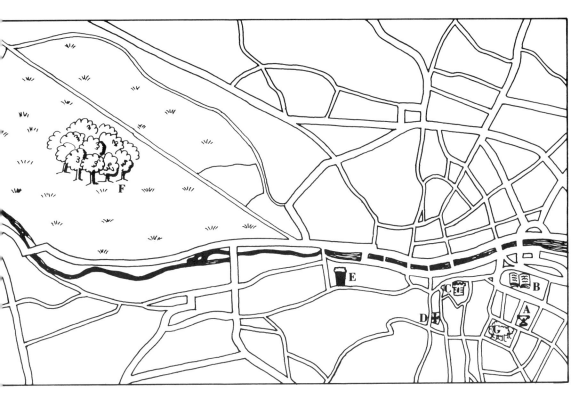

Working with a partner or group—

1. Find out and fill in the missing information on the maps.

2. Discuss the merits of the various itineraries; what has each to offer in the way of places to see and things to do? Choose the one you like best. You may, of course, decide to make out your own route, but keep in mind distances and condition of roads!

3. Discuss how best to plan each day's timetable. You will obviously have to be selective in deciding what to do; trying to achieve too much in a short time will only make everybody tired—and probably bad-tempered.

4. Write your daily timetable and itinerary in the space provided. Then compare yours with the other members of the group. Who would make the best guide?

A. .... [1] Museum; particularly want them to see the .... [2] Chalice and .... [3] Brooch.

B. Library in .... [4] College; .... of .... [5] a *must*. Fingers crossed a good page will be on view.

C. .... [6]—home of the English viceroys. Full of history and drama. See James .... [7] room (wounded 1916 leader kept prisoner here before being shot).

D. .... [8] Cathedral, where .... [9], author of *Gulliver's Travels*, was once dean.

E. St James's Gate. Can't miss .... [10] and the chance of a free pint!

F. .... [11]. The largest enclosed park in Europe. We can see the deer—and call at Áras an Uachtaráin for a cup of tea with the .... [12]! Or visit the zoo.

G. .... [13]. Weather permitting, good place for a picnic lunch. And visit .... [14], where Joyce went to university.

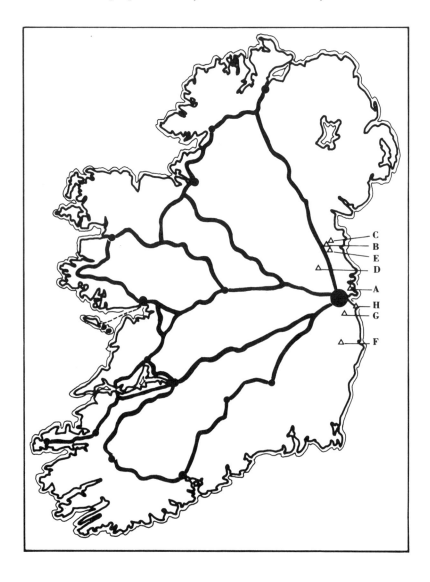

A. Norman .... [15] and beautiful gardens worth a visit here. ....
[16] itself a very pleasant little village.

B. .... [17] Abbey, founded by the Cistercians. Interesting for its
Romanesque architecture.

C. Sixth-century monastic site at Monasterboice. Good example of a
typical decorated high .... [18].

D. Hill of .... [19]—ancient seat of High .... [20] of Ireland.

E. Neolithic .... [21] graves at .... [22] and Knowth a priority
stop. And go back five thousand years in time!

F. St Kevin's monastery at .... [23] with most perfect round ....
[24] in Ireland. Real beauty spot, with wooded valley and lakes. Ideal for
picnic.

G. Lovely gardens at .... [25]. Even better, magnificent waterfall.

H. .... [26] tower where Joyce lived briefly. Now his museum.

DIARY NOTES

Thursday
10 am. Meet ferry. Let's make a day of
it and stop along the way. Loads of
interesting places to see between Rosslare
and Dublin. If we hit Dublin around 7 p.m.,
just time to settle in B&B and go out
for a meal. Early night then, I'd say!

Friday
Leave car at guesthouse. Sightseeing in
Dublin. What about food? Theatre in
evening, perhaps. Must find out what's on.

193

Saturday

Day trip. Take car (and picnic) and head for Newgrange. What else could we do? Evening — eat somewhere, and then Irish music.

Sunday

Head for where — south, west, north? Where do we stop and where do we stay overnight?

Monday

On tour — somewhere!

Tuesday

Still travelling. Have to be back at guesthouse by 6 o'clock. Evening? No thoughts yet.

Wednesday

Morning for leisurely coffee and shopping. Then early lunch before they set off for Rosslare — 2 p.m. at the latest.

ITINERARY

Day 1 (Thursday)

Day 2 (Friday)

_____
_____
_____
_____

Day 3 (Saturday)

_____
_____
_____
_____

Day 4 (Sunday)

_____
_____
_____
_____

Day 5 (Monday)

_____
_____
_____
_____

Day 6 (Tuesday)

_____
_____
_____
_____

Day 7 (Wednesday)

_____
_____
_____
_____

TRAVELLING LIGHT

One of the friends who are coming to visit Ireland is having a problem about what to pack, as there won't be room in the car for more than a travelling bag or small suitcase. In desperation he or she sends you a fax telling you all the things he or she has thought of (apart from essential toiletries, night attire, and underwear) and asking you to fax back with a list of only *ten* items.

1. Tick the ten items you consider either essential or appropriate. You may choose one item more than once (but you must count it as more than one!) and you may write in up to four items not already mentioned.

2. When you have made your choice, compare and discuss your list with the rest of the class.

3. Now fax back your message in the space provided.

Dear ....,

Help! Don't know what I'll really need in Ireland. Please choose for me and fax me back as soon as you can.

1: sunglasses
2: pair of sandals
3: swimming gear
4: pair of shorts
5: umbrella
6: light mac
7: quilted anorak
8: chunky sweater
9: something smart for evenings
10: tee-shirt
11: bottle of aspirins
12: hot water bottle
13: water purifier
14: pair of wellington boots
15: pair of fleece-lined gloves
16: pair of sneakers
17: pair of jeans
18: thermal vest
19: sunburn cream
20: bilingual dictionary
21: mosquito net
22: warm dressing-gown
23: ....
24: ....
25: ....
26: ....

See you next week.
Yours,

....

Dear ....,

A mosquito net in Ireland? You idiot! Bring the following and you'll be okay.

1. ....   6. ....
2. ....   7. ....
3. ....   8. ....
4. ....   9. ....
5. ....   10. ....

And a bit of advice:
....
....
....
....
....
....
....

See you next Thursday.

....

WRITING

Choose one of these subjects to write about but discuss them both before you make your decision.

1. Because you have spent some time in an English-speaking country or countries, the school or college you attend (or attended) has asked you to talk to a group of students who are interested in improving their English.

(*a*) Discuss with a partner or group the various experiences you have had; there will probably have been embarrassing and frustrating ones as well as the good ones!

(*b*) What advice would you give to a student intending to come to Ireland to improve his or her English?

Write your speech making maximum use of your experiences. Keep your audience in mind—they want to be informed, but they also want to be entertained.

2. Your local newspaper is running the usual new-year series of articles on holidays. The editor has asked you to write about being a student in Ireland. Apart from the essential hard facts (travel arrangements, cost, etc.) he wants you to give information and advice based on your own experience, to suggest a title for the article, and to supply a suitable photograph to accompany it.

(*a*) With your partner or group, discuss what facts are essential and what information and advice you can give that will be of value. You are not being commissioned by a student travel agency, so you are free to express your own views.
(*b*) What is the best approach? An arresting beginning and an interesting presentation of material are essential if you want to catch and hold the readers' attention.
(*c*) Write your article in not more than 350 words, give it a title, and, if you can't actually produce a suitable accompanying photograph, suggest what it might be.

PHRASAL VERBS

In the preceding units you have come across a number of phrasal verbs. How many of them can you remember?

Complete the following twenty sentences by choosing one of the verbs given below. (The verbs indicated can be used more than once.)

belt	get	put (2)	turn
bring	hold	set (2)	wipe
cater	look (4)	take (2)	work
come	pull		

1. What a coincidence! It .... out that the fellow you introduced me to last night was at school with my brother.

2. I've been living in Dublin for years now, but I was .... up in the North.

3. When she inherited some money from her aunt, she decided to .... up her own travel agency.

4. I can tell you, it was no fun .... after my sister's three children while she was in New York on business!

5. We were able to .... out the chorus of 'A Nation Once Again' with the rest of the audience because we had learnt the words that morning.

6. How she .... up with that husband of hers I don't know. She must have the patience of a saint!

7. The climbers are trapped somewhere near the top of the Mourne Mountains. We hope they'll be able to .... out till the rescue team arrives.

8. What I need is a good long walk to .... off that enormous dinner!

9. If you happen to .... across a reasonably priced second-hand fiddle on your travels, would you please buy it for me?

10. How can you expect children to .... up to their teacher if the teacher doesn't show any respect for them?

11. The whole house .... on an atmosphere of gloom when Mary's at home. She's a most depressing person to live with.

12. The school's social programme has tried to .... for all ages and interests. It includes everything from pub crawls to cultural tours.

13. It's been nice talking to you, but you'll have to excuse me. If I don't .... on with my work I'll never have it finished on time.

14. I wonder who's going to .... over the boss's job when she retires at Christmas.

15. If you're going to Donegal, I advise you to .... off really early. It may not look all that far on the map, but the road's bad and you can't make any speed.

16. It's unfair of Patrick to .... out of the camping holiday at the last minute. We were banking on him to share the driving.

17. A snob is simply a person who .... down on people who are superior to him! It's a sign of an inferiority complex.

18. The ruthless way the rebellion was .... down was, in fact, self-defeating. It only caused even greater unrest.

19. Over half the population of Ireland was .... out by famine in the nineteenth century.

20. When I .... back on my childhood now, I realise how unhappy and insecure I was.

FIND THE IDIOM

(a) pulling up one's socks
(b) meeting one's Waterloo
(c) damning with faint praise
(d) being at odds with
(e) drawing a blank

(f) lying low
(g) dampening one's enthusiasm
(h) taking by storm
(i) rocking the boat
(j) paving the way

The following situations are examples of the above idiomatic expressions. Match each situation with the corresponding idiom, and then rephrase it using the idiom appropriately. The first one has been done for you.

1. When I asked him if he liked the new dish I'd specially cooked for him, he said it was all right! (c) When I asked him if he liked the new dish I'd specially cooked for him, he *damned it with faint praise*.

2. I was doing so well till I got to the last fence in the cross-country, and then, when my horse stumbled, I fell off and broke two ribs.

3. We were all perfectly happy till you came along and started threatening to bring in the union if we didn't get a rise.

4. Seán seems to be making a greater effort to be on time these days. The warning I gave him has obviously worked.

5. Damn you! I was looking forward to taking my car to Ireland till you started going on about how I'd be sick on the ferry and wouldn't get used to driving on the left …!

6. Emer's furious with me for going to the dance with her former boy-friend, so I'm trying to avoid her till she cools off.

7. I wouldn't be surprised if they got divorced. Every time one of them says something, the other disagrees.

8. Their music is a cross between traditional Irish and punk rock. Their instant popularity will no doubt encourage other groups to be more innovative.

9. All I know is that her name begins with Mac and she lives in Howth. But I've been through all the Macs in the telephone directory a dozen times and I still can't find her number.

10. When Friel's play was put on in the West End, it was such a success that the whole of London was raving about it.

WHO IS IT?

You can do this quiz on your own or with a partner or group or by making it a competition between two class teams.

What you have to find out are the names of twelve people who have appeared in the preceding units of the book. Follow these instructions:
(*a*) The names are all mixed up: the first names have been linked with the wrong surnames. Unscramble as many as you can, and then proceed to the next stage.

Grace Heaney
Bob Kelly
Samuel Gonne
Mícheál Parnell
Jonathan de Valera
Charles Stewart Beckett

Maud Yeats
Paddy Mac Liammóir
Grace Geldof
William Butler O'Malley
Séamus Moloney
Éamon Swift

(*b*) To help you further, here are two sets of clues that should enable you to identify the people. Some will be instantly recognisable, others may need a little research. Match the pairs of descriptions with the correct person.

FIRST SET OF CLUES

1. He doesn't like Mondays
2. He is the son of an Ulster farmer.
3. Her husband was shot for being a rebel.
4. The little people of Lilliput were his invention.
5. He wrote his own epitaph: *Cast a cold Eye/On Life, on Death./Horseman, pass by!*
6. Her name is one of the most common ones in the telephone directory.

7. Called 'Ireland's uncrowned king'.
8. When asked about the meaning of his best-known play he replied, 'I meant what I said.'
9. He lived in the Phoenix Park from 1959 to 1973.
10. His most memorable performance was his one-man show *The Importance of Being Oscar*.
11. Her other name is Granuaile.
12. His work has taken him from the Great Wall of China to the White House.

SECOND SET OF CLUES

(i)   He hadn't a drop of Irish blood in his veins.
(ii)   The love of his life was Katharine O'Shea.
(iii)   He worked for the French Resistance during the Second World War.
(iv)   His good deeds earned him a title.
(v)   She gave up a Hollywood career for the man she married.
(vi)   A famous poet was infatuated with her.
(vii)   He was American by birth.
(viii) She was a queen of the sea.
(ix)   He prefers a pen to a spade.
(x)   He pipes for a living.
(xi)   His friends were the poor of Dublin, his enemies the victims of his lacerating satire.
(xii)   The Abbey Theatre owes its existence largely to him.

ANSWERS

Now write the number of the second clue after the number of the first clue, and then the person's correct name.

1. ...... Name: ....
2. ...... Name: ....
3. ...... Name: ....
4. ...... Name: ....
5. ...... Name: ....
6. ...... Name: ....
7. ...... Name: ....
8. ...... Name: ....
9. ...... Name: ....
10. ...... Name: ....
11. ...... Name: ....
12. ...... Name: ....

GREEDY-GUTS SPECIALS!

Below you have the ingredients for three recipes, but what do you do next? The instructions have somehow got mixed up. Can you work out which instructions belong to which recipe, and the order in which they should appear?

Write in the numbers of the appropriate steps in the spaces provided beside each recipe.

BROWN BREAD   METHOD

350 g wholemeal   ....
150 g white flour   ....
½ tsp salt   ....
¾ tsp bicarbonate of soda (bread   ....
soda)
300 ml buttermilk or sour milk   ....
—Deep, rectangular bread tin

IRISH STEW   METHOD

1 kg breast or neck of lamb   ....
1 kg potatoes   ....
5 medium-sized onions   ....
400 ml cold water   ....
Salt and pepper   ....
1 tsp chopped parsley
—Heavy-bottomed saucepan or
cooking pot

IRISH COFFEE   METHOD

1 measure Irish whiskey   ....
Strong black coffee   ....
2 tsp brown sugar   ....
Lightly whipped cream   ....
—Irish coffee glass   ....

1. Turn dough into the tin and bake for about ¾ hour.
2. Peel and slice the onions, peel the potatoes and cut the large ones in two.
3. Cut the meat into neat pieces and remove superfluous fat.
4. Pour in the whiskey and almost fill the glass with coffee.

5. Turn the oven to 215 °C.
6. Rinse a glass in hot water to warm it.
7. Add chopped parsley just before serving.
8. Grease and flour baking tin.
9. Arrange the meat, onions and potatoes in layers in the saucepan, season with salt and pepper, and add the water.
10. Mix the dry ingredients with the buttermilk or sour milk to an elastic consistency.
11. Pour on the cream over the back of a spoon so that it floats on top.
12. Stir in the sugar until it is dissolved.
13. To test if thoroughly baked, turn out of tin and tap bottom of loaf with your fingers. It should make a hollow sound.
14. Sieve flour and bread soda into a bowl and add wholemeal and salt.
15. Bring to the boil and simmer for 2½ to 3 hours, until meat is really tender.

WORD RACE

The missing words in these sentences are all ones you have come across in the preceding eleven units. How many do you remember? To help you, the first letter has been given as a clue in each case.

1. I found it a terrible w_____ leaving home after the Christmas holidays.

2. The only way I can tell the difference between those twin sisters is by the m____ one of them has on her neck.

3. I got a bit of g____ in my eye while I was out on my bicycle and it's so sore now I can't open it.

4. It was a typical morning in early autumn and the island was shrouded in m____.

5. The standard f__ charged by a dentist these days is so high that you think twice before you make an appointment!

6. The d_____ alleged he was at home watching television at the time the crime was committed.

7. I wouldn't vote for that party. One of their policies is to bring back the death p_____ for capital murder.

8. Our feet made a loud s_____ as we struggled across the boggy field.

9. Imagine her p_____; her five-year-old son had appendicitis while her husband was away on business, the phone was out of order, and the car had a flat tyre!

10. I've got awful hunger p____. If I don't eat soon, I'll die of starvation!

11. Every week he hands over his w____ to his wife, and she gives him just enough for a couple of pints a day.

12. He may not be a particularly bright student but he's certainly no s_____ at playing poker. He always wins!

13. That singer isn't gay at all. Dressing up as a woman is just a g_____ he uses to attract attention.

14. She's set her s_____ on being the first woman to win that motorcycle race, and she's so determined she'll probably do it!

15. So neither of us got the job. Come on, we might as well go out and drown our s_____!

16. To get to the site for the new apartment block, the architect had to clamber over the r_____ left after the demolition of the old house.

17. She kicked up such a s____ when the hotel receptionist said there was no reservation in her name that they had to give her the bridal suite!

18. Like me, your husband wants to go somewhere hot and sunny for a holiday. And mine wants to go mountain climbing in Donegal, like you. So why don't we do a s___!

19. I caught a g_____ of the bride and groom as they drove past in a white Rolls-Royce.

20. What a s_____ over which channel to turn the television to! You're behaving like two-year-olds instead of adults!

A NOTE TO YOUR SUCCESSOR

It's your last day in Ireland and you discover a fantastic singing pub five minutes' walk from where you're living, or somebody tells you where you can hire a car or moped or bicycle for half the going rate, and you say, 'If only I'd known!'

So you sit down and make out a list of information and advice you think will be appreciated by the student who is due to arrive as you are about to leave—a compatriot, as it turns out. Think of the problems you had, the things it was assumed you should know or understand, and the valuable discoveries you made—anything, in fact, that will save your successor time, energy and hassle and, moreover, make his or her time in Ireland more interesting and pleasurable. Some ideas have already been suggested for you below.

(*a*) Fill in the missing information.

(*b*) Discuss with a partner or group what else a new student might find useful, and write it down in the spaces provided.

(*c*) Use the rest of the page to add anything else of help or interest.

Dear Successor,
You may find the following information helpful:

1.
In case of emergency:
Embassy: ....
Hospital/doctor: ....
Police: ....

2.
Phone code to home: ....
Phone code from home: ....
Nearest coin-box phone: ....
Coins needed—Local call: .... Call to home: ....

3.

How to get to town: ....

Last bus/train at night: ....

If you miss it: ....

4.

Want to eat out? I recommend ....

....

5.

Entertainment/night life ....

....

6.

Thinking of travelling? ....

....

....

....

7.

....

....

8.

....

....

9.

....

....

10.

....

....

Here's hoping you have an enjoyable time in Ireland.

Your Predecessor

GRAMMAR

UNIT 1 · DEFINING AND NON-DEFINING RELATIVE CLAUSES

A *defining clause* defines the noun or pronoun it refers to. It is essentia[l] information, and is therefore not separated by commas; e.g. 'The man wh[o] spoke to you on the phone is my father.'

The relative pronoun used to introduce it depends on whether the noun o[r] pronoun being defined is a person or an object, and its position in the clause.

(*a*) For people, and in subject position: **who** (or sometimes **that**)

(*b*) For things, and in subject position: **that**

(*c*) For people, and in object position: **whom** or **that**—but it is more natural to omit it altogether.

(*d*) For things, and in object position: **that**—but again it is better to omit it.

(*e*) For both, and in possessive: **whose**

208

EXERCISE 1

Look at these examples and say which of the above types they are.

(i)   Nationality is something you are born with.

(ii) Many people who are born on this island do not consider themselves Irish.

(iii) The country that has the highest rate of chronic psychosis is also said to be the least neurotic.

(iv) The people whose photographs appear in unit 1 are all Irish.

(v)   The people he saw hadn't the slightest intention of doing what they said they'd do.

A ***non-defining clause*** gives non-essential information about the already defined noun, pronoun or even clause it refers to. It is therefore separated by commas in writing (and pauses in speech); e.g. 'My father, who spoke to you on the phone, would like to meet you.'

It tends to be more formal and less frequently used in spoken English. The relative pronouns used are as follows:

(*a*) For people, as subject: **who**

(*b*) For things, as subject: **which**

(*c*) For people, as object or with preposition: **whom**

(*d*) For things, as object or with preposition: **which**

(*e*) For both, as possessive: **whose**

(*f*) For the preceding clause: **which**

EXERCISE 2

Look at these examples and say which of the above types they are:

(i)   Mícheál Mac Liammóir, who spoke beautiful Irish, was English by birth.

(ii) *The Playboy of the Western World*, whose author is now a literary hero, was greeted with riots on its first performance.

(iii) James Joyce, about whom countless books have been written, spent most of his adult life in exile.

(iv) Although Edna O'Brien escaped from Ireland, she feels deeply Irish, which is somewhat paradoxical.

(v)   Northern Ireland, for which 'Ulster' is a misnomer, is usually referred to as 'the Six Counties' by southerners.

(vi) Ulster, which has nine counties, is one of the four provinces of Ireland.

In each case, what does the relative pronoun refer to?

EXERCISE 3

Put the following pairs of sentences together to form one sentence using a defining or non-defining clause and leaving out the relative pronoun where it is not needed. Then say which kind of clause you have used and whether commas are necessary or not.

You will find in some cases that more than one way of joining the sentences is possible; e.g. Fintan O'Toole writes for the *Irish Times*; he is also literary adviser to the National Theatre: 'Fintan O'Toole, who is literary adviser to the National Theatre, writes for the *Irish Times*.' Or: 'Fintan O'Toole, who writes for the *Irish Times*, is literary adviser to the National Theatre.' (Both are non-defining clauses.)

(i)   The portrait is of the poet W. B. Yeats. You saw it at the beginning of unit 1.
(ii)   De Valera's father was Spanish. De Valera was president of Ireland for fourteen years.
(iii) The Gate Theatre is at the end of O'Connell Street. One of the founders of the Gate Theatre was Mícheál Mac Liammóir.
(iv)   Joyce wrote a novel after Ulysses. This later novel is much more difficult to understand.
(v)   You see statues outside Trinity College. One of them is of the poet Oliver Goldsmith.
(vi)   It tends to rain rather a lot in Ireland. That's why the grass is so green.
(vii) The horse was ridden by a seventeen-year-old jockey. It won the race.
(viii) Grace Kelly often visited Ireland. When she married Prince Rainier of Monaco she became Princess Grace.
(ix)   You saw me talking to a man a few moments ago. He comes from Donegal.
(x)   A defining clause is different from a non-defining clause. It is more commonly used in spoken English.

EXERCISE 4

Make up your own relative clauses to add to the following sentences, and say which kind you have used in each case; e.g. Mrs Thatcher called Bob Geldof 'a true Brit': 'Mrs Thatcher called Bob Geldof, who was born in Dublin, "a true Brit".' Or: 'Mrs Thatcher, who was the fist woman to become British Prime Minister, called Bob Geldof "a true Brit".' Or: 'Mrs Thatcher called Bob Geldof "a true Brit", which is rather funny considering he's Irish.'

(i) Who wrote the play?
(ii) Oysters should be eaten with Guinness and brown bread.
(iii) Jonathan Swift was a misogynist.
(iv) A misogynist is a man.
(v) People are mad.

EXERCISE 5

You are walking through Dublin with an Irish friend, who is pointing out interesting sights. This is what he or she tells you when you come to O'Connell Street. In each space use an appropriate relative pronoun, but omit it whenever possible. You will also need to insert commas to indicate non-defining clauses.

The street .... you are now walking along ...., in fact, used to be called Sackville Street is Dublin's main thoroughfare. When Ireland became independent, it was renamed after the man .... won emancipation for Catholics in the eighteenth century, Daniel O'Connell. That's his statue .... you can see there, and the wide bridge .... takes you over the Liffey and into the south side is also called after him. The sign on the bus .... has just gone past says An Lár .... means 'city centre'. The monument to Admiral Nelson .... used to dominate the whole street was Dublin's greatest landmark for many years. In those days all the buses .... were going to the city centre simply said Nelson Pillar. Then in 1966 .... was the year the fiftieth anniversary of the Easter Rising was celebrated poor old Nelson was blown up by people .... resented the presence of a British lord in an Irish street. Talking of the Rising, the building .... you're standing in front of right now, the GPO, is the one .... the republican forces used as their headquarters. The Proclamation of the Republic .... signatories were all executed was read out from these steps by Patrick Pearse on Easter Monday 1916. Let's go inside. You can buy stamps for the postcards .... you wrote this morning and see the statue of Cú Chulainn; that's the legendary hero .... adventures your English teacher was telling you about.

EXERCISE 6

Both of the following exercises are based on structures, phrases, expressions etc. that you have met in unit 1. Similar exercises relevant to each unit appear at the end of each grammar section.

1. Finish each of the following sentences in such a way that it means the same as the sentence before it; e.g. 'There is a lot of truth in this notion.—This notion **has a lot of truth in it.**'

   (i) It is hard to encapsulate that essence in words.—What that ....
   (ii) Generally speaking, we can say that Irish people are tall and have pale complexions.—Generally speaking, Irish people can ...
   (iii) It isn't just immigrants to Ireland who have to make up their minds whether or not to choose Irish nationality.—Immigrants to Ireland are not ...
   (iv) Ireland contributed more to Live Aid than any other country.—No other country contributed as ...
   (v) The visitor may happen to like Ireland so much that he or she decides to stay here.—It ...

EXERCISE 7

In each case make a new sentence, as similar as possible in meaning to the original one, using the word printed after it (*you must not alter the word in any way*); e.g. 'The great majority of us have to decide what we want to be.—**almost**—Almost all of us have to choose what we want to be.'

(i) Ireland is a state of mind as well as an actual country.—**both**
(ii) These mythological invaders were eventually replaced by their historical counterparts.—**way**
(iii) The weather tends to be unreliable here, even in the summer.—**has**
(iv) You enjoy teasing me about being overweight, don't you?—**kick**
(v) I don't care what you do as long as you stop annoying me.—**give**

UNIT 2	ACTIVE–PASSIVE TRANSFORMATIONS

The most common uses of the *passive voice* are as follows:

(*a*) When the agent (i.e. the person or thing responsible for the action) is either not known or not important. It is therefore widely used in news reports; e.g. 'Tomorrow's bus strike has been called off.' 'The famine in Africa is reported to be worsening.'
(*b*) For greater formality. Compare the following:
   (i) Wine is drunk at mealtimes in France.—They drink wine at mealtimes in France.
   (ii) Not many skinheads are to be found these days.—You don't find many skinheads these days.

(c) When the agent is new information. Look at this dialogue:

> 'Dad, I've been robbed! My bag's been stolen!'
> 'Calm down and tell me what happened.'
> 'It was in Henry Street, about an hour ago. **I was surrounded by a gang of kids**. They stole my bag.'

The basic rules for changing from the active to the passive are very straightforward. Use the same tense of the verb 'to be' and the past participle of the relevant verb. Look at these examples:
Active: We **know** little. *Passive:* Little **is known.**
Active: They **have found** bronze products. *Passive:* Bronze products **have been found.**
Active: The scribes **wrote** them **down.** *Passive:* They **were written down** by the scribes.

Remember to make the verb agree with the new subject where there is a change from singular to plural, and vice versa; e.g. 'They **are** interviewing John for the job at the moment.—John **is being** interviewed for the job at the moment.'

Apart from the present and past continuous, the continuous tenses are not used in the passive, because they are too awkward; e.g. 'Her teacher has been telling her that for years.—She has been being told that for years'! The simple tense could be used here ('She has been told'), but the best idea is to avoid such a construction altogether.

If the verb is a prepositional or phrasal verb, don't forget the preposition or adverb particle when changing to the passive. Compare the following pairs of sentences:
Active: Did he pay the window-cleaner? *Passive:* Was the window-cleaner paid?
Active: Did you pay **for** the drinks? *Passive:* Were the drinks paid **for**?

EXERCISE 1

Change the following sentences from the passive to the active voice as instructed; e.g. 'Large sums of money should not be carried round by sightseers.—**Sightseers should not carry round large sums of money.**

(i)   I was assured that the matter would be thoroughly investigated.—The police …
(ii) The Mesolithic settlers were followed by waves of Neolithic colonists.—Waves …

(iii) You will be fascinated by the what the guide at Newgrange has to say.—What …
(iv) The beautiful ornaments could not have been made without tin.—The Bronze Age people …
(v) I've no idea where he is. When I last saw him in the coffee bar he was being chatted up by a couple of women!—I've no idea where he is. When I last saw him in the coffee bar, a couple …

EXERCISE 2

Now change these sentences from the active to the passive. This time you have no instructions to help you. Only mention the agent (i.e 'by …') where the information is important; e.g. 'Somebody once told me that you can see Scotland from here on a clear day.—I was once told that Scotland can be seen from here on a clear day.'

(i) Dr Ryan is to operate on you tomorrow morning.
(ii) They are going to knock down that derelict house and replace it with a new apartment block.
(iii) You can bet your bottom dollar that if the Government lowers tax rates, the banks will increase interest on loans.
(iv) You must be more careful! That car might have run over you!
(v) Did they tell you where you could find the dolmen?

Look at these ways of expressing what is or was said (reported, considered, thought, etc.) when the source of the information is vague, unimportant, or too obvious to need mention. Note how the time difference, if any, between the reporting verb and what is reported is indicated. Which is the least formal and which the least informal in each case?

(i) People **think** that red hair **is** very common in Ireland.—It **is thought** that red hair **is** very common in Ireland.—Red hair **is thought to** be very common in Ireland.
(ii) They **say** that Ireland **became** Celticised in the last centuries BC.—It **is said** that Ireland **became** Celticised in the last centuries BC.—Ireland **is said to have become** Celticised in the last centuries BC.
(iii) They **considered** that she **was** the best person for the job.—It **was considered** that she **was** the best person for the job.—She **was considered to be** the best person for the job.
(iv) People **believed** that he **had murdered** his wife.—It **was believed** that he **had murdered** his wife.—He **was believed** to **have murdered** his wife.

EXERCISE 3

Nearly all the verbs in the following newspaper report (adapted from the *Irish Times*, 22 November 1991) are in the active voice. Change them into the passive. Where the subject is X, it means that you don't need to mention the agent (i.e. 'by …'), since the person or persons are either unimportant or obvious. Begin: 'Three men are feared to have died …'

X fears [1] that three men died in the collision between two cargo vessels—the Dublin-based MV *Kilkenny* and the German-registered *Hasselwerder*—in Dublin Bay early this morning.

X recovered [2] one body as **X continued** [3] the search for the other two missing men. **X says** [4] that metal-cutting equipment has been ordered after **X heard** [5] knocking from inside the *Kilkenny*. **X rescued** [6] eleven of the fourteen crew members on board the ship and **took** [7] them to hospital. **X reported** [8] that the eight men on board the *Hasselwerder* had been in no danger at any time.

X airlifted [9] a crew of firefighters with special metal-cutting equipment onto the *Kilkenny* at 4 a.m. But although **X has been continuing** [10] the search since then, **X now considers** [11] there is little hope of **X finding** [12] the missing men alive.

X reports [13] that the *Kilkenny* has been floating towards the open sea and **X fears** [14] that cargo lost overboard **will endanger** [15] other vessels. **X reported** [16] later this morning that Howth lifeboat was searching for loose containers from the ship. **X said** [17] that the vessel had been carrying over 120 containers, up to half of which would have been stored on deck.

The Minister for the Marine, Mr Wilson, said that **X was doing** [18] everything that **X could do** [19].

VERBS FOLLOWED BY THE GERUND AND INFINITIVE

Which form of the verb in brackets would you use to complete the following sentences?

(i)   The Celts started [arrive] here as early as the sixth century.
(ii) Not to pay the penalty would mean [be] deprived of honour and normal society.

Grammatically it is possible to use either the gerund or the infinitive after 'start' and 'mean'. But while you could use either form in sentence (i) without any significant difference in meaning, only the gerund makes sense in sentence (ii). When 'mean' is followed by the gerund it can be replaced by 'result in', 'involve', or 'necessitate', but followed by the infinitive it denotes intention. Compare 'Blast, I forgot my umbrella! That **means getting** soaked and **sitting** in wet clothes all morning.' and 'Damn! **I meant to bring** my umbrella, but I forgot.'

Other verbs like 'start' are 'begin', 'propose', 'attempt', 'intend', 'continue', and 'can't bear'. Verbs like 'mean' are 'forget', 'go on', 'need', 'regret', 'remember', 'try', and 'stop'. Their meaning depends on whether they are followed by the gerund or the infinitive.

EXERCISE 4

In the following exercise, examples of usage are given of verbs whose meaning depends on whether they are followed by the gerund or infinitive. The questions are designed to make you think about the difference in meaning.

(i) **I'll never forget camping** in Connemara in the rain and **trying to** get warm by drinking hot whiskeys in the pub! We would have had some hilarious photographs to show you if Katie **hadn't forgotten to take** her camera with her.

What did you do in Connemara? What, as a result, will you now never do? What did Katie not do, and why? What, as a result, have you not got now?

(ii) Apparently this telegram arrived for me this morning, but I've been out all day so I've only just got it. Listen, it's from Auntie Jane; she says: '**Regret to tell** you great-uncle Sam died yesterday. Funeral today.' Oh, dear, it'll be over now. I'd better send a telegram saying **I regret not being able** to attend. Great-uncle Sam was a millionaire, you know. I **regret not going to visit** him more often now!

What is it that Auntie Jane is sorry she has to do? What are you sorry you were unable to do? And what are you sorry you didn't do more often?

(iii) **I've tried** my very best **to get** tickets for Brian Friel's new play at the Abbey. **I tried ringing** every theatre agent in town, and I even **tried standing** in a queue outside the Abbey for hours. But I had no luck, I'm afraid. I'm just off to see my cousin Paddy; he's an actor, so I'm going to **try asking** him. When everything else fails, **try pulling** strings! Keep your fingers crossed!

What have you so far not managed to do despite your efforts? What two things did you do without success? What third thing are you going to do to see if that works? What, in fact, is it a good idea to do when everything else you've done has been unsuccessful?

(iv) The guest speaker at the dinner last night was marvellous. He began by telling us how bad he was at public speaking, and then **went on to entertain** us with the most fascinating stories about his life as a television journalist. At one stage the fire alarm went off accidentally, but it didn't seem to worry him. He just made a joke about it and **went on talking** about his experiences in Beirut.

What did the guest speaker do first? What did he do next? What had he been doing when the fire alarm went off? What did he do when the fire alarm went off? And then what did he do?

(v) The journey to Killarney was never-ending. First we had to **stop to get** petrol, and then Carol insisted on **stopping to buy** ice-cream. By the time we reached Limerick we were all so tired and hungry we **stopped** at a pub **to have** a sandwich and a pint. Seán, of course, had three pints, so we had to **stop** four more times **to let** him go to the loo. He **should stop drinking** so much, but he's so funny when he has a couple of pints on him. We **couldn't stop laughing** all the way to Killarney.

How many times did they stop on the journey to Killarney? In each case why did they stop and what were they doing when they stopped? What habit should Seán stop? What did they do all they way to Killarney? Why?

(vi) *A:* Hi, come on in. I've just started to make the *coq-au-vin.* I hope you **remembered to bring** that bottle of cheap wine you said you had.

B: Oh, hell! I'm afraid I didn't! I distinctly **remember leaving** it out on the kitchen table so that I wouldn't forget it, but Frank called just as I was about to leave … Oh, dear, I'll have to go back for it.

A: Well, you'd better get a move on. Look, I'm up to my eyes here in the kitchen. If I give you the key of the front door, please **remember to leave** it in the hall with the other keys.

B: Of course I will! I'm not normally so unreliable! And by the way, I seem to **remember having to climb** through the bathroom window one time you were staying in my house because you **didn't remember to leave** the key under the flower-pot outside!

217

What did B not do, and why not? What does he know he **did** do, and why does he know this? When A offers B her front-door key, what does she want him to do? What happened in the past that B sarcastically reminds A of?

(vii) Now, let me make out a list of the things we **need to do** today. The grass is so long, we **need to mow** the lawn. And we really **need to do** something about the car; it's filthy after that long drive back from Killarney in the rain. The house-plants **need watering**, and we'd better do some shopping because the fridge **needs restocking**.

What four things do we need to do? What four things need doing? (Instead of saying that these things 'need doing', you could say they 'need to be done'. Give the alternative form in each case.)

EXERCISE 5

Now put the verb in brackets in the following sentences in the correct form—gerund or infinitive; e.g. 'I'm sorry I interrupted you. Please go on [work].—I'm sorry I interrupted you. Please go on **working**.'

(i)   Do you remember [have] your nappy changed when you were a baby?
(ii)   If you spill red wine on the carpet, try [spread] some salt on it. It's supposed to absorb it.
(iii)   It's often better to answer a question in English spontaneously. If you stop [think] you can get confused.
(iv)   I pressed the wrong key on the word-processor and erased the whole morning's work! That means [do] it all over again.
(v)   Will you ever forget [hide] the teacher's briefcase and [watch] him getting madder and madder when he couldn't find it?
(vi)   She studied medicine at university but gave it up in her final year and went on [become] one of the most successful rock singers of the day.
(vii)   We regret [inform] you that your application for the position as computer programmer in our firm has been unsuccessful.
(viii) I really tried very hard to [get] the coffee stain out of your good blouse. You can't see it any more, can you?
(ix)   This house is a disgrace! It badly needs [redecorate].
(x)   Remember [switch] the lights off when you're leaving the room.
(xi)   Would you please stop [talk] while I'm explaining this complicated grammar point to you?

(xii) Damn, I meant [go] to the bank before it closed, but it went clean out of my mind.

(xiii) If you hope to pass your exams in June, you'll need [pull] your socks up. You've done no work this term.

(xiv) Looking back on it, I've done a lot of things in my life I wish I hadn't done. But I'll never regret [marry] Mary and [have] such a wonderful family.

(xv) What do you mean you forgot [tell] me you crashed the car? How could you possibly forget something as important as that?

EXERCISE 6

Finish each of the following sentences in such a way that it means the same as the sentence before it; e.g. 'There is a lot of truth in this statement.—This statement **has a lot of truth in it.**'

(i) We need to know something about the different people who came and settled here.—It is …

(ii) Court cairns were probably built by immigrants from the Loire estuary.—Immigrants …

(iii) Court cairns are not as impressive as portal dolmens.—Portal dolmens …

(iv) The country was united by a common culture and language, despite the frequent faction-fighting.—Although …

(v) Not to pay the penalty would mean the defendant's being boycotted by society.—If the defendant …

EXERCISE 7

In each case make a new sentence, as similar as possible in meaning to the original one, using the word printed below (*you must not alter the word in any way*); e.g. 'The great majority of us have to choose what we want to be.— **almost**—Almost all of us have to choose what we want to be.'

(i) Besides the tools they used, their greatest legacy is the monuments they constructed.—**from**

(ii) The Neolithic tombs served not only as burial sites but also as shrines.—**both**

(iii) It seems that copper was introduced around 2000 BC.—**have**

(iv) It's so hot we could have a picnic in the garden today.—**enough**

(v) I don't think it's important to mention that particular point.—**worth**

THE MODALS—I: 'MAY'/'MIGHT'

'May' and 'might' are used in the following ways:

(*a*) To express future possibility, with varying degrees of probability. Look at these examples: 'I **might** go away for the weekend' (I haven't made up my mind yet). 'A diet of half-cooked flesh **may** not sound very appetising by modern standards' (I'm fairly certain it doesn't). 'The six-pints-a-night man **might/may well** not keep any liquor at home' (while I can't state this as a fact, I'm pretty sure this is the case).

(*b*) 'may' + the perfect infinitive to express an action that possibly happened in the past. (Native speakers often use 'might' + the perfect infinitive with the same meaning.) Again, 'well' can be added to increase probability. 'The cause of his death **may (well) have been** an overdose of poitín.'

(*c*) 'might' + the perfect infinitive to express an action that was possible in the past but didn't happen: 'If Joyce hadn't frequented the pubs of Dublin, he **might** never **have written** *Ulysses*.'

(*d*) 'might' to express reproach for actions not being performed: 'You **might give** me a hand with the washing-up!' And with the perfect infinitive for actions not performed in the past: 'You **might have remembered** it was my birthday today!'

EXERCISE 1

Use one of the above forms to re-express each of the following. You can be quite free in the changes you make; the important thing is to convey the meaning of the original sentence; e.g. 'Why don't you look in your room for your English book? You were reading it in bed this morning, so I expect you left it there.—Why don't you look in your room for your English book? You were reading it in bed this morning, so you **may (well) have left** it there.'

(i)   It's been a rotten summer so far, but you never know—it's just possible that we'll have a heat-wave in August.
(ii)   That's funny; they said they'd be at home this afternoon if I called. Perhaps they've just gone out to the shops.
(iii) I'm feeling rather tired, so I'll very likely be in bed when you get home.
(iv)   It's an awful pity you didn't tell me you were going to see that film. You knew I badly wanted to see it.
(v)   If the Victorian age hadn't been so prudish, perhaps Oscar Wilde wouldn't have died so young.

(vi) Hey, why don't you look where you're going! You've just knocked a full pint of Guinness out of my hand!

(vii) Don't wait for me outside the restaurant. Go on in and sit at a table. It's just possible that it'll be raining by lunchtime.

(viii) Of course nobody can actually prove it, but it's highly probable that St Brendan was the first European to set foot on American soil.

(ix) Keep Saturday night free, will you? The chances are we'll have a few people in for dinner and I'd like you to be there.

(x) Mary was complaining of a sore throat yesterday, so she's probably decided to stay in bed today.

THE MODALS—II: 'SHOULD'

'Should' can be used in the following ways:

(*a*) To express what is the right, advisable, sensible or responsible thing to do: 'All good customers **should be** conspicuous by their absence at closing time.' 'Ought to', as an alternative, suggests that the action is not or will not be carried out. Compare the following: 'People **should travel** by taxi when they've been drinking' (this is a sensible thing to do). 'People **ought to travel** by taxi when they've been drinking' (unfortunately they don't). 'Had better' is similar in meaning but can only be used of specific situations to express advice or warning: 'You**'d better take** a taxi if you're going to drink.' (Note that this is the contracted form of 'had better'.)

(*b*) 'should' (or 'ought to') + the perfect infinitive means that the right or sensible thing was not done in the past: 'I **should/ought to have worked** harder for my exams. Then I wouldn't have failed.'

(*c*) To express strong probability in the present or future (with 'ought to' as an alternative): 'It's eight o'clock. They **should be (ought to be)** up by now.' 'It **should be (ought to be)** a lovely weekend. The forecast is good.' And with the perfect infinitive to express actions probably completed in the past: 'They **should have (ought to have) finished** dinner by now. After all, it's 10 o'clock.'

EXERCISE 2

Re-express each of the following, using 'should' in one of the ways indicated above. As in the previous exercise, feel free to make changes or leave out words, as long as you retain the meaning of the original sentence; e.g. 'I left your umbrella in the hall this morning, so **unless something has happened to it, it's there**.—I left your umbrella in the hall this morning, so it **should be** there.'

(i)   If you're feeling tired, the sensible thing would be to go to bed early.

(ii) It's not very wise of her to be smoking. She's six months pregnant.

(iii) Ask Séamus about that sign in Irish. He speaks Irish so he'll probably know what it means.

(iv) Unless I'm very much mistaken, Tom and Mary are having the time of their life on their Caribbean holiday.

(v)   I feel bad that I didn't ring my mother last night. I know she was expecting to hear from me.

(vi) It's not good manners to speak with your mouth full.

(vii) If it's just a service you want, you can call back for your car at about two o'clock. Unless something unforeseen happens, it'll be ready by then.

(viii) I'm beginning to get really worried. If he left the office an hour ago, there's no earthly reason for him not to be here by now.

(ix) It's all right for little children to be seen but not to be heard, according to the nineteenth-century attitude!

(x)   I don't care what excuses he makes, it was wrong of him to shout at me like that in front of customers.

EXERCISE 3

Finish each of the following sentences in such a way that it means the same as the sentence before it; e.g. 'There is a lot of truth in this statement.—This statement **has a lot of truth in it**.'

(i)   Ireland is by no means unique in this regard.—By no means …

(ii) The Irish are *the* tea-drinkers of Europe.—Nobody else in Europe …

(iii) Although the situation has changed considerably in recent years, drinking is still considered an activity quite separate from eating.—Despite …

(iv) The Irish are the most enthusiastic dog-lovers in Europe.—The Irish love dogs …

(v)   We are an indoor society because of our climate.—Our climate …

EXERCISE 4

In each case make a new sentence, as similar as possible in meaning to the original one, using the word printed below (*you must not alter the word in any way*); e.g. 'The great majority of us have to choose what we want to be.—*almost*—Almost all of us have to choose what we want to be.'

(i)   Drink has long been considered the curse of the Irish nation.—**looked**

(ii) Drinking is both a serious business and a national pastime.—**not only**

(iii) Drink has long been considered an essential aid to the creative muse.—**time**

(iv) I need someone to correct my English pronunciation.—**have**

(v) Many Irish people seldom keep any liquor at home.—**hardly**

<table>
<tr><td>UNIT 4</td><td></td></tr>
</table>

UNIT 4   PAST AND PRESENT PERFECT TENSES

The past tense is used when a past time is either stated or implied, while the present perfect (as its name denotes) is concerned with the present, i.e. the situation now, even though the action happened at some unspecified time in the past.

Compare these two possible answers to the question, 'Where's Seán?'
(*a*) 'I **saw** him **just a moment ago**.' ('A moment ago' = a past time).
(b) 'I've **just seen** him.' (That is the present situation.)

Or the answers to the question, '**Have you ever been** to Limerick?'
(*a*) 'Yes, I **was** there last year.' (Past time stated.) (b) 'Yes, **I've been** there several times.' (*When* is not important.)

And compare these statements: (*a*) 'Oscar Wilde **wrote** six plays' (i.e. when he was alive). (b) 'Brian Friel **has written** eighteen plays' (he is still alive, and he may well write more).

EXERCISE 1

Put each of the verbs in brackets in the following sentences into the past or present perfect simple, active or passive; e.g. *A*: 'St Patrick [get rid of] all the snakes. That's why you won't see any in this country.' *B*: But I [see] one! In fact I [see] lots of them in the zoo last week!'—*A*: 'St Patrick **got rid of** all the snakes. That's why you won't see one in this country.' *B*: 'But **I have seen** one! In fact **I saw** lots of them in the zoo last week!'

(i) Although much [say] about the Celtic civilisation on the Continent in detail, little is known about the Celts in Ireland.

(ii) When the Romans [invade] Britain they [record] what they saw there.

(iii) The brehon laws [pass on] orally from the first century BC and eventually [write down] in the seventh century. They [survive] almost unchanged up to the seventeenth century.

(iv) Artefacts that [make] by Bronze Age people [find] as far away as the eastern Mediterranean.

(v) A beautiful Early Christian chalice, which [lie] buried in a field at Derrynaflan for hundreds of years, [discover] as recently as the 1980s.

Now look at the following uses of the **past continuous** and the **present perfect continuous** compared with the simple forms of the tenses.

(i)   While the Romans **were imposing** their legal system on Britain, Ireland **was establishing** a Celtic identity.—When the Romans **left** Britain, the seeds of Christianity **were being sown** in Ireland.

(ii) You**'ve been drinking** all evening. Look, you**'ve drunk** the six-pack of beer I bought this morning! And you **drank** all yesterday evening too.—You **were drinking** when I **left** you at seven o'clock and you **were still drinking** when I came home from the cinema!

EXERCISE 2

In the following dialogue, put the verbs in brackets into a suitable tense—past or present perfect, simple or continuous. *You may need to make some changes in the word order.* In two cases, two tenses are equally correct; e.g. *Mary:* 'I [see]^{11} Seán several times in the pub recently.'—*Mary:* **'I saw/I've seen** Seán several times in the pub recently.'

Mary: Hi, Emer! Where on earth you [be]^{1}? I [try]^{2} to get in touch with you for the last couple of weeks! And where you [get]^{3} that sun-tan? I never [see]^{4} you looking so brown and healthy!

Emer: Well, actually, I just [come]^{5} back from our holiday cottage in west Cork. The sun never [stop]^{6} shining all the time I [be]^{7} there. I [be]^{8} very lucky really, because I [get]^{9} the only good weather we [have]^{10} so far this summer.

Mary: I [see]^{11} Seán several times in the pub recently. I take it he not [go]^{12} with you, then.

Emer: Oh, yes. But you know we [try]^{13} to sell the house for the last year, so the poor man [have to]^{14} keep coming back to Dublin every time the estate agent [ring]^{15} him. I feel a bit guilty, because while I [lie]^{16} on the beach sunning myself, he [sit]^{17} in the car in the sweltering heat. By the end of the holiday he [be]^{18} so exhausted I [decide]^{19} he [need]^{20} a proper break, so I [plan]^{21} a surprise for him ever since.

Mary: And what you [decide]^{22} to do?

Emer: Well, we finally [sell]^{23} the house last Monday. We [have]^{24} a late breakfast on the veranda when a prospective buyer [call]^{25}. He [be]^{26} so keen to have the house that he [offer]^{27} us £5,000 more than we [ask]^{28} for it. So, since we not [have]^{29} a decent honeymoon when we [get]^{30} married and we [mean]^{31} to ever since, I just [look]^{32} at some brochures for holidays in the Caribbean!

A NOTE ON 'SPECIALLY' AND 'ESPECIALLY'

Compare the use of 'specially' and 'especially' in the following sentences:

(i)   St Patrick's Day is celebrated with **specially** imported high-school
      bands and majorettes.
(ii) The high status of women in Celtic Ireland is worth noting, **especially**
      when compared with their position under the Romans.

'Specially' means 'for that particular purpose'. It is often used with a past
participle in such phrases as 'a cake baked **specially** for your birthday'
or 'shoes that have to be specially made'. 'Especially' is simply a
synonym for 'particularly'.

EXERCISE 3

Decide which is the correct word to complete each of the following
sentences;
e.g. I hope you didn't buy those cream buns .... for me! ....
since I'm on a diet!—I hope you didn't buy those cream buns **specially**
for me! **Especially** since I'm on a diet!

(i)   It's been a long day, but we've had such a good time that I'm not
       .... tired. I'm actually looking forward to the disco!
(ii)   Irish people have fair skin with lots of freckles—............. in the
       summer if they've been out in the sun.
(iii) 'I hope you didn't open that bottle of wine .... for me!' 'Stop
       worrying. To tell you the truth, I'm glad of the excuse! I wouldn't
       normally drink wine at lunchtime, but it's nice to indulge yourself
       once in a while, ... since we don't have to work this afternoon.'
(iv)   They had their conservatory .... designed so that it gets the sun
       all day long. It's .... useful in the winter, when it's too cold to sit
       outside.
(v)   'Tom has a bad back so he had this ridiculously expensive chair
       installed in his office .... for him.' 'Does it help?' 'Not ....!'

INVERSION AFTER NEGATIVE ADVERBIALS

Note the word order in this sentence: '**No sooner had Patrick gained**
his freedom than he heard a voice begging him to go back to Ireland.'
What would the normal word order be? 'Patrick ....'

If a negative or restrictive adverbial is placed before the subject and verb,
inversion (i.e. the interrogative form) follows. Negative adverbials are words
like 'never', phrases like 'in no way', and even clauses, like 'not since I was a

225

child'. Can you think of any more? Examples of restrictive adverbials are 'hardly', 'hardly ever', 'seldom', 'only when the economy recovers'.

Note that this is a rather formal, uncolloquial structure. When it is used in spoken English it is emphatic and attention-seeking.
The angry teacher might say:

'**Never in all my teaching career have I had to deal with** such lazy, good-for-nothing students!'
The priest rouses his sleepy congregation by declaring:
'**Only by repenting your sins will you be worthy of entering** the kingdom of Heaven.'
Or the chairman addressing a meeting stresses the urgency of the financial situation:
'**Not since operations began has this company shown** such a poor turnover.'

EXERCISE 4

In the following sentences, put the word (or words) in bold type before the subject and verb, and make the necessary alterations; e.g. 'Darling, you should **not** stop to talk to strange men on your way home from school **for any reason**.—Darling, **for no reason should you** stop to talk to strange men on your way home from school.'

(i) The fire alarm had **no sooner** gone off than the fire engine was speeding down the street.
(ii) You are **not** to talk or otherwise communicate with each other during the exam **on any account**. (Begin: On no account ...)
(iii) I know it's not worth much, but I wouldn't part with this ring **even if you gave me a thousand pounds**. (Say: Not even ...)
(iv) I remarked that it looked like rain, and I had **hardly** said the words when the heavens opened and there was an almighty downpour.
(v) In the mid-eighties we **little** thought that such dramatic changes in world relationships would **take place** in the space of a few years.

EXERCISE 5

Finish each of the following sentences in such a way that it means the same as the sentence before it; e.g. 'There is a lot of truth in this notion.—This notion **has a lot of truth in it**.

(i)   It is sometimes claimed that St Brendan was the first European to set foot on American soil.—St Brendan ...

(ii) The monks who travelled to the Continent in the Dark Ages looked like 'spiritual hippies', according to one writer.—In one ...

(iii) Although the weather was atrocious, everybody seemed to enjoy the St Patrick's Day celebrations.—Despite ...

(iv) A writer has seldom been less appreciated by his fellow-countrymen than Joyce was during his lifetime.—Seldom ...

(v)   His charming manner enabled him to get the job.—His charming manner made ...

EXERCISE 6

In each case make a new sentence, as similar as possible in meaning to the original one, using the word printed below (*you must not alter the word in any way*); e.g. 'The great majority of us have to choose what we want to be.—**almost**—Almost all of us have to choose what we want to be.'

(i)   We travelled from one end of the country to the other looking for new recruits for the company.—**length**

(ii) Even though it's pouring rain, she takes her dogs for a long walk.—**if**

(iii) She rarely arrives late for work.—**hardly**

(iv) It took me all my time but I eventually managed to finish my thesis.—**succeeded**

(v)   So great was Patrick's impact on Ireland that the whole country was Christianised by the time he died.—**such**

UNIT 5   **THE MODALS—III: 'MUST'**

'Must' can be used in the following ways:

(*a*) To express absolute necessity or obligation (a stronger form of 'ought to'); e.g. 'Fox hunting is a tradition that **must be preserved** at all costs.' 'Have to' is a weaker form; compare 'I **must ring** my wife' (it's a matter of great urgency/I promised I would, etc.) and 'I **have to ring** my wife' (I'm explaining where I'm going/Can you tell me where there's a phone?' etc.)

Past and future forms are 'had to' and 'will have to', but 'must' is used to express present obligation to do something in the future; compare 'I **must ring** my wife tomorrow' (I feel the need to do this as I speak) and 'I'll **have to ring** my wife every night when I'm in Paris' (there's no need for me to think about this until I go there).

Note that necessity or obligation not to do something is expressed by 'must not/mustn't', while absence of necessity or obligation is expressed by 'don't have to', 'don't need to', or 'needn't'; compare 'You **mustn't waken** the children if they're asleep' (if you waken them I'll kill you!) and 'You **don't have to/don't need to/needn't waken** the children if they're asleep' (There is no reason to waken them).

(*b*) To express the speaker's certainty by inferring from the known facts; e.g. 'Hurling **must be** the fastest and most dangerous game in the world.' The negative equivalent of this is 'can't', and the past may be expressed by using 'must have' and 'can't have'; e.g. 'Patricia **must be** sick' (she's not at work today and I know she wasn't in good form yesterday); 'Seán **can't be working** late' (I rang the office a few minutes ago and there was no reply); 'James **must have gone** home' (his car isn't in the car park); 'Sheila **can't have had** her baby yet' (she told me last week it was due in two months' time).

Note that 'mustn't (have)' is a weaker form of 'can't (have)'; compare 'He **can't be** in Galway' (I'm convinced of this because I saw him in the pub this evening) and 'He **mustn't be** in Galway' (it's unlikely, because his friends there haven't seen him recently).

EXERCISE 1

(*a*)

must	can't	had to
must have	can't have	will have to
mustn't have	have to	don't have to

Use one of the above to complete the following sentences, and put the verb in brackets into its appropriate form. Where a choice is possible, what difference in meaning is there?

(i)   Ouch! This tooth has been giving me hell all weekend. I .... [ring] the dentist first thing on Monday morning.

(ii) You won't have your mother to get you out in the morning when you go to university, my boy! You .... [get up] and make your own breakfast then.

(iii) Now listen carefully, darling. You ...., under any circumstances, [accept] sweets from strange men.

(iv) 'Is question 1 on the exam paper compulsory?' 'Yes, in fact you .... [answer] the first three questions or you'll lose valuable marks. Questions 4 and 5 are optional, so you .... [answer] them.'

(v)   I .... [do] some shopping on my way home this evening. Is there anything you want from the supermarket?

(vi) 'I .... not [forget] to buy some more coffee today. We're completely out of it.' 'We .... [be] out of coffee; I bought half a kilogram only two days ago!'

(vii) 'Why weren't you at the party last night? Your boy-friend was.' 'He .... not [be]! When I left him at six o'clock, he was on his way to bed with a bad dose of flu. It .... [be] his twin brother you saw.'

(viii) 'I'm sorry I'm late but there was an accident on the road this morning and I .... [make] a detour.' 'Humph, it .... [be] a very long detour. It's now half past ten!'

(ix) 'I think we should go on without them. We've waited twenty minutes for them so they .... not [come].' 'Oh, look, there they are now! They .... [hold up] in the rush hour traffic.'

(x)   'I've got two tickets for the hurling match next Sunday. Will you come with me?' 'You .... [joke]! I'm not remotely interested in ball games. Anyway, you know I .... [visit] my grandmother every Sunday afternoon.'

'MIGHT/MAY AS WELL'

'Northerner and Southerner are united in their support for the Irish team at an international rugby match, and the day this fails to happen, **the politicians might as well give up**.' This is an elliptical comparison, the implied missing information being considered too obvious to state. It could be fully expressed thus: 'The politicians **might as well give up as carry on working towards a solution to the Northern problem**.'

The thinking behind this is as follows: as long as Northerners and Southerners can be united at a sports event, there is some hope for a political solution to the Northern problem. But if ordinary people can't be united in this way, what hope will the politicians have? The answer, of course, is that they will have so little hope of finding a solution that to give up trying would probably be better than to carry on working (which would only be a waste of time and energy).

In other words, 'might as well' (or 'may as well', which is exactly the same) is a very quick and useful way of expressing indifference, resignation or lack of enthusiasm when you want to say that one alternative is slightly preferable to another. In informal speech the second alternative is frequently left unstated, as the following examples show.

(i) 'I've been waiting for her for nearly an hour. Continuing to wait for her seems pointless. I **might as well go home** (as go on waiting for her).'

(ii) 'I've been waiting for her for nearly an hour, but she's bound to come within the next five minutes. I **might as well wait another five minutes** (as go home at this stage).'

(iii) 'There's nothing much on television tonight. Boxing, which we both hate, and *The Sound of Music*, which I've already seen twice. We **might as well watch *The Sound of Music*** again (as watch boxing).' Equally, a person might say in this situation: 'We **might as well watch boxing**. I couldn't bear to see **The Sound of Music** again!' or 'We **might as well go to bed early/catch up on our English homework/write that letter we've been putting off writing.**' (Since the alternative is to watch something on television we're not enthusiastic about, it seems slightly better to do one of these things.)

EXERCISE 2

Use 'might as well' to express the speaker's attitude to each of the following situations. Make full use of any colloquial and idiomatic expressions you are familiar with; e.g. 'Class stops at one o'clock. It's five to one and we've just finished what we were doing. It's not worth starting a new exercise, so we **might as well stop for lunch/call it a day/leave the work we haven't done till tomorrow**, etc.'

(i) We have five minutes before the end of class. It would be a pity to waste the time and we haven't corrected last night's homework yet, so we ...

(ii) Mr O'Brien's at a meeting. You won't be able to see him for at least fifteen minutes. There's a comfortable chair beside you, so you ...

(iii) I know you're not interested in the art exhibition I'm going to, but sitting here on your own won't be much fun, so you ...

(iv) Tim gave me a delicious box of chocolates for my birthday. I've just eaten one and I'm supposed to be on a diet. Oh, well, now that I've broken the diet I ...

(v) It's eleven o'clock. I'm not particularly tired but there's nothing decent on television and I've been working all evening, so I ...

(vi) Here we are in Limerick with no money and nothing to do all evening. I have a cousin who lives here. He's an awful bore, but in the circumstances we ...

(vii) There's another half hour before closing time and we've finished our pints. It would be a shame to sit here chatting with nothing to drink, so we ...

A NOTE ON 'DARE'

'Dare I say it, they still do things in style at Dublin Horse show.' 'They shush anybody who dares to clap during the round.'

The most common uses of the verb 'dare', meaning 'have the courage to do something' or 'not be afraid to do something', are shown in the following examples.

(i) **Dare I say it**, they still do things in style at Dublin Horse Show. (I'm somewhat hesitant about what I'm going to say as it might be considered offensive.)

(ii) They shush anybody who **dares to clap** during the round (i.e. anybody who has the audacity to do so).

(iii) I **daren't have another drink**. (I'm driving, so I'm afraid another drink will put me over the limit.)

(iv) **Don't (you) dare touch that cake** I've just baked! (I'm warning you!)

(v) **How dare you call me a liar**! (I am most indignant!)

(vi) **I dare you ask the teacher** who was kissing her in the car this morning. (I'm challenging you to do this.)

(vii) **I dare say** it'll start raining as soon as we get to the beach. (This is simply another way of saying 'I expect/imagine/suppose that's what will happen.')

'I dare say' can be used to show agreement: 'Fianna Fáil are bound to win the election.' 'I dare say.'

'Dare' (like 'need': see unit 10) can be used in two ways, in its negative and interrogative forms—like a modal and like an ordinary verb. The rule may be summarised thus: If you use 'do', use 'to'. If you don't use 'do', don't use 'to'!

It is, however, also possible to use 'to' but not 'do', and it should be noted that in the third person singular the –s ending is dropped. Look at these examples:

I don't dare (to) ask him. **I daren't ask** him.
Do you dare (to) ask him? **Dare you ask** him?
Dare he ask him?

EXERCISE 3

Rephrase each of the following sentences, using the instructions given after each; e.g. 'Perhaps I shouldn't tell you, but I saw your expensive new dress in a sale yesterday for half price! (Use 'dare') **Dare I say it**, I saw your expensive new dress in a sale yesterday for half price!'

(i)   It's eleven o'clock, so she's probably gone to bed. (Use 'dare say')
(ii)   You borrowed my new jeans without asking me! I can't believe it! (Begin: How …)
(iii)   He's so worried he might lose his job he doesn't dare to ask the boss for a rise. (Omit 'to' and make two sentences)
(iv)   I'm not sure if I should say it, but your hair was much nicer before you had it permed. (Begin: Dare …)
(v)   If you say anything about me getting drunk last night, I'll kill you! (Begin: Don't …)
(vi)   Would it be wise of him to tell the Gardaí about the drug pushers? After all, they might implicate him too. (Begin: 'Dare …)
(vii)   People didn't dare to criticise the regime when he was dictator. (Begin: Nobody …)
(viii) She lost the diamond brooch her husband gave her for Christmas, but she doesn't dare to tell him. (Omit 'doesn't')
(ix)   Go on, let's see if you have the guts to tell him what a bastard he is! (Use 'dare')
(x)   A slice of Black Forest gateau? Oh, no thank you! I'm terrified of putting on any more weight. (Use 'daren't')

EXERCISE 4

Finish each of the following sentences in such a way that it means the same as the sentence before it; e.g. 'There is a lot of truth in this statement.—This statement **has a lot of truth in it**.'

(i)   Sport is not so much a pastime as a way of life in Ireland.—Sport is more …
(ii)   Because it requires such a degree of skill, hurling is only played well in certain counties.—Such …
(iii)   Gaelic football is more popular than any other field sport.—The …
(iv)   There were no fewer than 50,000 spectators at the match.—There were at …
(v)   If it weren't for the work of the local hunt, the farmer would have to use his own method of exterminating vermin.—The farmer would be …

EXERCISE 5

In each case make a new sentence, as similar as possible in meaning to the original one, using the word printed below (*you must not alter the word in any way*); e.g. 'The great majority of us have to choose what we want to be.—**almost**—Almost all of us have to choose what we want to be.'

(i) Apparently Garret FitzGerald would rather study a train timetable than watch a football match.—**prefer**

(ii) My mother is a very skilful knitter.—**dab**

(iii) She used every method she could think of to get an interview with the rock star.—**book**

(iv) We're going to be too late for the beginning of the film now, so let's just go to the pub instead.—**might**

(v) Dublin Horse Show is not just a rosette-winning affair. It's a sale as well.—**much**

UNIT 6	**THE MODALS—IV: THE VERB 'TO BE'**

'St Stephen's Green **was to be** the pattern for eighteenth-century Dublin.'

The verb 'to be' + the infinitive can be used as follows:

(*a*) To express the idea of destiny, i.e. things we are now aware of but were not known at the time. It is generally used in the past tense in this way; e.g. 'Swift **was to die** after a slow and painful illness.' 'The arrival of the Normans in Ireland **was to be** the beginning of centuries of trouble.' Exceptions are where people claim to have a psychic and spiritual insight into the future, e.g. when the fortune teller says, 'You **are to become** rich and famous!' or the prophet says, 'This man **is to become** the saviour of the world.'

(*b*) To express orders or future arrangements; e.g. 'You **are to start** English classes on 16 October.' 'You **are not to waken** the baby!' 'She **was to go** to the dentist this morning' (that's probably why she's not in class/at work). 'He **was to put the** baby to bed before he went out' (I hope he remembered).

If a past order or arrangement was unfulfilled, the perfect infinitive is used. 'She **was to have gone** to the dentist this morning, but she has such a bad cold she had to cancel the appointment.' 'He **was to have put** the baby to bed, but he forgot all about it and went out to the pub. That's why I had to do it!'

EXERCISE 1

Rephrase the following, using the verb 'to be' + the infinitive in one of the above ways; e.g. 'The President had agreed to open the garden fête, but she had to cancel at the last moment because she had a sore throat.—The President **was to have opened** the garden fête ...'

(i) The Chieftains have been contracted to play in the National Concert Hall on Saturday week.
(ii) You mustn't go outside the gate when you're playing in the garden.
(iii) I had said I'd play in the match next Saturday, but I can't now because I have to go to a funeral.
(iv) It was your turn to do the washing up. I hope you did it!
(v) Mr O'Reilly says he wants you to go to his office immediately.
(vi) According to the weather forecast, the heat-wave will continue for the next week.
(vii) What are you doing here? I thought you had planned to go to Galway.
(viii) I predict that this man will have a profound influence on the next generation.
(ix) I had an appointment with Dr Harte, but as he was recovering from a coronary, Dr Foot saw me.
(x) My instructions are that you should keep a close watch on anybody entering or leaving the building.

PAST HABITUAL: 'USED TO'/'WOULD'

'The monks **would retreat** to their round towers when an attack was threatened.'

This is an event that happened regularly in the past but no longer happens. The habitual past can be expressed by 'would' or 'used to'. They are often interchangeable (as they are in the above statements); but—

(a) 'would' is not used for long-lasting states: 'Irish people **used to believe** in fairies';

(b) 'would' is commonly used when details of a past event or state are being given, particularly with a time clause beginning 'when'/'whenever'/'every time', etc. (but 'used to' is also possible here). 'When I was a student I **would** frequently **skip** boring lectures.' 'I **used to go out with** a wimp. Every time I suggested doing something interesting he **would say** he had to go to bed early.'

(c) note that the negative and question form of 'used to' can be formed in two ways: 'I **didn't use to do** it' or 'I **usedn't to do** it.' ' **Did you use to do** it?' or '**Used you to do** it?' Since the regular form using 'do' is more common nowadays, it is perhaps simpler to to use it.

EXERCISE 2

In the following passage, change each of the numbered verbs to the past habitual, i.e. using either 'used to' or 'would' (use 'would' whenever possible). Where there is an adverbial, you may have to change the word order. The first one has been done for you as an example.

When I was a little girl we **would**[1] always go to Portrush on the north Antrim coast for our summer holidays. Year after year we [stay][2] in the same austere boarding-house. It wasn't exactly the Ritz or the Hilton, but I [not mind][3]; I [spend][4] all my time in the water or making sandcastles or having donkey rides on the beach.

At the beginning of every August when I saw my mother packing the big trunk with our holiday clothes, I [get][5] so excited that I [not be able to][6] sleep at night. As soon as she tucked me up in bed I [get out][7] again and [start][8] wrapping up all my toys in newspaper and brown paper bags. Whenever she came in to waken me up in the morning she [find][9] the floor littered with neat little parcels.

By the time the first day of the holidays arrived, my excitement was so great that I always [get][10] sick in the car. The same thing [happen][11] at Christmas. I [go][12] to bed at about five o'clock on Christmas Eve to wait for Santa Claus. In all the years of my childhood I never saw him; he always [manage][13] to sneak in during the brief five minutes when I was actually asleep. Then I [lie][14] awake for the rest of the night examining and re-examining the contents of the stocking he had filled with goodies. On Christmas Day I always [be][15] so sick with excitement and tiredness that they [have to][16] put me to bed again.

I [be][17] a bit of a nuisance when I was a child, I think. I seem to have spent most of the time being sick!

PAST PERFECT TENSES

'The native Irish **had already established** themselves on the mouth of the River Liffey.' 'The same process of assimilation that **had characterised** all previous invasions began to take effect.'

The past perfect is used—

(*a*) After reporting verbs when the direct speech is in the past or present perfect tense; e.g. 'I **was** an awful fool.—I realised what an awful fool I **had been**.'

(*b*) In the 'if' clause of a conditional type III; e.g. 'I would have rung her if you**'d reminded** me.'

(*c*) As the past equivalent of the present perfect; e.g. 'I**'ve never been** to a hurling match before' (now). 'I**'d never been** to a hurling match before' (then). 'It's/this is the first time I**'ve drunk** Guinness' (now). 'It/that was the first time I**'d drunk** Guinness' (then).

(*d*) To indicate the relationship between the 'before past' and the past, especially when there would be ambiguity if the tense did not clarify the sequence of events. Where the sequence is obvious or the time gap between the actions or situations is almost non-existent, native speakers don't bother to use the past perfect; e.g. 'As soon as he **(had) finished** one cigarette he **lit up** another.' 'He **had no** sooner **got into** bed than the phone **rang**.' 'After he **(had) left** the pub, he went to a disco.' 'When she**'d had** her breakfast, she **read** the paper.' 'Although he **hadn't seen** her before, he **recognised** her immediately.'

However, the past simple is frequently used in a dependent clause that comes after a past perfect tense; e.g. 'He told me he **had seen** her when he **was** in Cork.' This avoids overuse of the past perfect, which would make the style seem awkward.

Basically the past perfect is used in relation to the past in the same way as the present perfect is used in relation to the present.

Note that in narrative style, when actions, events or situations about the past are being expressed in simple sentences or main clauses, the past tense is used. Compare 'He **booked** himself into the hotel and **went** to his room. Then he **switched** on the television, **poured** himself a stiff drink, and **lay down** on the bed to watch the news.' and 'After he **had booked** himself into the hotel, he went to his room. When he **had**

switched on the television and **poured** himself a stiff drink, he **lay** down on the bed to watch the news.'

EXERCISE 3

Put the verbs in brackets into an appropriate past tense. Only use the past perfect where you feel it's necessary for the sense, using the examples above as a guide.

(i)   When she [do] the washing up, she [wash] the tea towels.

(ii)   At one stage they [talk] about separating. Then apparently they [get] on very well together for several years when she [discover] he [have] an affair with her sister!

(iii)   As soon as I [see] her I knew she [cry], because her eyes were red and puffy.

(iv)   You'd have really enjoyed yourself if you [see] the play on television last night.

(v)   Immediately we [reach] Belfast we [ring] the journalist Tom [put] us in touch with. We arranged a time and a place for the interview he [agree to] when we first [contact] him, and then [go] off to a pub for lunch.

(vi)   Considering she [be] up since six o'clock that morning and [work] all day, it's hardly surprising she [fall] asleep during the concert.

(vii) He found *Dubliners* so interesting he [not able to] put the book down. It was the first time he [read] anything by Joyce. In fact he never [read] anything by an Irish writer before.

(viii) I [be] convinced I [invite] him for dinner. When he [not turn up] an hour after the other guest [arrive] I [be] so annoyed that we started without him. You can imagine how I felt when he [ring] me at ten o'clock and told me he [be] in an accident on the way to my house.

(ix)   She heard that her book [be] accepted by the publisher in the afternoon post. Up to that time she [not be able to] concentrate on anything because she [be] so tense.

(x)   He now wishes he [do] medicine instead of economics. I remember when I was in my first year at university I [wish] I [not choose] economics either. I [decide] I really [want] to do philosophy, so I [change].

A NOTE ON 'MOST' AND 'MOST OF THE'

'For **most people** Northern Ireland means violence.' 'The landlords have already devoured **most of the parents**.'

We use 'most' in a general sense and 'most of the' in a restrictive sense, i.e. when only a certain group is being referred to. 'Most people' in the first sentence above means people anywhere, while in the second sentence 'most of the parents' means only the parents of the poor children, i.e. the ones Swift recommends eating! In other words, if the noun is restricted by a stated or implied 'of' phrase or defining clause, 'most of the' is used. A preceding adjective does not have this influence; compare '**Most Irish songs** are ballads' and '**Most of the Irish songs** I know are rebel songs.'

The same applies to 'some', 'several', 'many', 'few', etc., and numbers; compare '**Ten people** were injured in the train crash' and '**Four of the people** injured in the train crash are still in hospital.'

EXERCISE 4

Use 'most' or 'most of the' to complete the spaces in the following sentences.

(i)   .... hardback books have a blurb about the author on the jacket.
(ii) .... books I have are paperbacks.
(iii) It's probably true to say that .... women nowadays would rather go out to work than be housewives, but in fact .... housewives I know are quite content to stay at home!
(iv) .... thoroughbred Irish horses are exported to other countries. In fact, ... horses ridden by the British show-jumping team were bred in Ireland.
(v)   They say that .... doctors nowadays are concerned with preventive rather than curative medicine. Mind you, ... doctors I've ever been to only want to send me away with a prescription.

EXERCISE 5

Finish each of the following sentences in such a way that it means the same as the sentence before it; e.g. 'There is a lot of truth in this statement.—This statement **has a lot of truth in it**.'

(i)   The name the Vikings gave the capital city is as not as old as the one used by the native Irish.—The name the native Irish used ...

(ii) Swift recommended that the babies be well fed so as to make them good food for the landlords.—In …

(iii) Strongbow not only came to Mac Murchú's aid but married his daughter as well.—Not only …

(iv) While the Normans made great changes, they eventually became more Irish than the Irish themselves.—Great changes though …

(v) The Duke of Leinster is said to have replied, 'They will follow me wherever I go.'—The Duke of Leinster is said to have replied that …

EXERCISE 6

In each case make a new sentence, as similar as possible in meaning to the original one, using the word printed below (*you must not alter the word in any way*); e.g. 'The great majority of us have to choose what we want to be.—**almost**—Almost all of us have to choose what we want to be.'

(i) How permanently they settled here is proved by the number of Norman names in today's telephone directories.—**dug**

(ii) Your disgraceful conduct at the conference was quite unacceptable.—**beyond**

(iii) The elderly couple who sold us the house didn't occupy half of it, but with our large family we'll soon be making the most of all the rooms.—**put**

(iv) I wish I hadn't done it. If they find out, I may well lose my job.—**risk**

(v) Our local TD hasn't done any of the things he promised to do. If he wants to be re-elected he'll have to make more of an effort.—**socks**

UNIT 7	THE MODALS—V: 'COULD'

'Could' is used in the following ways:

(*a*) For general ability in the past; e.g. 'In a very small area they **could grow** enough potatoes to support a whole family.' But note that where the ability to perform an action was fulfilled in specific circumstances, 'could' cannot be used; instead we must use 'was/were able to' or, to express greater effort involved, 'managed to do' or 'succeeded in doing'; e.g. 'Captain de Cuellar **was able to write** about the food the Irish ate in the sixteenth century.'

'Could' is used with a negative, however, to express inability to perform a specific action in the past; e.g. 'Those who **could no longer pay** their rents were evicted.'

(b) For general permission in the past; e.g. 'They **could grow** potatoes on land owned by the landlord. Of course they had to pay exorbitant rents.'

(c) As part of a type II conditional to express the ability to do specific things in the present. The 'if' clause is sometimes stated but more often implied in colloquial English; e.g. 'What'll we do now?' 'We **could have** a cup of coffee' (if you liked).

(d) With the perfect infinitive to express specific ability in the past, *not* fulfilled. This is also a way of expressing reproach; e.g. 'The corn grown in Ireland at the time of the Great Famine **could have alleviated** the suffering of the destitute.' 'You **could have told** me you were going to be late!'

EXERCISE 1

Rephrase each of the following sentences using 'could' where possible. Otherwise use 'was/were able', 'managed', or 'succeeded', whichever seems most appropriate; e.g. 'I learnt to swim when I was six.—I **could swim** when I was six.'

(i)   The children were allowed to watch television once they'd finished their homework.
(ii)   I don't know why you're laughing. I almost got run over!
(iii) It took the mechanic the whole afternoon to find what was wrong, but she finally got the car going again.
(iv)   'I'm fed up sitting at home.' 'Well, what about sitting in the pub for a change?'
(v)   I've never been so embarrassed in my life! Why didn't you warn me my ex-husband was going to be at the party?
(vi)   Mary is obviously much better at maths than I am. She did her homework with no bother, but although I spent hours at it I failed to get the right answer. (Two changes.)
(vii) At one time he was set to become a brilliant brain surgeon, but when his wife died suddenly he took to the bottle and never recovered.
(viii) 'Would it be possible for you to lend me a fiver?' 'Sorry, I'm broke right now. Try asking Séamus; he got paid yesterday.' (Two changes.)
(ix)   O'Carolan was a very gifted musician. He had the ability to compose an air on the harp impromptu.
(x)   We saw your documentary on emigration, even though we were staying in a cottage in the wilds of Donegal at the time. The local hotel had a television and they very obligingly let us watch it whenever we liked. (Two changes.)

EXPRESSING PREFERENCES

Look at this statement: 'Many Irish people **prefer** shop-bought white bread **to** home-made brown.' When expressing general preferences, we can 'prefer' one thing or action 'to' another *or* 'like' one thing or action 'better than' another *or* 'would rather' have etc. one thing or action 'than' another.

Look at the following constructions: 'I **prefer** coffee/going for a walk **to** tea/sitting in a pub.—I **like** coffee/going for a walk **better than** tea/sitting in a pub.—I'**d rather** have coffee/go for a walk **than** tea/sit in a pub.'

To express a preference in a specific situation we can use 'would rather', 'would prefer', or 'would like'. So while your preference is *normally* for going for a walk, *today*, perhaps because it's cold and wet outside, you say: 'I'**d prefer to sit** in the pub.' (Note the infinitive form of the verb after 'would prefer'.)—'I'**d like to sit** in the pub.—I'**d rather sit** in the pub.'

Note that in spoken English we don't normally bother to state the alternative, as it is usually understood in context. Where it is considered necessary to do so, 'would prefer' + the infinitive presents a problem, since the construction 'I'd prefer to sit in the pub to to go for a walk' is ugly and awkward. We could say, 'I'**d prefer to sit** in the pub **rather than (to) go** for a walk,' but it's much easier to say, 'I'**d rather sit** in the pub **than go** for a walk'!

When the preference is for someone else to perform the action, for example in answer to the question 'Will you ask the boss for a rise or will I?' we say: '**I'd prefer** you **to ask** him.—I'**d like** you **to ask** him.—I'**d rather** you **asked** him.'

Note these ways of expressing preferences about the past: 'I'**d prefer to have gone** for a walk' (rather than sat in the pub).—'I'**d rather have gone** for a walk' (than sat in the pub). 'I'**d prefer you to have asked** the boss for a rise.—I'**d rather you had asked** the boss for a rise.'

EXERCISE 2

Use the above ways of expressing preferences to complete the following monologue. In each case the number of spaces indicates the number of words needed. (Contracted forms—e.g. 'd rather, 'd prefer—count as two words.) The first two are done for you as examples.

Seán and I were at Kevin's party last night. We knew it wouldn't be a very good party, so we**'d rather have stayed** [1] at home. As soon as we arrived Kevin gave me a glass of wine, which he kept topping up. He knows I **prefer** wine **to** [2] anything else, but this was such horrible cheap plonk that really I'd rather he (3) .... [3] me water out of the tap! Seán likes beer .... [4] wine, but there wasn't any, so he had to drink the cheap plonk too. There were about forty guests all crammed into one small room, and it was uncomfortably hot and noisy. I .... [5] to a small intimate dinner party than that sort of thing. I .... [6] sitting round the table having interesting conversations better .... in a crowd of people all pushing and shoving and spilling wine. We were just about to leave at midnight when supper was announced. By this stage I was tired and, as I wasn't particularly hungry, I told Seán I'd rather we .... [7] home. He .... [8] to have left too, but he thought it wouldn't be very polite. There was a choice of lamb curry or sweet and sour pork. Normally I .... lamb .... [9] pork, but in this case I thought I .... the sweet and sour .... [10] the curry, so that's what I had. But it was horribly fatty and it gave me a bad dose of indigestion. As I said to Seán when we got home, I .... [11] a plate of boiled rice than that greasy mess. All he said was that he .... us .... [12] at home and watched the football match on television!

EXERCISE 3

Finish each of the following sentences in such a way that it means the same as the sentence before it; e.g. 'There is a lot of truth in this notion.—This notion has a lot of truth in it.'

(i)   Provided the potato crops thrived, there was no cause for alarm.—As ...

(ii) Despite the forewarning, nothing was done to prevent eventual calamity.—In ...

(iii) People rejected anything associated with the famine so vehemently that many of the old traditions were lost.—So ...

(iv) Brendan prefers accompanying himself on the guitar when he's singing to being accompanied by someone else.—Brendan would rather ...

(v)   I know he's at home. I was speaking to him on the phone only a moment ago.—I know he's at home. I've ...

In each case make a new sentence, as similar as possible in meaning to the original one, using the word printed below (*you must not alter the word in any way*); e.g. 'The great majority of us have to choose what we want to be.— **almost**—Almost all of us have to choose what we want to be.'

(i)   He kept a horse in case he would be unable to marry off his daughters if he only had a donkey.—**fear**
(ii) If you can't give up cigarettes altogether, you should at least try to reduce the number you smoke.—**cut**
(iii) To a certain extent it's understandable why the Irish language went into a decline.—**point**
(iv) Captain de Cuellar regarded the people he saw in the west of Ireland as savages.—**upon**
(v)   The great majority of people barely managed to keep body and soul together by living on a diet of potatoes.—**succeeded**

UNIT 8

CONDITIONALS

Few learners of English can have reached an advanced stage in the language without being well versed in the three basic types of conditional statement! These examples will remind you of them:

(1) If I **win** the lotto I'**ll/may/can buy** a Rolls-Royce. (This is a future possibility.)
(2) If I **won** the lotto I'**d/might/could buy** a Rolls-Royce. (I am only imagining it.)
(3) If I'**d wo**n the lotto I'**d/might/could have bought** a Rolls-Royce. (But this didn't happen.) Note the movement from real possibility to impossibility.

Variations of types I and II to express reduced probability can be added to this pattern. The movement from possibility is more subtle and gradual. Study the following.

(1) If my horse **wins** the race I'**ll drink** a bottle of champagne. (Perhaps he will.) (1a) If my horse **should win** the race I'**ll drink** a bottle of champagne. (1b) **Should** my horse **win** the race I'**ll drink** a bottle of champagne. (I don't think he will.)
(2) If my horse **won** the race I'**d drink** a bottle of champagne. (I'm only imagining it.) (2a) If my horse **were to win** the race I'**d drink** a bottle of champagne. (2b) **Were** my horse **to win** the race I'**d drink** a bottle of champagne. (Even in my imagination I consider it an unlikely event.)

(3) If my horse **had won** the race **I'd have drunk** a bottle of champagne.
(3a) **Had** my horse **won** the race **I'd have drunk** a bottle of champagne. (But of course he didn't. Nor did I drink the champagne.)

Note that the inverted forms ('should I', 'were I to', 'had I') are more stylistic and therefore more formal alternatives.

EXERCISE 1

Re-express each of the following according to the instructions, using one of the above variations; e.g. 'He could make a greater effort to get on with his boss. Then he might get promoted.' (I've tried telling him that but he doesn't seem to give a damn what his boss thinks of him.)—'If he **were to make** a greater effort to get on with his boss he **might** get promoted' or '**Were** he **to make** a greater effort to get on with his boss he **might** get promoted.'

(i)   If I'm late for the meeting, please start without me. (I don't expect to be late.)
(ii)   Nothing would ever get done if we all took the attitude she takes. (We wouldn't dream of it, of course.)
(iii)   If Paul doesn't ask Sonya to marry him she'll be devastated. (He did!)
(iv)   If Sonya accepts Paul's proposal, he won't emigrate to Australia. (She did!)
(v)   If you happen to come across that book I've been looking for when you're in town this afternoon, please get it for me. (It's out of print and practically impossible to find.)
(vi)   He's got an interview for a job tomorrow. He's going to get his hair cut. (His hair's still long and he didn't get the job.)
(vii)   Imagine selling the house and buying a caravan. We could travel round the world. (Well, I know it's hard to imagine!)
(viii) If she took my advice and smartened herself up a bit, her husband might not be so interested in the au pair. (But she'd never listen to me, of course.)
(ix)   You might see Mary in the pub tonight. Will you ask her to give me a ring? (I doubt it, though. Mary hasn't been seen in the pub for weeks.)
(x)   It looks as though it's going to be a lovely evening. We'll have a barbecue in the garden. (What a pity! The weather's turned cold and wet.)

Now look at these further variations and how they are used.

Type I

(*a*) If you **drink** too much, you **get** a hangover. (A general truth.)

(*b*) If you**'re twisting** my arm, **I'll have** another drink. (A particular situation at the moment of speaking.)

(*c*) If you **decide** to come with us, **ring** me before lunchtime. (Imperative form.)

(*d*) **Provided/providing/as long as** you **behave** yourself, **I'll buy** you an ice-cream. (The condition is stressed.)

Type II

(*a*) If it weren't for (or But for) the rain, we could go for a walk. (This is the only factor involved.)

Type III

(*a*) **If it hadn't been for** (or **But for**) Joyce's familiarity with Dublin pubs, much of *Ulysses* **would/might** never **have been written**. (This is the only factor involved.)

(*b*) If Joyce **hadn't been** so familiar with Dublin pubs, *Ulysses* **would be** a very different book. (Note the different times involved here: the 'if' clause refers to the past while the main clause refers to the present. This is a mixture of types II and III.)

EXERCISE 2

Re-express each of the following using one of the above forms; e.g. 'I had previous experience, you see. That's why we knew how to behave.—But **for my previous experience, we wouldn't have known how to behave**.'

(i)   Water always boils when heated to 100 °C.—If you …

(ii)   The only thing that stopped me from giving in my notice was your advice.—If it …

(iii)   I hit my young sister yesterday, so now my dad won't let me go to the disco.—If I …

(iv)   Yes, you can watch television, but it's absolutely essential that you finish your homework first.—Provided …

(v)   I have the most awful hangover. I drank too much at the party last night.—I wouldn't …

(vi)   All that prevents her from leaving her husband is her two-year-old child.—But …

(vii)   You must promise not to laugh at me. On that condition, I'll give you a demonstration of Irish dancing.—As long …

(viii) Records tend to warp. They do this when they are left in a damp place.—If you …
(ix) Why is this part of Ireland so sparsely populated? Well, the answer is starvation and emigration as a result of the famine.—Had it …
(x) 'Are you going for a pint?' 'Yes.' 'Then I'm going.'—'If …

EXERCISE 3

Finish each of the following sentences in such a way that it means the same as the sentence before it; e.g. 'There is a lot of truth in this statement.—This statement **has a lot of truth in it**.'

(i) The movement was so infectious that it even crossed the political divide.—So …
(ii) The Dubliners were both competent performers and good entertainers.—Not only …
(iii) 1951 was the first time that a concerted effort was made to promote traditional music.—It was not …
(iv) Up to the 1960s they did almost nothing to promote Irish music.—Little …
(v) More exotic music was considered to be better.—The more …

EXERCISE 4

In each case make a new sentence, as similar as possible in meaning to the original one, using the word printed after it (*you must not alter the word in any way*); e.g. 'The great majority of us have to choose what we want to be.—**almost**—Almost all of us have to choose what we want to be.'

(i) Any time you walk down Grafton Street you pass at least half a dozen buskers.—**without**
(ii) The Chieftains are undoubtedly the most celebrated folk group of all time.—**must**
(iii) When normal forms of entertainment were banned during Lent, the Church habitually made an exception for Irish dancing on St Patrick's night.—**would**
(iv) There are signposts in Irish all over Ireland.—**wherever**
(v) Ó Riada did the same thing for music as Joyce did for literature.—**what**

246

'I **wish** people in the North **could learn** to live together.' The speaker here regrets that this does not seem to be possible; in other words, the situation seems to be that people in the North *can't* live together.

The verb 'to wish' can be used to express certain feelings about present and past situations, as follows:

(*a*) To express discontentment or regret about present or near future realities, the unlikelihood of a change in the situation being implied. The subjunctive form of the following verb can only be detected by the use of 'were' for all cases of the verb 'to be', but in fact in colloquial English this is often replaced by the indicative 'was'. The best rule is to use the past tense but in formal situations retain the subjunctive for the verb 'to be':

> **I'm fat/poor/unemployed**, etc.—**I wish I wasn't/weren't** …
> He **talks** too much.—I wish he **didn't talk** so much.
> He **doesn't speak** Spanish.—**I wish he spoke** Spanish./**I wish he did**.
> They **can't learn** to live in peace.—I wish they **could learn** …

(*b*) To express annoyance, irritation or disapproval about actions or behaviour, especially when they are persistent, repetitive, or wilful:

> He **will call** Catholics Taigs./He **keeps (on) calling** Catholics
> Taigs./He **persists in calling** Catholics Taigs./He's **always**
> **calling** Catholics Taigs.—I wish he **wouldn't**.
> They **won't listen** to reason.—**I wish they would** …

Note the difference between these statements: 'I wish he **didn't call** Catholics Taigs.—I wish he **wouldn't call** Catholics Taigs.' Which expresses resignation and which annoyance?

(*c*) To express regret about the past:

> My house **was destroyed** by a bomb.—**I wish it hadn't been** …
> I **didn't learn** Irish at school.—**I wish I had learnt** …

In all the above cases the exclamatory form' if only' can replace 'I wish' to express greater emotional intensity:

> **If only** people in the North **could learn** to live together!
> **If only** they **would listen** to reason!
> **If only** I'd **learnt** Irish at school!

Apart from the above, 'wish' can be used:

(*a*) As a more formal alternative to 'would like/'d like'. Compare 'I'd like to speak to the manager' (there's something I want to tell/ask/discuss with him) and 'I **wish to see** the manager' (this is a matter of urgency so I expect your prompt attention—i.e. I demand to see him).

(*b*) To convey good will on certain occasions. Nowadays you can find special greetings cards to do this for you:

> **Wishing you** a merry Christmas and a happy New Year.
> **To wish you** success in your new job/in your exam, etc.
> **This is to wish you** health and happiness.

EXERCISE 1

Rephrase each of the following sentences using 'wish' and an appropriate verb form; e.g. 'You're annoying me. Go away and leave me alone!—I wish **you'd stop annoying** me./I wish **you'd go away** and **leave** me alone.'

(i)   Oh dear, I have a dreadful hangover. I shouldn't have gone to that party last night.—I wish …
(ii)   Do you have to blow smoke into my eyes?—I wish …
(iii)   Why don't you listen when I'm speaking to you?—I wish …
(iv)   It'd be lovely to spend a weekend in the most expensive hotel in Paris. But I know I can't afford it.—I wish …
(v)   Oh, do stop behaving like a two-year-old and grow up!—I wish …
(vi)   It's his own fault that he failed the exam. I bet he's sorry now that he didn't work harder.—I bet he wishes …
(vii)   Brr, I'm so cold and miserable. Wouldn't it be lovely if we were sitting in front of a nice turf fire drinking hot whiskey right now!—I wish …
(viii) Oh, my head! They're making the most awful noise next door. I can't stand it!—I wish …
(ix)   Ireland's a lovely country. It's just a pity it rains so much.—I wish …
(x)   Why does it have to rain every time I want to sit in the garden!—I wish …

EXERCISE 2

What would you say in these situations?

Use 'I wish' or 'if only' and a suitable verb form to respond to these situations; e.g. 'You look in the mirror. Frankly, you don't like what you see!—I wish/if only I **hadn't had** my hair cut so short!' *or* 'I wish/if only my face **wouldn't keep breaking** out in spots!' *or* 'I wish/if only I **didn't have** such a big nose.' *or* 'I wish/if only I **looked** like Madonna/the fellow next door!'

(i)   While you're very fond of your boy-friend or girl-friend, he or she has an irritating habit, e.g. a silly laugh, talking with food in his or her mouth, or biting his or her nails. You can't stand it any longer!

(ii) Your car has let you down again. You look at it; it's old and badly rusted. In brief, it's seen better days. But you are up to your eyes in debt.

(iii) You live so far from the city centre that it takes you an hour and a half to get to school or work every morning. It's an awful waste of time and energy.

(iv) It's three o'clock on a Sunday afternoon. You're tired and thirsty after a long walk and you've just reached a pub. Pub opening hours on Sundays are 12.30–2 p.m. and 4–11 p.m.

(v)   You could have gone to the Bahamas with your family. Instead you came to Ireland. It's wet and cold outside, you haven't made any friends here, and, frankly, you're feeling pretty miserable!

A NOTE ON COMPARISONS

Note the use of 'as ... as' (or the alternative 'so ... as' with negatives) and 'more ... than' in the following sentences and how one form can be changed to the other.

(a) I am **as** mature **as** I'm ever going to be.—I'm never going to be **more** mature **than** I am now.

(b) They have **more** sagacity in their little toe **than** I am ever likely to have.—I am never likely to have **as** much sagacity **as** they have in their little toe.

(c) Strabane is about **as** far away from Belfast **as** you can get.—You can't get any **further** from Belfast **than** Strabane.

(d) Sport is not **so/as much** a pastime **as** a way of life.—Sport is **more** a way of life **than** a pastime.

(e) Gaelic football is **more** popular **than** hurling.—Hurling is not **as** popular **as** Gaelic football.

EXERCISE 3

Change the following from the form given to the other form by completing the new sentence in each case; e.g. 'I'm fatter than I've ever been before.—**I've never** been as fat as this before/as I am now.'

(i) I haven't got as much money as I thought I had.—I thought I had …
(ii) Nobody could have done any more than she has done.—She has done …
(iii) When it comes to standing up for one's rights, I'm not nearly as assertive as you are.—You are far …
(iv) I wish you'd let me explain the instructions myself. You're more a hindrance than a help.—I wish you'd let me explain the instructions myself. You're not …
(v) She may be very hard-working but she's not nearly as intelligent as her sister.—She may be very hard-working but she's far …

A NOTE ON COMPARATIVES AND SUPERLATIVES

'The **Lower** Main Street was the **humbler** end.' 'The **less** important people lived in numbers.' 'Strabane could win the Who's Got the **Highest** Unemployment Contest.' 'Why is Esso the **best** petrol?'

The comparative ('more …/–er', or irregular forms like 'less') is used when only *two* ideas are implied or expressed, i.e. there is only one alternative. In the above examples, 'Upper' is the alternative of 'Lower', 'posher/smarter' etc. is the alternative of 'humbler', and 'more' the alternative of 'less'. The superlative ('most …/–est', or irregular forms like 'best') is used when there are *more than two*. Strabane is only one of many towns; Esso is only one of many types of petrol.

EXERCISE 4

Here is a page of the diary you are keeping while staying in Ireland. Put each of the words in brackets into an appropriate comparative or superlative form. The first one has been done for you as an example.

The second day of our holidays in Donegal. I wish the weather was a bit **less chilly**[1] or at least that I'd brought my [warm][2] clothes with me, but I didn't think I'd need winter woollies in the middle of August! The drive from Dublin yesterday took much [long][3] than we'd expected, so by the time we got here all I felt like doing was falling into the [comfortable][4] armchair—only three for four people! Considering I had done [some][5] of the driving, I don't think it was the [little][6] bit selfish of me! The others slept off and on during the journey, so they had [some]⁷ energy to unpack the car, light the turf fire, and make up the beds. At one stage Kathleen put a glass of the [strong]⁸ hot whiskey I've had since I came to Ireland into my hand. That and the heat of the fire must have made me doze off, for next thing, in the middle of the [fantastic]⁹ dream, I was woken up by Pat shaking me and complaining, 'You're the [loud]¹⁰ snorer I've ever heard! You're even [loud]¹¹ than my eighty-year-old grandmother! We've decided you'll have to sleep out here on your own.' I was secretly much [happy]¹² with this arrangement than they knew. There was a double bed in each of the two bedrooms; one was short and lumpy and the other, while [big]¹³, was even [lumpy]¹⁴! I am the [tall]¹⁵ of the four of us and I knew I would be [comfortable]¹⁶—and [warm]¹⁷—in my sleeping-bag in front of the fire. I was right! One look at the bleary eyes of the other three this morning told me that, by comparison, I had slept [long]¹⁸ and [soundly]¹⁹. I'm now looking forward to a long walk and, perhaps, a swim. But it looks as if I'll be on my own, unless Pat and Kathleen and Mary are a bit [bad-tempered]²⁰ by the time they've had their breakfast. Perhaps I should make them all hot whiskeys!

REPORTED STATEMENTS AND QUESTIONS

Note how the tense changes from direct to reported statements or questions. 'Which shops **are** ours?'—He wanted to know which shops in the street **were** ours. '**I'll be** a piper in an Orange band.'—'I decided **I'd be** a piper in an Orange band.'

When the reporting verb (e.g. 'wanted to know', 'decided') is in the past tense, the verb in the indirect statement changes, as illustrated by the following examples.
(*a*) 'I'm tired.'—He said he was tired.
(*b*) 'I'm going home.'—He said he was going home.
(*c*) 'I've had lunch.'—He said he'd had lunch.
(*d*) 'I had a problem.'—He said he'd had a problem.
(*e*) 'I'd never seen one before.'—He said he'd never seen one before.
(*f*) 'I'll enjoy myself.'—He said he'd enjoy himself.
(*g*) 'I can do it.'—He said he could do it.
(*h*) 'I must/have to go.'—He said he'd have to go.
(*i*) 'It may rain.'—He said it might rain.

Note that 'must' for inference, 'could', 'should/ought to/had better' and 'might' do *not* change, as shown in the following examples:

'There's the phone ringing. It **must be** Paul.'—He said the phone was
   ringing and that it **must be** Paul.
'We **could go** to the theatre.'—She said we **could go** to the theatre this
   evening.
'We **should/ought to/had better go**.'—She said they **should/ought
   to/had better go**.
'It **might snow** before the week's out.'—He said it **might snow** before
   the week was out.

And note that there are no changes when reporting conditionals type II
and III.

'**Will** you **help** me if **I'm** in trouble?'—She asked me if I **would help**
   her if she **was** in trouble.
'**Would** you **help** me if I **was/were** in trouble?'—She asked me if I
   would help her if she **was/were** in trouble.
'**Would** you **have helped** me if **I'd been** in trouble?'—She asked me if
   I'd have helped her if she**'d been** in trouble.

In reported questions, unless there is an introductory *wh–* word, the
indirect question is introduced by 'if' (or 'whether', especially when an
alternative is expressed), and the affirmative word order is used. Hence:

He asked (me) **who was going**.—He asked (me) **if/whether I was
going** (or not).—He asked me **whether/if I was going or staying at
home**.

Native speakers often don't bother to make such changes in informal
speech if the reporting is in roughly the same time zone as the actual
statement or question. Hence:

(*a*) I didn't hear what he said.—He said he**'ll meet us** in this pub **this
   evening**.
(*b*) What did she ask him?—She asked him **if he wants to go home**.

Similarly, people often don't make changes in time adverbials, and in fact
it would be wrong to do so if the reporting takes place in the same time
zone as the direct statement or question. Compare (*a*) above with:
What did he say when you saw him **last week**?—He said he**'d meet** us
in the pub **that evening**.

Here is a guide to the changes in some common time adverbials.

Today		
Tonight		
This morning	}	that day/night/morning/afternoon
This afternoon		

Yesterday etc.—the day before/the previous day, etc.
Tomorrow etc.—the next/following day, etc.

Note also that when a statement or question is reported in a different place, 'this' changes to 'that', or simply 'the', and 'here' changes to 'there', etc.

EXERCISE 5

Change the following from direct to indirect speech. In each case imagine that the statement or question is being reported at a different time and in a different place; e.g. 'I can't go to the theatre on Thursday night. I think I have to babysit for my sister.'—Paul said **he couldn't go to the theatre on Thursday night because he thought he had to/would have to babysit for his sister.**

(i)   'What would you do if you were in my shoes?'—She asked me ...
(ii)   'Katie's going to start Irish classes next Monday.'—Neil told me that ...
(iii) 'Should we switch off the electricity at the mains before we leave?'—He wanted to know if ...
(iv)   'You'll have to pull your socks up if you want to pass the exam.'—The teacher advised him that ...
(v)   'Will they ever learn to live together in peace in this part of the world?'—He wondered if ...
(vi)   'You mustn't, on any account, leave the room until you have finished your exam.'—The invigilator instructed the students that ...

Orders, requests and advice can be reported by simply using the infinitive. Which two of the above can be changed in this way?

EXERCISE 6

Now decide what was actually said in the following; e.g. 'He told me not to tell anybody that he was getting married.'—'**Don't tell** anybody **I'm getting married**'.

(i)   The lecturer explained that even if more help had been forthcoming during the famine years, thousands of Irish people would still have emigrated.

(ii) They advised her to send them her curriculum vitae that day if she wanted to be considered for the job.

(iii) He wondered if he should tell his wife that he was having an affair with her best friend.

(iv) He warned his daughter not to accept a lift from anybody she didn't know and to go home immediately the concert had finished.

(v)   They told him during the meal that if they'd had any idea how expensive the restaurant was going to be they'd never have dreamt of going there.

EXERCISE 7

Finish each of the following sentences in such a way that it means the same as the sentence before it; e.g. 'There is a lot of truth in this statement.—This statement **has a lot of truth in it**.'

(i)   We were honoured to be part of the United Kingdom, detached from the mainland though we might be.—Although …

(ii) Another reverend gentleman directed me to be polite but not too friendly towards any Catholics I met.—Another reverend gentleman said, '…

(iii) The questions, because there were no straight answers, continued to grow.—Because of …

(iv) I can't tell you any more than that.—That's …

(v)   I've never met a smugger, more conceited so-and-so than your brother.—Your brother …

EXERCISE 8

In each case make a new sentence, as similar as possible in meaning to the original one, using the word printed after it (*you must not alter the word in any way*); e.g. 'The great majority of us have to choose what we want to be.— **almost**—Almost all of us have to choose what we want to be.'

(i)   I expanded my repertoire of known facts simply by sitting in the classroom.—**dint**

(ii) The muted conversation of the corner boys was regularly my lullaby at bedtime.—**used**

(iii) Since I was too young to understand the situation, it didn't worry me.—**being**

(iv) If only they'd stop fighting and start talking reasonably.—**wish**

(v)   'Will you talk to us when you grow up?' one of them once asked me.—**would**

254

'BE'/'GET USED TO'

'Queen Maeve **was used to taking** as a lover any fellow she fancied.'

'To be used to' is a less formal equivalent of 'to be accustomed to', and 'to get used to' is a similar equivalent of 'to become accustomed to'. All four are prepositional verbs and are followed by a noun, noun phrase, or clause, or the gerund form of a verb:

I have become accustomed to	—the weather
I have got used to	—people's eating habits here
I am accustomed to	—the way the buses operate
I am used to	—eating potatoes every day

Be careful not to confuse the past habitual, where the 'to' is part of the following infinitive, with this form, where the 'to' is part of the verb itself; compare 'I used **to do** it' and 'I'm used to **doing** it.'

Foreign speakers have a tendency to use 'to be used to' when a native speaker would simply say 'usually' or 'normally'. 'To be/get used to' implies that a habit, which was perhaps a little strange or difficult or uncomfortable to begin with, has been formed or is in the process of being formed. 'Usually', on the other had, simply states that an action occurs frequently enough to be considered routine: 'Irish people **usually eat** potatoes every day.—Most foreigners who come to Ireland **are not used to eating** potatoes every day. They **have to get used to it/doing so**. By the time they're ready to leave, they **usually** say, **'I'm used to eating** potatoes every day!'

Now while Queen Maeve may not have had much trouble forming her amorous habit, she would no doubt have found it difficult to give it up! The problem of changing habits formed over long periods is often expressed by 'be used to' and 'so ... that'. Look at this conversation between two women:

A: My son Brian is starting university in October. He's going to share a flat with some friends. I'm a bit concerned, because he**'s so used to me waiting on him hand and foot that I don't know how he'll manage.**

B: Oh, don't worry. He**'ll soon get used to looking after** himself, and it'll do him all the good in the world!

EXERCISE 1

Look at the following situations and in each case make three appropriate statements using 'usually' or 'be/get used to'; e.g. 'In Spain they have their evening meal as late as ten o'clock. Here in Ireland it's normal for people to eat at six o'clock. Juan is a Spanish **student who has just arrived in Ireland**.—(a) The Spanish usually eat at ten o'clock in the evening. (b) The Irish **usually eat at six o'clock**. (c) Juan **will find it difficult/will have to get used to eating so early**.

(i) It's customary for the French to drink wine with their meals. Most Irish people drink tea, whether they're having a meal or not! Rose, from Tralee, has been working in Paris for years.—(a) The French … (b) The Irish … (c) Rose …

(ii) Pat the postman gets up at five o'clock most mornings. When he started the job twenty years ago he found this rather difficult, but now it's second nature to him.—(a) Pat the postman … (b) When he started the job … (c) Now …

(iii) My mother used to do all the ironing in our house. When I got married a couple of years ago my wife told me I'd have to iron my own shirts unless she had time to do it. At first I resented this, but now I'm rather fussy about the way my shirts are ironed. The odd time she does it for me, I do it again!—(a) I … (b) When I first got married … (c) Now I'm so …

(iv) Jesper's Danish. As you know, in Denmark they have a preference for lager. Guinness is supposed to be an acquired taste, so he probably won't like his first pint. But I bet by the time he goes back to Copenhagen he won't want to change back to lager!—(a) Danish people … (b) Jesper will have to drink a couple of pints before he … (c) When he goes home, he'll be so …

THE CAUSATIVE 'HAVE' AND 'GET'

'The parents **had the new science teacher removed** because she was a Catholic.' 'Pearse **got himself executed** by firing squad.'

We use 'have/get something done' to denote that an action was, is or will be performed by someone else. 'Get' is more colloquial and quite definitely implies that the subject causes the action to be performed; e.g. 'I'd better **get that leak fixed** before the whole house is flooded' (I will presumably employ a plumber to fix it.) '**Get your hair cut**, or I'll cut it myself!' (this is a father ordering his son to go to the hairdresser's).

Look at the first two examples again. By saying that Pearse got himself executed, the writer does not, of course, mean that Pearse went to the British authorities and told them to execute him! You should already have discussed this, but remind yourself: by using this construction, what does the writer suggest?

In the other example, the parents were instrumental in the removal of the science teacher by putting pressure on the headmaster. 'Having something done', like 'getting something done', can mean asking, telling or employing somebody to perform an action; e.g. 'They **had/got the house rewired** before they moved in' (the electricians did the job). But what about this statement? 'They **had their house burgled** while they were in Spain.' Naturally they didn't employ somebody to do this! This simply means that something unpleasant happened to them. 'Get' would be quite wrong here.

EXERCISE 2

Use 'have/get something done' to respond to the following situations. The prompts given after each will guide you; e.g. 'I'm afraid you can't leave the country. Your passport is out of date.—**should/passport/renew**— You **should have had your passport renewed**.'

(i)   The outside of the Kellys' house is a disgrace; the walls are dirty and the paint is peeling. A van has just pulled up outside and two men in white overalls are taking a ladder and tins of paint out of it.— **they/must/the outside/do up**

(ii)   The neighbours' dog keeps him awake all night by barking. If it doesn't stop he'll have a nervous breakdown, lose his job, divorce his wife, etc. 'Take him to the vet,' he shouts over the garden fence, 'and don't bring him back, or I'll shoot the lot of you!'—**if/dog/put down/shoot**

(iii) The last time I was at the dentist's he warned me that this tooth might give me more trouble. It's been excruciatingly painful for the past week. Oh dear!—**suppose/have to/take out**

(iv)   Excuse me, but my colleagues and I are finding it difficult to work because we're so cold. I know it's only September, but it is rather chilly. We'd all be much happier if there was some heat …— **wonder/we/central heating/turn on**

(v)   That evening she parked her car outside her apartment block as usual, but when she went out the next morning, it had gone.—her **car/steal/night**

(vi)   You shouldn't be driving so fast; there's a general speed limit of 96 km per hour in Ireland. You know what'll happen if the police catch you.—**if/licence/endorse**

(vii) Just look at those windows! They're so dirty you can't see through them. But they're too high up for me to get at them. I have visitors coming to stay at the weekend. I hope the window cleaner comes before then.—**hope/windows/by the time**

(viii) You've been complaining about back pains for the last year. For goodness' sake stop moaning and do something about it!—**go/back/see to!**

(ix) Listen, you ill-mannered lout, we don't put up with bad language in this pub. And if you don't behave yourself immediately I'll make sure you won't be able to drink in any pub in town.—**if/behave/bar/every pub**

(x) 'This is disgraceful! I'm on my honeymoon and I expressly asked for a double-bedded room with a view of the sea. Instead you give me a room overlooking the back yard and the rubbish bins!'—'I do apologise, sir, there must have been some mistake.' **room/change/at once**

'IT'S TIME …'

'Maeve would scold her husband saying that **it was high time he realised** she could match him any day.' Maeve's probable words to her husband were: '**It's high time you realised** I can match you any day.' '**It's about time Lizzie was put** in her place, Grace thought.' Maeve is admonishing her husband for not realising something she thinks he should have realised long ago, and Grace feels that somebody should have put Queen Elizabeth in her place long ago.

In other words, we use 'it's (high/about) time' + the past tense when we want to indicate that an action is urgent and should have been performed at an earlier time; e.g. '**It's time you grew up!**' says an irate father to a teenage son or daughter. 'You're behaving like a two-year-old! And **it's high time you got up**! Your mother had your breakfast ready ten minutes ago! In fact,' he might add, '**it's about time you learnt** to make your own breakfast and give your mother a rest!'

'It's high time' stresses the speaker's anger or irritation, while 'it's about time' tends to express exasperation or sarcasm. If you have had to wait at the bus-stop for twenty minutes in the rain, you might well mutter when you see the bus coming, '**And about time, too!**'

'It's time (for somebody) to do something' is simply a factual statement, meaning the right or arranged or appointed time has arrived for an action to be performed. Compare the following dialogues:
A: What time did we arrange to leave at?
B: Half past ten.

258

A: It's half past ten now, so **it's time (for us) to leave**.

C: What time did we say we'd be there at?

D: Two o'clock.

C: Oh, lord! It's after one now and it'll take us at least an hour to get there. **It's time we left/were leaving**.

EXERCISE 3

What would you say in the following situations? Use 'it's time/about time/high time' as shown above (and your imagination!); e.g. 'You are a teacher. Séamus is an intelligent student who wants to go on to university to study medicine. He has exams in two months but he hasn't done a tap of work all year.—**It's high time you did some work/got down to some work/pulled your socks up**/etc. if you want to go to university/study medicine/pass your exams …'

(i) Mickey Mooney has been the leader of the political party you support for the last twenty years. He's now seventy-two. There are several younger people in the party who would be capable leaders if they were given the chance.

(ii) You're having difficulty putting on your old but freshly laundered jeans; they're so tight that the zip breaks and they split at the back. Either the jeans have shrunk or you've put on weight!

(iii) You are a guest at a dinner party. You've been drinking brandy and coffee and chatting for the last hour or so. Then you notice the hostess stifling a yawn and that the glasses and the coffee-pot have been empty for some time.

(iv) As you're cycling to work, your bicycle goes into yet another pot-hole. Ouch! You hurt—in a very delicate place! This road is in a disgraceful condition, but despite your repeated complaints the council don't seem to be doing anything about it.

(v) You are an exasperated teacher of English as a foreign language. Every day since this class started you've corrected your students for saying 'people is …' Mario has just said, 'Irish people drinks a lot of Guinness.'

A NOTE ON 'NEED'

'Elizabeth **needn't have bothered** offering to make Grace a lady.' 'As a married woman, you **didn't need** to to earn money and therefore **no longer needed to work**.'

Elizabeth *did* offer to make Grace a lady, an act that proved unnecessary, since Grace rejected the offer. A married woman, however, *didn't* work

259

and *didn't* earn money, because it was unnecessary (i.e. because she was supported by her husband). The tone, of course, is heavily ironic!

We use 'needn't have (done)' when an action was performed unnecessarily, and 'didn't need (to do)', like 'didn't have (to do)', when the action was not performed because there was no necessity to do so; compare 'I **needn't have watered** the garden—it's raining!' 'I **didn't need to water** the garden—it was raining.'

'To need to do' something is often used as an alternative to 'to have to do' something; e.g. 'I've no cash left. I **need/have** to go to the bank.'

As indicated in unit 5, in the interrogative and negative forms of the present tense, 'need' can be used like 'dare' (note the question tags); e.g. 'I **don't need to** do it, **do I**?' 'I **needn't do** it, **need I**?' '**Do I need to do** it?' '**Need I do** it?' In other words, the basic rule applies here: If you use 'do', use 'to'. If you don't use 'do', don't use 'to'!

Like 'dare' too, the –s ending is dropped in the third person singular when the auxiliary 'do' is not used; e.g. 'He **needn't do** it.—**Need he do** it?' Since the form omitting 'do' tends to be used for immediate necessities only, while the 'do' form is always correct, perhaps the best advice is to use 'do'! Compare 'You **needn't go/don't need to go** to work today. It's a public holiday.' 'Married women whose husbands are earning good salaries **don't need to go out** to work.'

EXERCISE 4

Use one of the above forms of 'need' and an appropriate form of the verb in the following monologue. The first one has been done for you as an example.

Oh, how I love Sunday mornings! It means I **needn't/don't need to get up**[1] early. I'll just stay in bed for another hour or so and plan what I'm going to do today. Oops, my head isn't feeling too good. It must have been four o'clock when I got home from the party last night. I [stay][2] so long, I suppose, and I [drink][3] so much, but I was having such a good time it's worth having a hangover. I was lucky I got a lift home with Conn and Emer and [call][4] a taxi. Now that Emer's pregnant, for the fourth time, she doesn't drink, so Conn [worry][5] when he's out for the evening; he's got his own private chauffeur! Now, what's on today's agenda? Conn and Emer have asked me to lunch so I [cook][6]. In fact I [buy][7] that leg of lamb yesterday. Never mind; that means I [do][8] any shopping again for another few days. One of the advantages of living on your own is that you [think][9] about anybody except yourself. Thank goodness I [feed][10] a family like Emer with her three children! You [get][11] married these days if you don't want to. Poor Flann: he proposed to me again last night. [Be]^{12} I so unkind every time he asks me to marry him? I really [feel]^{13} so guilty, I suppose. He knows I have no intention of ever accepting him, so he [make]^{14} a fool of himself every time I turn him down. There's the phone ringing. It'll be Flann, I bet. [Answer]^{15} it? I [answer]^{16} it if I don't want to, but then if I don't I'll be telling myself all day I [behave]^{17} so heartlessly. Maybe I'll invite him round for supper tonight … and have the leg of lamb. After all, he's a nice fellow. I [stop]^{18} being friends with him just because he's in love with me, [ ]^{19} I? Here goes … Oh, hi, Emer. You don't feel like cooking today?—Oh, you [apologise]^{20}. I quite understand … in your condition. Look, as it happens, I have a leg of lamb in the fridge, so why don't you come to me for lunch?—Oh, yes, do bring the children with you.

EXERCISE 5

Finish each of the following sentences in such a way that it means the same as the sentence before it; e.g. 'There is a lot of truth in this statement.—This statement has a lot of truth in it.'

(i)   Home rule was as far away as it had ever been.—Home rule had never …
(ii) It wasn't by any means the first time arms had been taken up against the British.—By no means …
(iii) The Easter Rising was so unpopular that people spat on the insurrectionists as they were led away to jail.—So …
(iv) The tide of opinion was turned by the ritual execution of sixteen of the leaders of the Rising.—It was …
(v)   It was less expensive to be a member of the weaker sex.—It wasn't …

EXERCISE 6

In each case make a new sentence, as similar as possible in meaning to the original one, using the word printed after it (*you must not alter the word in any way*); e.g. 'The great majority of us have to choose what we want to be.— **almost**—Almost all of us have to choose what we want to be.'

(i)   I'll excuse his behaviour because he's so young.—**account**
(ii) It really wasn't necessary of you to go to such trouble. Mary's already given me the information.—**gone**
(iii) Of course they'll be annoyed. We're going to be an hour late for their dinner party.—**stands**
(iv) Mary and I have just sorted out our problems, so please don't make trouble by talking about the past!—**rock**
(v)   More than anything else I want you to be here on time tomorrow.— **above**

A. Samuel Beckett; **B.** Grace Kelly **C.** John F. Kennedy; **D.** W. B. Yeats; **E.** Bob Geldof; **F.** James Joyce

UNIT 1   INVENTING A SENSE OF BEING IRISH (page 5)

1. (*a*) Nationality is something a person is born with. (*b*) He can deny it. (*c*) He can choose to give it up or retain it. (*d*) He can adopt a different one.

MULTIPLE-CHOICE QUESTIONS: (page 6 and 7)

1. (*b*); 2. (*d*); 3. (*c*); 4. (*d*); 5. (*b*).

THE IRISH AND IRISHNESS (page 7)

There is room for interpretation here, but the point is that students should be able to explain their choices.

(*a*) Kennedy	(*b*) Northern Protestants
(*c*) Geldof	(*d*) O'Brien
(*e*) Joyce	(*f*) Shaw
(*g*) O'Brien	(*h*) Visitors

WHAT LOOKS CAN TELL (pages 10–11)

A. Switzerland; **B.** Japan; **C.** Burundi; **D.** Italy; **E.** Iceland; **F.** Pakistan.

A GOOD SALAD (page 12)

1. A good salad is composed of many ingredients. Irish people are a composition of different racial types.
2. Tall, pale complexion, light-coloured eyes (probably blue) and brown hair.
3. Difficult to describe because of its paradoxical nature.

COMPREHENSION QUESTIONS (pages 14–15)

1. *Paragraph 1*: wiry; hotch-potch; *paragraph 3*: spot; hunch; brogue; joggled; *paragraph 4*: motley; pinch; *paragraph 5*: honed; paying one's last respects; did him a power of good; clamber; boast.
2. They are so totally different from each other in looks.
3. The mythological tribes. Both were invaders of Ireland.
4. Because of their isolation, the people of these countries did not mix with other racial types. Yes, since the Irish are said to be a mixture of

many different types. For long periods the country was left undisturbed, unlike mainland Europe where there was constant movement of tribes.

5. Both are composed of different parts: pieces or ingredients.
6. The 'national essence'. The contrasting descriptions of the Irish character.
7. The assertion that the Irish are 'such a nation of paradoxes …'
8. The first sentence of the paragraph.

IDENTIFY THESE! (pages 15–16)

A. Seán MacBride; **B.** Bono; **C.** Maud Gonne; **D.** Brendan Behan; **E.** Mary Robinson; **F.** Lady Gregory; **G.** Mícheál Mac Liammóir; **H.** Éamon de Valera; **I.** Ian Paisley.
A (ii); **B** (viii); **C** (iii); **D** (iv); **E** (i); **F** (v); **G** (vii); **H** (ix); **I** (vi).

VOCABULARY PRACTICE (pages 17–19)

1. (*b*); 2. (*d*); 3. (*a*); 4. (*c*); 5. (*b*); 6. (*d*); 7. (*a*); 8. (*d*); 9. (*d*); 10. (*a*); 11. (*a*); 12. (*d*); 13. (*c*); 14. (*a*); 15. (a).

CLOZE (page 19)

1. that	7. whom	12. blood	17. deny/reject
2. on	8. lay	13. themselves	18. because/
3. than	9. example/	14. other	since/as
4. what	instance	15. whose	19. order
5. all	10. it	16. for	20. living
6. outside	11. like		

UNIT 2   **THE MELTING-POT** (page 21)

1. (*a*) Mesolithic—hunters, food-gatherers, blood group O; (*b*) Neolithic—settled farmers; builders of monuments; (*c*) Bronze Age people—metalworkers and traders.
2. No written records of the period.
3. Uniformity and control versus individuality of small social units.
4. Before the Romans there was already a linguistic division between British and Irish Celts. During the Roman occupation the British Celts were pushed into Wales; hence the linguistic distinction was between

Welsh and Irish. After the Romans the Germanic tribes pushed the Celts further into the extremities of Britain, which is why the language survives only in those areas.

COMPREHENSION QUESTIONS (page 24)

1. The different people and cultures that mixed together to make the Irish what they are today.
2. Mesolithic people lived by hunting; Neolithic people were settled farmers.
3. The Late Stone Age.
4. To bury their dead and to worship nature.
5. Tin had to be imported to make bronze; artefacts found in other countries.
6. They both gave accounts of the Celtic civilisation …
7. The fact that there was often faction-fighting.
8. The common culture of the country.
9. They both pushed the Celts into the remoter areas of the country.
10. Irish is the only one that is an official language of a country.

THE CELTIC WORLD (pages 27–28)

1. From Portugal in the west to eastern Turkey, including France, Britain, Ireland, Belgium, the Netherlands, Switzerland, Austria, most of Germany, part of Poland, Czechoslovakia, Hungary, and parts of the Baltic countries.
2. Ireland (Irish), Wales (Welsh), Scotland (Gaelic), France (Breton).

LISTENING (pages 24–26)

Newgrange
1.A. 2.C. 3.A. 4.B, C, D, F. 5. True c and f. False a, b, d, e.

WHAT'S IN A LANGUAGE? (page 28)

fir: 'men'; mná: 'women' (seen on public toilets)
sláinte: literally 'health' (used as a toast)
an lár: 'the (city) centre' (seen on buses)
oifig an phoist: 'post office'

LAWS IN ANCIENT IRELAND (page 31)

1. (b); 2. (c); 3. (b); 4. (d); 5. (a)

PHRASAL AND PREPOSITIONAL VERBS (pages 36–37)

1. cater	4. embarrassed	7. imposing	9. took
2. took	5. comply	8. pull	10. brought
3. named	6. stripped		

VOCABULARY PRACTICE (pages 37–39)

1. (*b*); 2. (*a*); 3. (*d*); 4. (*d*); 5. (*a*); 6. (*d*); 7. (*a*); 8. (*b*); 9. (*b*); 10. (*c*); 11. (*c*); 12. (*d*); 13. (*d*); 14. (*c*); 15. (*a*)

CLOZE (page 39)

1. how	6. though/	10. set	16. Because
2. at	although/	11. off	17. themselves
3. called	while	12. where	18. against
4. fell	7. refuse/reject	13. only	19. himself
5. later/	8. would	14. but	20. so
afterwards	9. make	15. other	

UNIT 3 **DRINK TALK** (pages 41–42)

1. hangover	7. hollow legs	11. under the
2. jar	8. drunk us	influence
3. plonk	under the	12. a hair of the
4. twisting my arm	table	dog
5. shorts	9. plastered	13. jar
6. knock back	10. barred	

GUINNESS AND GAS (page 42)

1. They have such a reputation for drinking, yet they do not consume as much alcohol as people in other countries.
2. Drinking is a serious business; hard drinkers are admired; there is a tolerance of excessive drinking.
3. (*a*) The need, due to the climate, to enjoy themselves indoors.
   (*b*) Their cleverness in using the distilling process to make whiskey (also Guinness and poitín).

4. So many Irish writers have had a reputation for drinking that drink has been considered essential to their creativity. Medical evidence proves that drinking does not help the creative process.

MULTIPLE-CHOICE QUESTIONS (page 45)

1. (*d*); 2. (*c*); 3. (*b*); 4. (*a*); 5. (*a*); 6. (*c*); 7. (*b*); 8. (*b*)

HOMAGE TO THE PINT (page 46)

1. 'your horse has also ran'—should be 'run'
2. 'is the only answer to all your troubles.'
3. Spends all his money on gambling and drink; no money left for food; gets into debt; finds solace to all his problems in drink.

A PINT OF PLAIN IS YOUR ONLY MAN (page 46)

1. right	2. can
3. get	4. change
5. bare	6. pan
7. life	

MORE DRINK TALK (page 47)

page 49 = C; page 51 = D; page 53 = A; page 54 = B.

TEENAGE DRINKING (page 49)

1. There was a considerable increase in alcohol consumption, because people had more money to spend.
2. There has been a general decrease in the amount of drink consumed, but people who never drank before (teenagers and women) are now doing so.
3. It used to be old men who were seen drunk on the streets. Now it is young people.
4. People of their own age.
5. Sarcastic and sceptical. 'A wonderful idea, although pigs will fly …'
6. Informal, witty, sarcastic …

7. The very early age at which people start drinking, and the number of young people who drink too much. So many of these young people had not been told about the dangers of alcohol.
8. It is a serious, factual report, compared with Liz McManus's article, in which opinions are expressed in a more personal style.

VOCABULARY EXERCISE (pages 51–53)

1. (*a*); 2. (*b*); 3. (*d*); 4. (*d*); 5. (*c*); 6. (*a*); 7. (*b*); 8. (*b*); 9. (*c*); 10. (*d*); 11. (*c*); 12. (*b*); 13. (*d*); 14. (*d*); 15. (*a*)

CLOZE (page 54)

1. always/ usually/ generally …	6. television	11. It	16. up
	7. to	12. could/ would	17. themselves
	8. not		18. kinds/sorts …
2. one	9. as	13. not	19. everything/ anything
3. involved	10. what/ something	14. medical	
4. Inside/In		15. bottles	20. little/no
5. who/that			

UNIT 4   A LAND OF SAINTS AND SCHOLARS (page 57)

1. It was a period of great learning and culture, particularly art.
2. Taken from Britain to Ireland as a slave; escaped and spent many years in Gaul preparing to go back to Ireland; devoted the rest of his life to converting the Irish to Christianity. A humble, caring, sensitive man.
3. It ranges from pure fiction to proven fact.
4. Embracing the older druidic practices of the Celts; monasticism.

MORE QUESTIONS (page 60)

1. *Paragraph 1:* plunged in the Dark Ages; *paragraph 2:* begging; *paragraph 3:* win over; *paragraph 4:* legion; *paragraph 5:* second nature; *paragraph 6:* hippies.
2. Almost/practically/virtually.
3. The virtual disappearance of Christianity in Britain.
4. They happened at the same time.
5. Growing up in Britain; slavery in Ireland; years in Gaul preparing for his mission; return to Ireland to convert Irish.
6. His diplomacy and respect for tradition.

7. The continuation of the old religious practices.
8. It is an example of how Christianity embraced paganism.
9. Completely fictitious; possible but not proved; proven fact.
10. Rural way of life; people not completely settled; society composed of small units.
11. Its real meaning implies aimlessness as well as distance covered; the monks had a very specific purpose for their travels.
12. They were all trained by Colm Cille.
13. It has not been proved.

LISTENING (page 62)

3.C; 4.B.

A GREAT DAY FOR THE IRISH (page 66)

1. 1. A and H; 2. C and B; 3. D and J; 4. G and E; 5. I and F.
2. 1. (d); 2. (a); 3. (e); 4. (c); 5. (b).
3. 13 March 1991: 2.
17 March 1991: 4.
18 March 1991: 1, 3, 5.

TREASURES OF THE GOLDEN AGE (pages 67–69)

Photograph—description
A (ii); B (i); C (iv); D (vi); E (v); F (iii).

Photograph—description—caption

F (iii) Gallarus Oratory   C (iv) High Cross
D (vi) Round Tower   A (ii) Page from book of Kells
E (v) Ardagh Chalice   B (i) Tara Brooch

THE SAINT OF GLENDALOUGH (page 70)

1. 1. C; 2. E; 3. A; 4. G; 5. F; 6. B; 7. D.
2. Women; fishing.
3. The importance of celibacy.

VOCABULARY EXERCISE (pages 71–73)

1. (*b*); 2. (*a*); 3. (*d*); 4. (*b*); 5. (*b*); 6. (*d*); 7. (*b*); 8. (*c*); 9. (*d*); 10. (*a*); 11. (*a*);
12. (*a*); 13. (*d*); 14. (*c*); 15. (*b*).

CLOZE (pages 73–74)

1. sort/kind/type	6. if	10.	15. own
2. the	7. reach	more/so	16. must
3. at	8. tried/	11. size	17. Out
4. touch/contact/	attempted/	12. far/much	18. As
communication	endeavoured	13. aboard/on	19. inured/used
5. by	9. none	14. by	20. physical

UNIT 5   **IT'S A GOAL!** (page 76)

1. Hurling and Gaelic football.
2. (*a*) The atmosphere of excitement and the way the spectators show their support. (*b*) Rival supporters not divided; no problem with violence.
3. It was part of the nationalist movement of the late nineteenth century and has always openly declared its political sympathies.
4. (*a*) Because the Irish team combines North and South it has a unifying influence. (*b*) The country is divided into two teams. Best talent goes to Britain. Great interest shown when Ireland competing internationally.

MORE QUESTIONS (page 79)

1. The important part sport plays in Irish life: Garret FitzGerald's remark lost him popularity, and a party conference was interrupted by sporting activities.
2. The fact that sport is more a way of life than a pastime in Ireland.
3. For a very long time/for hundreds of years …
4. The speed, the number of points and goals scored, and the mental and physical skill of the players.
5. It is so frequently the scene of furious activity.
6. Soccer fans.
7. Support for the rival teams takes the form of clever remarks rather than physical violence.

8. The fact that the GAA was a powerful morale-booster …
9. Its former ban on members attending or playing foreign sports; the fact that it prohibits members of the British army and RUC from membership; the notices of sympathy on the deaths of the IRA hunger-strikers.
10. Few, if any, such people would want to join the GAA.
11. It is a pun on the word 'green'. A green light indicates permission to do something, but the colour has nationalist associations in Ireland.
12. If people from the North and the South can't be united in their support for the Irish rugby team, the politicians will have little hope of uniting them.
13. Since the best talent has gone to Britain, people tend to follow teams there. When Ireland is playing internationally there is a sudden interest in and support for the Irish team.
14. His success with the Irish soccer team has won him such popularity.

SPORTING PICTURES (pages 80–81)

2.

A. Hurling   B. Golf
C. Greyhound racing   D. Show-jumping
E. Rugby   F. Fishing/angling
G. Betting

G (betting) is the odd one out: it is not a sport.

A (iv)   B (iii)   C (ii)   D (vi)
E (v)   F (i)   G (viii)

HORSE TALK (page 83)

1. Eventing   2. dressage
3. cross-country   4. gymkhana
5. race meeting   6. point-to-point
7. show-jumping   8. faults
9. clear round   10. faults

DUBLIN HORSE SHOW (pages 85–86)

1. (*d*); 2. (*a*); 3. (*c*); 4. (*c*); 5. (*b*).

VOCABULARY PRACTICE (pages 89–91)

1. (*b*); 2. (*b*); 3. (*d*); 4. (*a*); 5. (*b*); 6. (*d*); 7. (*b*); 8. (*a*); 9. (*c*); 10. (*a*); 11. (*c*); 12. (*d*); 13. (*a*); 14. (*a*); 15. (*c*).

CLOZE (pages 91–92)

1.after	8. came/became	15. stood
2. win	9. having	16. there
3. like	10. As	17. time
4. comes	11. made	18. windows
5. draw	12. home	19. showed/revealed
6. brought	13. which	20. except/save
7. last	14. in	

UNIT 6   **CONQUEST** (page 95)

1. They founded towns, built ships, promoted trade with other countries, and introduced coins.
2. Building of cathedrals, abbeys, castles, and boundary walls. Introduction of feudal system, and inheritance through first-born male.
3. They both became assimilated through intermarriage with the native Irish.
4. Through time the Normans in Ireland adopted the Irish way of life and became estranged from the English Normans. Their shared Catholicism led to their persecution during and after the Reformation.

MORE QUESTIONS (page 97)

1. Arriving in their boats, they attacked the settlements and seized anything of value, particularly the treasures of the monasteries.
2. To make it more difficult for the Vikings to enter them.
3. Their defeat was in military terms only.
4. The victory of the Irish at the Battle of Clontarf.
5. The Irish lost a powerful unifying force, and it weakened their resistance to the Norman invasion.
6. Considering his behaviour, the term is hardly appropriate. The tone is sarcastic. He can be held responsible for the Norman invasion and the ensuing struggle between England and Ireland.

7. They were not united among themselves, and the Normans were better armed.
8. Signified/symbolised.
9. They all indicate a person's descent.
10. They defied the rule from England by adopting the Irish way of life. They spoke Irish, used Irish names, married into Irish families, dressed like the Irish, adopted Irish laws, and played hurling.
11. The passing of the Statutes of Kilkenny. It doesn't require explanation.
12. They had settled, i.e. made a permanent home for themselves.
13. Its aim was to subdue the Irish by any means they could. Those who weren't killed lost their property, were persecuted because of their religion, lost their pride by surrendering to the English, or had to leave the country.

LISTENING (page 99)

1. Spanish	4. 1641	7. 1690	10. 22
2. 1607	5. Hell	8. 12 (th)	11. France
3. Scotland	6. 1688	9. 1691	12. 14

THE MAKING OF A CAPITAL CITY (pages 101–103)

2 (photographs): A (iv); B (vi); C (i); D (ii); E (v); F (iii)
3 (chronological order): 1. F; 2. C; 3. D; 4. E; 5. A; 6. B

THE MAKING OF A MAN (page 104)

(i) crouching	(v) lash	(ix) catcalls
(ii) seedy	(vi) disclaim	(x) cute
(iii) squalor	(vii) wallowed	(xi) arid
(iv) bravado	(viii) dreary	

POEMS (page 106)

1. MacDonagh: 'Dublin made me,' and continues by describing the provincial areas that have had no influence on him. MacNeice: 'I was not born nor bred/Nor schooled here.'
2. Decaying grandeur; charm, elegance and gentility combined with poverty … He is both detached and irresistibly attracted to the city.

3. To show, by contrast, the places that have not profoundly influenced him. The west: the harshness of life. The south: the cunning of the people who fail to recognise that they are ruled by Dublin. The north: atmosphere of fear and repression. Obvious contrast of last two lines indicate the superiority of Dublin over the provinces (age, permanence, pride …).
4. MacDonagh identifies with Dublin; MacNeice is fascinated but detached. They both attribute to it a sense of pride.

AN IRISH SOLUTION TO AN IRISH PROBLEM (pages 108–109)

1. (*a*) false; (*b*) true; (*c*) true; (*d*) false; (*e*) false; (*f*) true; (*g*) true; **2.** (*d*); **3.** (*c*); **4.** (*b*); **5.** (*b*).

VOCABULARY PRACTICE (pages 109–111)

1. (b); 2. (a); 3. (d); 4. (b); 5. (d); 6. (a); 7. (c); 8. (b); 9. (a); 10. (d); 11. (a); 12. (d); 13. (c); 14. (c); 15. (a).

CLOZE (page 111)

1. course
2. from
3. however/ nevertheless
4. which
5. laid
6. just/simply
7. back
8. established/ founded
9. for/of
10. can/may
11. There
12. except/besides
13. greatly/ considerably
14. out/well/far
15. Following/After
16. as
17. in
18. over/nearly
19. pace/rate/speed
20. although

UNIT 7 THE STORY OF THE SPUD (page 112)

1. It became the staple diet of the great majority of the people, because of their enforced poverty and lack of other resources. At the same time the population increased, so when the potato crop failed, the result was death, homelessness, and emigration. This led to the rise of nationalism and the struggle for independence.
2. A large quantity could be grown in a small area, and, with milk, potatoes provided all the necessary nutrition. But when the potato crop failed, people had nothing else to eat.
3. Starvation, fever, death, and emigration.
4. The rise of nationalism, the further decline of the Irish language, and the loss of traditions that people came to associate with poverty.

1. He admired their physiques but despised the coarseness of their manners.
2. Total dependence on the potato meant monotony of diet and way of life.
3. In any other way.
4. Eating undercooked potatoes. People could survive provided there was a good supply of potatoes.
5. Something edible that has a definite taste. The word has not got its normal dictionary meaning here. Potatoes have a bland taste; people had a strong desire for something with flavour.
6. The disastrous consequences of the failure of the potato crop.
7. It is enough to say.
8. The corn grown in Ireland could have been used to feed the people; people who couldn't afford to pay their rents were made homeless.
9. Politically it led to the struggle for independence. Socially it caused major changes in the way of life.
10. It questions the real meaning of the word: people who suffered such hardships can hardly be considered fortunate.
11. By choosing to live in towns and cities rather than rural areas, which were more like the places they had left.
12. New bungalows built beside the old cottages; a preference for shop-bought white bread; and the high consumption of meat.
13. The writer is making a pun on the word 'root', which refers both to the source of the problem and to the type of vegetable that grows underneath the soil.
14. Reference to Captain de Cuellar as 'this civilised Spanish gentleman' a little sarcastic. Underlines arrogance and patronising tone of his observations. Writer's sympathy for the plight of the poor conveyed by: 'as if the destruction of the vital food supply were not enough'; 'to earn a few miserable pence'; 'the establishment indifference and downright callousness'; 'what point was there in speaking Irish?'; 'those who were "fortunate" enough'.

PICTURES OF DISASTER (page 117)

2. A (ii); B (iii); C (i); D (iv).

CHILDREN OF THE DEAD END (page 121)

1. (c); 2. (b); 3. (b); 4. (b); 5. (c).

SPADE WORK (page 122)

1. (*a*) curt; (*b*) gravelly; (*c*) rasping; (*d*) soggy; (*e*) snug; (*f*) sloppy; (*g*) squat.
2. (*a*) bog; (*b*) turf; (*c*) shaft/lug; (*d*) rump; (*e*) squelch.
3. (*a*) nestled; (*b*) stooped; (*c*) heaving; (*d*) nick.

DIGGING (page 124)

1. Three types: in the garden, for potatoes, and for turf.
2. Verse 3: 'his straining rump …/Bends low, comes up twenty years away.' Seeing his father working in the garden, he remembers him twenty years younger, digging for potatoes.
3. 'By God, the old man …'
4. Different: 'But I've no spade …'; similar: 'I'll dig with it [the squat pen]'. He sees both digging and writing as skills, different but of equal value (admiration for father's and grandfather's ability).
5. Satisfied: the pen is comfortable ('snug') in his hand. Short lines at the end, especially the last one, indicate the poet's resolve and sense of contentment.

VOCABULARY PRACTICE (pages 125–126)

1. (d); 2. (b); 3. (a); 4. (c); 5. (b); 6. (d); 7. (c); 8. (c); 9. (b); 10. (c); 11. (c); 12. (a); 13. (b); 14. (b); 15. (d)

CLOZE (page 127)

1. person	7. most/many	14. from
2. what	8. on	15. until
3. answer/response/ reply	9. over	16. this
	10. apart	17. little/no
4. which	11. way	18. into
5. well	12. to	19. minority
6. back	13. used	20. left

UNIT 8   (page 130) 5. A. (iii); B. (iv); C. (ii); D. (i); E. (vi); F. (v)

Wind: D and F
Percussion: A and E
String: B and C

LETTING THE MUSIC SPEAK FOR ITSELF (page 131)

1. Because people associated with poverty, they tended to despise it. They thought it was old-fashioned and unsophisticated.
2. A small number of enthusiastic people kept it alive by playing it and teaching their children.
3. Setting up of Comhaltas Ceoltóirí Éireann. International interest in folk music. Ballad singing popularised by groups like the Dubliners. Traditional music finally made acceptable to public, especially through work of Seán Ó Riada and the Chieftains.

MORE QUESTIONS (pages 134–135)

1. The street is crowded.
2. They are both forms of Irish music, one old and traditional, the other new and innovative.
3. They were both despised because of their associations with the past. Much was done to revive the language but very little to revive the music.
4. Indifference: 'barely tolerated céilí music …'; hostility: 'a form of low-life entertainment …'
5. Nobody knew what a disco was at that time.
6. The women felt they were on display. The men had been drinking and were waiting for it to take effect, i.e. to give them the courage to ask the women to dance.
7. It had originated in Ireland, developed as a particular style in America and, as such, became popular in Ireland.
8. The lack of popularity of Irish music before the 1960s.
9. Positive: it was played and taught with such enthusiasm. Negative: it was so limited in popularity and there was no real effort made to promote it.
10. They are both idiomatic. 'Tipped the balance': the ballad groups were the decisive factor in making Irish music popular. 'Hitting the big time': the Beatles were famous/popular/successful.
11. They were good entertainers.
12. 'Instead of being ignored, the country cousin was all of a sudden the centre of attention.'
13. By popularising the ballad they made people more receptive to traditional music.
14. The way they look and dress is at variance with the activity they are engaged in. 'A cluster of civil servants.'
15. A type of music that …
16. The massive following for a kind of music that was not considered commercial.

LISTENING (pages 135–137)

A.

1.
A. 8–10 pm; B. Free; C. Abbey Theatre; D. £10; E. 9 pm; F. £4; G. 9 pm; H. Free; I. Kerry; J. 1 pm; K. £60; L. country rock; M. £6.

2.
A. False; B. False; C. False; D. False; E. True.

B.
1. b; 2. b; 3. d; 4. c.

BREAKING NEW GROUND (page 139)

1. C and D; 2. A; 3. C; 4. A; 5. C.

WHOSE KIND OF MUSIC? (page 141)

2. A. (ii); B. (vi); C. (iii); D. (vii); E. (i).

IN PRAISE OF THE HARP (pages 143–144)

1. walls	2. days
3. more	4. tells
5. breaks	6. lives

1. Beauty, grandeur, dignity, glory … of Ireland's past.
2. Soft and slow. The mood is sad and sentimental.

VOCABULARY PRACTICE (pages 144–146)

1. (*a*); 2. (*b*); 3. (*c*); 4. (*a*); 5. (*a*); 6. (*a*); 7. (*d*); 8. (*a*); 9. (*b*); 10. (*c*); 11. (*c*); 12. (*b*); 13. (*a*); 14. (*b*); 15. (c).

CLOZE (pages 144–147)

1. Like	8. for	15. dates
2. up	9. as	16. whom
3. flying	10. for	17. like
4. means	11. it	18. would
5. without/no	12. it	19. as
6. may/might	13. can/may	20. who
7. such	14. old/ancient	

UNIT 9   WHAT'S IN A NAME? (pages 149–150)

A. Ulster	B. Ulster
C. the (wee) North	D. the six counties
E. Ulster	F. Northern Ireland

FACES OF THE NORTH (pages 151–153)

A (vi); B (iv); C (ii); D (iii); E (i); F (v).

A POTTED VERSION (pages 154–155)

1. (a); 2. (a); 3. (b); 4. (c); 5. (d).

THE COLOUR ORANGE (page 155)

(a) 1. stem; 2. blowing; 3. beam; 4. glowing; 5. both; 6. flourish;
    7. growth; 8. nourish.
(b) The two traditions are symbolically united by the lily, whose blossom
    is orange and stem is green.

ORANGE TALK (page 156)

'To turn' here means to change religion.

GOODBYE TO INNOCENCE (pages 156–160)

(A) She is now middle-aged, doesn't feel particularly wise or
    knowledgeable; was brought up as a middle-class Protestant in a
    largely Catholic town in Northern Ireland; … the town ugly, with
    chronic unemployment.
   1. Be able to explain the Northern situation because of her
      background and experience.
   2. The other people in the street needed numbers on their houses to
      show where they lived.
   3. A market town; high proportion of Catholics; chronic
      unemployment; unemployed people standing idly in the streets.
   4. It implies a criticism of the people who couldn't find jobs. They
      were considered useless, although they were unemployed through
      no fault of their own.
   5. Favourite places that people frequent. 'Stamping' literally means
      putting the feet down heavily. One can imagine the corner boys,
      who have been standing in one place for a long time, doing this.

6. By describing her reluctance to go to school at the end of the previous paragraph ('dragged my feet').
7. It was mixed only as regards the sexes, not religion.
8. She was naïve; she wasn't aware of the difference between the two traditions.

(B) She was protected by her innocence and naïveté. Her aunt's remark led her to question what she had unthinkingly accepted.
   1. True
   2. True
   3. False
   4. False

(C) She saw that what people said and did was at variance with the values she was brought up to believe in. Their bigoted attitudes led her to adopt an extreme position, without any real understanding of the situation. The destruction of her family home, as an indirect result of an IRA bomb, so disillusioned her that she abandoned the North.

MULTIPLE-CHOICE QUESTIONS

1. (b), (c), (d); 2. (a), (b), (c); 3. (c), (d); 4. (b), (c), (d).

VICTIM (pages 161–162)

1. (a) grin; (b) bland; (c) culvert; (d) perched; (e) side-whiskers.

ENEMY ENCOUNTER (page 163)

1. Personal response.
2. Pathetically small, lonely, vulnerable ('perched hiding'; 'weenie-bopper's boy-friend'; 'Like a lonely little winter robin'; 'he is afraid/That I have come to kill him').
3. 'Lovely day./Are you enjoying yourself? …' He didn't react at all.
4. Personal view.

VOCABULARY PRACTICE (pages 164–165)

1. (b); 2. (d); 3. (a); 4. (b); 5. (d); 6. (b); 7. (a); 8. (c); 9. (b); 10. (d); 11. (b); 12. (a); 13. (c); 14. (d); 15. (d).

CLOZE (pages 165–166)

1. film	8. from	15. at
2. seats	9. anthem	16. such
3. another	10. to	17. too
4. being	11. than	18. example/instance
5. screen	12. followed	19. name
6. stood	13. that	20. for
7. seated	14. neither	

UNIT 10   POETS, PATRIOTS, AND POLITICIANS (page 169)

1. It was the last in a series of risings. It was a failure in itself, since it lacked general support and the leaders surrendered; the execution of the leaders won popular sympathy for their cause.
2. Direct rule from Westminster; persecution of Catholics; injustices suffered under landlords; famine. O'Connell won emancipation for Catholics; Parnell was partially successful in gaining land reform.
3. The influence their actions and words have had on the country with regard to the struggle for freedom.

MORE QUESTIONS (pages 171–172)

1. Ironic.
2. Simply 'was executed'. It suggests that this was the purpose of his actions, that it was something he had planned.
3. They knew they had little or no hope of succeeding.
4. Not complete failures. Although each one was put down, the leaders became heroes and inspired future generations.
5. The Act of Union, which placed Ireland under direct rule from Westminster.
6. The scandal of his affair. A deep and bitter split between his supporters and those who turned against him, probably causing his early death and certainly putting an end to the hopes for an independent parliament.
7. 'With what frightening passion they held their positions.'
8. After Parnell the politicians failed to unite the country, but the writers were able to inspire feelings of nationalism in the people.
9. The founding of the National Theatre.
10. That he was prepared to fight for the freedom of his country.
11. They felt sure they would soon have an independent parliament and there were so many Irish soldiers fighting for Britain in the First World War.

12. They all refer to the dramatic change in popular opinion brought about by the execution of the 1916 leaders.
13. It was achieved only after much violence and bloodshed. The fighting has not stopped (in the North).
14. Suggested answers only: '… what would have happened?/… what would the situation be now?'

THE ALTERNATIVE REVOLUTION (page 176)

1. takes the biscuit
2. drawn a blank
3. lie low
4. on the dole
5. met his Waterloo
6. on the grapevine
7. hit by storm
8. rock the boat

MORE QUESTIONS (page 179–180)

1. (a) Maud; (b) Eva; (c) Constance; (d) Maeve; (e) Grace.
2. (a) False; (b) false; (c) true; (d) true; (e) true; (f) false.
3. (c) and (f).
4. (a) and (d).
5. (a) True; (b) true; (c) false; (d) true; (e) false.

LISTENING (pages 180–182)

A. 1. (a) 1865; (b) 1903; (c) 1916; (d) 1953.
   2. (a), (b), (e), and (g).

B. 1. 1868
   2. art
   3. Polish
   4. Dublin
   5. magazine
   6. 1916
   7. prison
   8. British MP
   9. Labour
   10. eight

C. 1. (c)   2. (a)

D. 1. (a), (c), (d) and (e).
   2. (a) and (b).
   3. (a), (b), (e), and (f).

VOCABULARY PRACTICE (pages 183–184)

1. (*b*); 2. (*a*); 3. (*c*); 4. (*a*); 5. (*d*); 6. (*a*); 7. (*c*); 8. (*a*); 9. (*d*); 10. (*a*); 11. (*d*); 12. (*c*); 13. (*b*); 14. (*c*); 15. (*c*).

CLOZE (page 185)

1. themselves	6. in	12. time	18. both
2. learnt	7. not	13. no	19. be
3. little/nothing	8. but	14. whose	20. when/where
4. as	9. the	15. to	
5. sleeping	10. the	16. voted	
	11. women	17. whom	

UNIT 11 **LISTENING** (pages 186–188)

A. True: 1, 2, 4, 7. False: 3, 5, 6, 8.

B. 1.A, D, E. 2.B. 3.D. 4.A.

NEVER MIND THE WEATHER (page 189)

A (ii). B (iv). C (i). D (iii).

CLOZE (pages 189–190)

1. It	6. time	11. can	16. who
2. travelling	7. head	12. clouds	17. Irish
3. rain	8. climate	13. as	18. climate
4. up	9. visitor/foreigner	14. rain	19. his
5. beside	10. seasons	15. already	20. stopped

PIT YOUR WEATHER WITS (page 190)

1. (*c*). 2. (*c*). 3. (*a*). 4. (*a*). 5. (*d*).

A GUIDED TOUR (pages 191–192)

Map of Dublin and area

1. National	6. Dublin Castle	11. Phoenix Park
2. Ardagh	7. Connolly	12. President
3. Tara	8. St Patrick's	13. St Stephen's Green
4. Trinity	9. Jonathan Swift	14. Newman House
5. Book of Kells	10. Guinness's brewery	

MAP OF IRELAND (page 192)

15. castle	19. Tara	23. Glendalough
16. Malahide	20. Kings	24. tower
17. Mellifont	21. passage	25. Powerscourt
18. cross	22. Newgrange	26. Martello

PHRASAL VERBS (pages 198–200)

1. turned	6. puts	11. takes	16. pull
2. brought	7. hold	12. cater	17. looks
3. set	8. work	13. get	18. put
4. looking	9. come	14. take	19. wiped
5. belt	10. look	15. set	20. look

FIND THE IDIOM (pages 200–201)

1. He damned it with faint praise.
2. I met my Waterloo.
3. You started rocking the boat.
4. He's pulled up his socks.
5. You've dampened my enthusiasm.
6. I'm lying low.
7. They're always at odds with each other.
8. It'll pave the way for other groups.
9. I've drawn a blank.
10. It took London by storm.

WHO IS IT? (pages 201–202)

1, (iv) Bob Geldof
2, (ix) Séamus Heaney
3, (vi) Maud Gonne
4, (xi) Jonathan Swift
5, (xii) William Butler Yeats
6, (v) Grace Kelly
7, (ii) Charles Stewart Parnell
8, (iii) Samuel Beckett
9, (vii) Éamon De Valera
10, (i) Mícheál Mac Liammóir
11, (viii) Grace O'Malley
12, (x) Paddy Moloney.

GREEDY-GUTS SPECIAL (pages 203–204)

Brown bread: 5, 8, 14, 10, 1, 13.
Irish stew: 3, 2, 9, 15, 7.
Irish coffee: 6, 4, 12, 11.

WORD RACE (pages 204–205)

1. wrench	2. mole
3. grit	4. mist
5. fee	6. defendant
7. penalty	8. squelch
9. plight	10. pangs
11. wages	12. slouch
13. gimmick	14. sights
15. sorrows	16. rubble
17. stink	18. swap
19. glimpse	20. squabble

GRAMMAR KEY

UNIT 1

EXERCISE 1 (page 209)

(i) (*d*); (ii) (*a*); (iii) (*b*); (iv) (*e*); (v) (*c*)

EXERCISE 2 (page 209)

(i) (*a*) (Mícheál Mac Liammóir) (ii) (*e*) (*The Playboy*)
(iii) (*c*) (James Joyce) (iv) (*f*) (the fact that she escaped from Ireland yet feels deeply Irish)

(v) (d) (Northern Ireland) (vi) (b) (Ulster)

EXERCISE 3 (page 210)

(i) The portrait you saw at the beginning of unit 1 is of the poet W. B. Yeats. (Def., *d*)
(ii) De Valera, whose father was Spanish, was President of Ireland for fourteen years. (Non-def., *e*)
(iii) The Gate Theatre, one of whose founders was Mícheál Mac Liammóir, is at the end of O'Connell Street. (Non-def., *e*)
(iv) The novel Joyce wrote after *Ulysses* is much more difficult to understand. (Def., *d*)
(v) One of the statues you see outside Trinity College is of the poet Oliver Goldsmith. (Def., *d*)

(vi) It tends to rain rather a lot in Ireland, which is why the grass is so green. (Non-def., *f*)

(vii) The horse that won the race was ridden by a seventeen-year-old jockey. (Def., *b*)

(viii) Grace Kelly, who became Princess Grace when she married Prince Rainier of Monaco, often visited Ireland. (Non-def., *a*) Grace Kelly, who often visited Ireland, became Princess Grace when she married Prince Rainier of Monaco. (Non-def., *a*)

(ix) The man you saw me talking to a few moments ago comes from Donegal. (Def., *c*)

(x)   A defining clause, which is more commonly used in spoken English, is different from a non-defining clause. (Non-def., *b*)

EXERCISE 4 (pages 210–211)

These are suggestions only.
(i) Who wrote the play **we saw last night**?
(ii) Oysters, **which are an acquired taste**, should be eaten with Guinness and brown bread.
(iii) Jonathan Swift, **who wrote Gulliver's Travels/who was Dean of St Patrick's Cathedral**, was a misogynist.
(iv) A misogynist is a man **who doesn't like women**.
(v) People **who parachute from aeroplanes** are mad.

EXERCISE 5 (page 211)

The street [ ] you are now walking along, **which**, in fact, used to be called Sackville Street, is Dublin's main thoroughfare. When Ireland became independent it was renamed after the man **who** won emancipation for Catholics in the eighteenth century, Daniel O'Connell. That's his statue [ ] you can see there, and the wide bridge **that** takes you over the Liffey and into the south side is also called after him. The sign on the bus **that** has just gone past says *An Lár*, **which** means 'city centre'. The monument to Admiral Nelson, **which** used to dominate the whole street, was Dublin's greatest landmark for many years. In those days all the buses **that** were going to the city centre simply said *Nelson Pillar*. Then in 1966, **which** was the year the fiftieth anniversary of the Easter Rising was celebrated, poor old Nelson was blown up by people **who** resented the presence of an English lord in an Irish street. Talking of the Rising, the building [ ] you're standing in front of right now, the GPO, is the one [ ] the republican forces used as their headquarters. The Proclamation of the Republic, **whose** signatories were all executed, was read out from these steps by Patrick Pearse on Easter Monday 1916. Let's go inside. You can buy stamps for the postcards [] you wrote this morning and see the statue of Cú Chulainn; that's the legendary hero **whose** adventures your English teacher was telling you about.

EXERCISE 6 (pages 211–212)

(i)   What that essence is is hard to encapsulate in words.
(ii) Generally speaking, Irish people can be said to be tall and to have pale complexions.
(iii) Immigrants to Ireland are not the only people/ones who have to make up their minds whether or not to choose Irish nationality.
(iv) No other country contributed as much to Live Aid as Ireland (did).
(v)   It may happen that the visitor likes Ireland so much that he or she decides to stay here.

EXERCISE 7 (page 212)

(i)   Ireland is both a state of mind and an actual country.
(ii) These mythological invaders eventually gave way to their historical counterparts.
(iii) The weather has a tendency to be unreliable here, even in the summer.
(iv) You get a kick out of teasing me about being overweight, don't you?/It gives you a kick to tease me about being overweight, doesn't it?
(v)   I don't give a damn what you do as long as you stop annoying me.

UNIT 2   EXERCISE 1 (pages 213–214)

(i)   The police assured me that the matter would be thoroughly investigated.
(ii) Waves of Neolithic colonists followed the Mesolithic settlers.
(iii) What the guide at Newgrange has to say will fascinate you.
(iv) The Bronze Age people could not have made the beautiful ornaments without tin.
(v)   When I last saw him in the coffee bar, a couple of women were chatting him up.

EXERCISE 2 (page 214)

(i)   You are to be operated on by Dr Ryan tomorrow morning.
(ii) That derelict house is going to be knocked down and replaced with a new apartment block.

(iii) You can bet your bottom dollar that if tax rates are lowered, interest on loans will be increased.

(iv) You must be more careful! You might have been run over!

(v) Were you told where the dolmen could be found?

EXERCISE 3 (page 215)

1. Three men are feared to have died (Also possible: It is feared that three men have died)
2. One body was recovered
3. the search was continued
4. Metal-cutting equipment is said to have been ordered/It is said that metal-cutting equipment has been ordered
5. knocking was heard
6. Eleven of the ... were rescued
7. taken
8. The eight men ... were reported to have been in no danger/It was reported that the eight men had not been in danger (had been in no danger)
9. A crew ... was airlifted
10. the search has been continued since then
11. it is now considered that there is little hope
12. of the missing men being found alive
13. The *Kilkenny* is reported to have been floating .../It is reported that the *Kilkenny* has been floating ...
14. it is feared that
15. other vessels will be endangered by the cargo lost overboard
16. Howth lifeboat was reported ... to be searching for/It was reported that Howth lifeboat was searching for ...
17. The vessel was said to have been carrying—It was said that the vessel had been carrying ...
18. everything was being done
19. could be done.

EXERCISE 4 (pages 216–218)

(i) **I'll never forget camping**—the action of camping occurred first, i.e. that's what I'll never forget. **hadn't forgotten to take her camera**—the action of forgetting occurred first, i.e. that's why she didn't have her camera.

287

(ii) **Regret to tell you**—I regret what I am going to tell you. **regret not being able etc.**—regret what has already happened.

(iii) **I've tried to get tickets**—I've made an attempt/effort. **I tried ringing etc.**—I did these things to see if they would work/be successful/produce a result.

(iv) **went on to entertain**—continued by doing something different. **went on talking**—continued what had already been in progress.

(v) **stop to get etc.**—stop (doing something) in order to get. **stop drinking etc.**—stop doing what was/is being done.

(vi) **remembered to bring etc.**—the action of remembering should occur first; if it doesn't, the action of the following verb doesn't happen. **remember leaving etc.**—the action of the following verb occurs first and as a result the person can remember it.

(vii) **need to do etc.**—the subject of 'need' is the same as the implied subject of the following verb. **need watering etc.**—there is a difference between the subject of 'need' and the implied subject of the following verb.

EXERCISE 5 (pages 218–219)

(i)   having
(ii) spreading
(iii) to think
(iv) doing
(v)   hiding/watching
(vi) to become
(vii) to inform
(viii) to get
(ix) redecorating
(x)   to switch
(xi) talking
(xii) to go
(xiii) to pull
(xiv) marrying/having
(xv) to tell

EXERCISE 6 (page 219)

(i)   It is necessary (for us) to know something about the different people who came and settled here.

(ii) Immigrants from the Loire estuary probably built court cairns.

(iii) Portal dolmens are more impressive than court cairns.

(iv) Although there was frequent faction-fighting, the country was united by a common culture and language.

(v)   If the defendant didn't pay the penalty, he would be boycotted by society/it would mean his being boycotted by society/it would mean he would be boycotted by society.

EXERCISE 7 (page 219)

(i)   Apart from the tools they used, their greatest legacy is the monuments they constructed.

(ii) The Neolithic tombs served as both burial sites and shrines/served both as burial sites and as shrines.

(iii) Copper seems to have been introduced around 2000 BC.

(iv) It's hot enough (for us) to have a picnic in the garden today.

(v)   I don't think that particular point is worth mentioning.

UNIT 3   **EXERCISE 1** (pages 220–221)

(i)   … we might have a heatwave.

(ii)   … they may have/might have gone out.

(iii) … I may/may well/might well be in bed when you get home.

(iv)   You might have told me …

(v)   Oscar Wilde mightn't have died so young …

(vi)   You might look where you're going …

(vii) … It might be raining by lunchtime.

(viii) … St Brendan may/may well/might well have been the first European to set foot on American soil.

(ix)   … We may have a few people in for dinner and I'd like you to be there.

(x)   … she may/might have decided to stay in bed today.

EXERCISE 2 (pages 221–222)

(i)   … you should go to bed early.

(ii)   She shouldn't be smoking …

(iii) … he should know what it means.

(iv)   … they should be having the time of their life on their Caribbean holiday.

(v)   I should have rung my mother last night …

(vi)   You shouldn't speak with your mouth full.

(vii) … it should be ready by then.

(viii) … he should be here by now.

(ix)   Little children should be seen but not heard …

(x)   … he shouldn't have shouted at me like that in front of customers.

EXERCISE 3 (page 222)

(i)   By no means is Ireland unique in this regard.

(ii) Nobody else in Europe drinks as much tea/likes tea as much as the Irish.

(iii) Despite a change in the situation in recent years, drinking is still considered an activity quite separate from eating.

(iv) The Irish love dogs more than anybody else in Europe/any other people in Europe.

(v) Our climate makes us an indoor society.

EXERCISE 4 (pages 222–223)

(i) Drink has long been looked on as the curse of the Irish nation.

(ii) Drinking is not only a serious business but a national pastime./Not only is drinking a serious business …

(iii) Drink has been considered an essential aid to the creative muse for a long time.

(iv) It's necessary for me/I need to have my English pronunciation corrected.

(v) Many Irish people hardly ever keep liquor at home.

UNIT 4 **EXERCISE 1** (page 223)

(i) has been said

(ii) invaded; recorded

(iii) were passed on; were eventually written down; have survived

(iv) were made; have been found

(v) lay; was discovered

EXERCISE 2 (page 224)

1. have you been
2. I've been trying
3. did you get
4. I've never seen
5. I've just come back
6. stopped
7. was
8. was
9. got
10. we've had
11. I've seen/saw
12. didn't go
13. we've been trying
14. had to
15. rang
16. was lying
17. was sitting
18. was
19. decided
20. needed
21. I've been planning
22. have you decided/did you decide
23. sold
24. were having
25. called
26. was
27. offered
28. were asking
29. didn't have
30. got
31. we've been meaning to
32. I've just been looking

EXERCISE 3 (page 225)

(i) especially. (ii) especially. (iii) specially; especially. (iv) specially; especially. (v) specially; especially.

EXERCISE 4 (page 226)

(i)   No sooner had the alarm gone off than …
(ii) On no account are you to talk …
(iii) Not even if you gave me £1,000 would I part …
(iv) I remarked that it looked like rain and hardly had I said the words when …
(v)   In the middle eighties little did we think that such …

EXERCISE 5 (pages 226–227)

(i)   St Brendan is sometimes claimed to have been the first European to set foot on American soil.
(ii) In one writer's opinion, the monks who travelled …
(iii) Despite the atrocious weather, everybody seemed …
(iv) Seldom has a writer been less appreciated by his fellow-countrymen than Joyce was …
(v)   His charming manner made it possible for him to get the job.

EXERCISE 6 (page 227)

(i)   We travelled the length of the country looking for …
(ii) Even if it's pouring rain, she takes …
(iii) She hardly ever arrives late for work./Hardly ever does she arrive late …
(iv) It took me all my time but I eventually succeeded in finishing my thesis.
(v)   Such was Patrick's impact on Ireland that …/Patrick made such a great impact on Ireland that …

UNIT 5   **EXERCISE 1** (page 228–229)

Where alternatives are given, the first one is preferable in context.

(i)   must/ 'll have to ring
(ii) 'll have to get up
(iii) must not accept
(iv) must answer; don't have to answer
(v)   have to/'ll have to/must do

(vi)   mustn't forget; can't be
(vii) can't have been; must have been
(viii) had to make; must have been
(ix)   mustn't be coming/can't be coming; must have been held up
(x)   must be joking; have to visit

EXERCISE 2 (page 230)

There are, of course many possibilities; these are simply suggestions.

(i)   … might/may as well correct last night's homework/make use of the time.
(ii)   … might/may as well sit down/have a seat (while you're waiting).
(iii) … might/may as well come with me.
(iv)   … might/may as well have another one/finish the box/eat the whole lot.
(v)   … I might as well go to bed/call it a day/hit the sack.
(vi)   … might/may as well go and see him/look him up/give him a ring.
(vii) … might/may as well have another pint/drink.

EXERCISE 3 (page 232)

(i)   … so I dare say she's gone to bed.
(ii)   How dare you borrow my new jeans without asking me!
(iii) He's worried he might lose his job. He doesn't dare ask for a rise/he daren't ask for a rise.
(iv)   Dare I say it, but your hair …
(v)   Don't (you) dare say anything … !
(vi)   Dare he tell the Gardaí … ?
(vii) Nobody dared criticise …
(viii) … she daren't tell him.
(ix)   I dare you tell him …
(x)   I daren't have a slice of Black Forest gateau (in case I put on more weight). I daren't put on any more weight.

EXERCISE 4 (page 232)

(i)   Sport is more a way of life than a pastime in Ireland.
(ii)   Such a degree of skill is required in hurling that it is only played well in certain counties./Such a degree of skill does it require that hurling …
(iii) The most popular field sport is Gaelic football.
(iv)   There were at least 50,000 people …
(v)   The farmer would be obliged/forced to use his own method of exterminating vermin if it weren't for the local hunt.

EXERCISE 5 (page 233)

(i)   Apparently Garret FitzGerald would prefer to study a train timetable rather than (to) watch a football match.
(ii) My mother is a dab hand at knitting.
(iii) She used every trick in the book to get …
(iv) … so we might/may as well go to the pub.
(v)   Dublin Horse Show is as much a sale as a rosette-winning affair.

UNIT 6   **EXERCISE 1** (page 234)

(i)   The Chieftains are to play …
(ii)   You are not to go outside …
(iii) I was to have played at the match …
(iv)   You were to do …
(v)   You are to go to Mr O'Reilly's office …
(vi)   The heat-wave is to continue … (according to the weather forecast).
(vii) I thought you were to have gone …
(viii) This man is to have …
(ix)   Dr Harte was to have seen me …
(x)   You are to keep …

EXERCISE 2 (page 235)

Keep in mind that 'used to' is always possible as an alternative to 'would'—and, obviously, overusing either form would be bad style. The aim here is to show where only one form ('used to') is possible.

1. would always go
2. would stay
3. didn't use to mind/I usedn't to mind
4. would spend
5. would get
6. wouldn't be able to
7. would get out
8. start
9. would find
10. would always get sick
11. would happen
12. would go
13. would always manage
14. would lie
15. would always be
16. would have to
17. used to be

EXERCISE 3 (page 237)

(i)   had done; washed
(ii) talked; had been getting on; discovered; had had/was having

293

(iii) saw; had been crying
(iv) had seen
(v) reached; rang; (had) put; had agreed to; contacted; went off
(vi) had been up; had been working; fell
(vii) wasn't able to; had read; had never read
(viii) was; had invited; didn't turn up; had arrived/arrived; was; rang; had been
(ix) had been; hadn't been able to; was
(x) had done; wished; had not chosen; decided; wanted; changed

EXERCISE 4 (page 238)

(i) most. (ii) most of the. (iii) most; most of the. (iv) most; most of the.
(v) most; most of the.

EXERCISE 5 (pages 238–239)

(i) The name the native Irish used for Dublin is older than the one the Vikings gave it.
(ii) In order to make them good food for the landlords, Swift recommended …
(iii) Not only did Strongbow come to Mac Murchú's aid but he married …
(iv) Great changes though the Normans made, they …
(v) The Duke of Leinster is said to have replied that they would follow him wherever he went.

EXERCISE 6 (page 239)

(i) How well/permanently they dug themselves in is proved …
(ii) Your disgraceful conduct … was beyond the pale.
(iii) …we'll soon put all the rooms to good use.
(iv) … if they find out, I risk losing my job/my job is at risk.
(v) If he wants to be re-elected he'll have to pull his socks up.

UNIT 7   EXERCISE 1 (page 240)

Where 'was/were able to do' or 'managed to do' or 'succeeded in doing' is given as the answer, either of the other two alternatives is equally possible. The suggested answer is simply more appropriate in context.

(i) The children could watch …
(ii) … I could have got run over.
(iii) … she finally succeeded in getting the car going again.
(iv) '… we could sit in the pub for a change.'

(v)   You could have warned me …

(vi)   She was able to do her homework …; … I couldn't get the right answer.

(vii) He could have become …

(viii) 'Could you lend …?'; 'You could ask Séamus …'

(ix)   … He could compose an air …

(x)   We managed to see …; … we could watch it whenever we liked.

EXERCISE 2 (pages 241–242)

1. 'd rather have stayed
2. prefer; to
3. had given
4. better than
5. 'd rather go
6. like; than standing
7. went
8. 'd prefer
9. like; better than
10. 'd prefer; to
11. 'd rather have had
12. 'd prefer; to have stayed

EXERCISE 3 (page 242)

(i) As long as the potato crops thrived …

(ii) In spite of the forewarning …

(iii) So vehemently did people reject anything associated with the famine that …

(iv) Brendan would rather accompany himself … than be accompanied by someone else.

(v) … I've just been speaking to him on the phone.

EXERCISE 4 (page 243)

(i)   He kept a horse for fear of being unable to …

(ii)   …you should at least try to cut down (on the number you smoke).

(iii) Up to a point it's understandable …

(iv)   Captain de Cuellar looked upon the people he saw in the west of Ireland as savages.

(v)   The great majority of people barely succeeded in keeping …

(i)   If I should be late/Should I be late …

(ii)   Nothing would ever get done if we were all to take the attitude she takes/were we all to take …

(iii)   Had Paul not asked Sonya to marry him, she would have been devastated.

(iv)   Had Sonya not accepted Paul's proposal, he would have emigrated to Australia.

(v)   If you should happen to come across/Should you happen to come across …

(vi)   Had he got/had his hair cut he'd have got the job.

(vii)   If we were to sell the house and buy a caravan/Were we to sell the house and buy a caravan we could …

(viii)   If she were to take my advice and smarten herself up a bit/Were she to take my advice and smarten herself up a bit, her husband might not …

(ix)   If you should see Mary/Should you see Mary in the pub tonight, will you ask her …

(x)   Had it not turned cold and wet, we could have had a barbecue in the garden.

EXERCISE 2 (pages 245–246)

(i)   If you heat water to 100°C, it boils.

(ii)   If it hadn't been for your advice, I'd have given in my notice.

(iii)   If I hadn't hit my young sister yesterday, my dad would let me go/I could go to the disco.

(iv)   Provided you finish your homework first, you can watch television.

(v)   I wouldn't have such an awful hangover if I hadn't drunk so much at the party last night.

(vi)   But for her two-year-old child she would leave her husband.

(vii)   As long as you promise not to laugh at me/don't laugh at me, I'll give you a demonstration …

(viii)   If you leave a record (records) in a damp place, it (they) warps (warp).

(ix)   Had it not been for starvation … this part of Ireland wouldn't be so sparsely/would be less sparsely populated.

(x)   If you're going for a pint, I'm going.

EXERCISE 3 (page 246)

(i)   So infectious was the movement that it …

(ii)   Not only were the Dubliners competent performers but they were also good entertainers.

(iii)   It was not until 1951 that a concerted effort …

(iv)   Little was done … before the 1960s.

(v)   The more exotic the music, the better it was considered (to be).

EXERCISE 4 (page 246)

(i)   You can't walk down Grafton Street without passing …

(ii)   The Chieftains must be the most …

(iii)   … the church would make an exception for …

(iv)   Wherever you go in Ireland there are signposts/There are signposts wherever you go …

(v)   Ó Riada did for music what Joyce did for literature.

UNIT 9   EXERCISE 1 (page 248)

(i)   I wish I hadn't gone …

(ii)   I wish you wouldn't blow …

(iii)   I wish you'd listen …

(iv)   I wish I could afford to spend …

(v)   I wish you'd stop … and grow up.

(vi)   … I bet he wishes he'd worked harder.

(vii)   I wish we were sitting … drinking …

(viii)   I wish they wouldn't make such an awful noise …

(ix)   … I wish it didn't rain so much.

(x)   I wish it wouldn't rain …

EXERCISE 2 (page 249)

These are suggested answers only. Variations are possible.

(i)   I wish/If only you wouldn't laugh in such a silly way …/I wish/If only you'd stop laughing …

(ii)   I wish/If only I could afford a new car …

(iii)   I wish/If only it didn't take me so long to get to work/school./I wish/If only I lived nearer the city centre.

(iv)   I wish/If only the pub was open; we could go in and sit down …

(v)   I wish/If only I'd gone to the Bahamas …/I wish/If only I was/were in the Bahamas …

EXERCISE 3 (page 250)

(i)   I thought I had more money than I have.

(ii)   She has done more than anybody could have done.

(iii)   You are far more assertive than I am when …

(iv)   …You're not so much a hindrance as a help.

(v)   …but she's far less intelligent than her sister.

EXERCISE 4 (pages 250–251)

1. less chilly
2. warmest
3. longer
4. most comfortable
5. most
6. least
7. more
8. strongest
9. most fantastic
10. loudest
11. louder
12. happier
13. bigger
14. lumpier
15. tallest
16. more comfortable
17. warmer
18. longer
19. more soundly
20. less bad-tempered

EXERCISE 5 (page 253)

(i)   She asked me what I would do if I were in her shoes.
(ii) Neil told me that Katie was going to start Irish classes the following Monday.
(iii) He wanted to know if they should switch off the electricity at the mains before they left.
(iv) The teacher advised him that he would have to/should pull his socks up if he wanted to pass the exam.
(v)   He wondered if they would ever learn to live …
(vi) The invigilator instructed the students that they must not, on any account, leave the room until they had finished their exam.

These are the two sentences that can be changed.

(iv) The teacher advised him to pull …
(vi) The invigilator instructed the students not to leave …

EXERCISE 6 (pages 253–254)

(i)   Even if more help had been forthcoming … thousands of Irish people would still have emigrated.
(ii) You should/had better send us your curriculum vitae today if you want to be considered for the job.
(iii) Should I tell my wife (that) I'm having an affair with her best friend?
(iv) Don't/You mustn't/You're not to accept a lift from anybody you don't know, and come home/you must come home/you're to come home immediately the concert has finished.
(v)   If we'd had any idea how expensive the restaurant was going to be, we'd never have dreamt of coming here.

EXERCISE 7 (page 254)

(i)   Although we might be/were detached from the mainland, we …

(ii)   Another reverend gentleman said, 'Don't be too friendly towards any Catholics you meet.'

(iii) Because of the lack of straight answers, the questions …

(iv) That's all I can tell you.

(v)   Your brother is the smuggest, most conceited so-and-so I've ever met.

EXERCISE 8 (page 254)

(i)   I expanded … by dint of sitting in the classroom.

(ii)   The muted conversation … used to be my lullaby …

(iii) Being too young …, I wasn't worried about it.

(iv) I wish they'd stop fighting …

(v)   One of them once asked me if I would talk to them when I grew up.

UNIT 10   EXERCISE 1 (page 256)

(i)   (*a*) The French usually drink wine … (*b*) The Irish usually drink tea … (*c*) Rose is used to/has got used to drinking wine.

(ii)   (*a*) Pat usually gets up at five o'clock. (*b*) When he started the job, he found it hard to get used to getting up so early. (*c*) Now he's so used to getting up at five o'clock, it's second nature to him.

(iii) (*a*) I usually iron my own shirts. (*b*) When I first got married, I wasn't used to ironing …/I found it difficult to get used to … (*c*) Now I'm so used to ironing my own shirts that when my wife does it for me, I do it again!

(iv) (*a*) Danish people usually drink lager. (*b*) Jesper … before he gets used to Guinness/drinking Guinness. (*c*) When he goes home, he'll be so used to Guinness/drinking Guinness he won't want to change back to lager.

EXERCISE 2 (pages 257–258)

(i)   They must be having/getting the outside of their house done up.

(ii)   If you don't have/get that dog put down, I'll shoot the lot of you.

(iii) I suppose I'll have to have it taken out.

(iv) I wonder if we could have the central heating turned on.

(v)   She had her car stolen during the night.

(vi) If the police catch you, you'll have your licence endorsed.

(vii) I hope I (can) have/get the windows cleaned by the time my visitors come.

(viii)Go and have/get your back seen to!

(ix) If you don't behave yourself I'll have you barred from every pub in town.

(x)   I'll have your room changed at once.

EXERCISE 3 (page 259)

Note that these are only suggestions. 'It's time', 'it's high time' and 'it's about time' are interchangeable, the only difference being one of stress and tone.

(i)   It's about time Mickey Mooney retired/stepped down/gave the younger people a chance …
(ii) It's time I bought a new pair of jeans/I lost some weight …
(iii) (I think) it's time I left/was leaving/went home …
(iv) It's high time they did something about this road …
(v)   It's high time you learnt that 'people' is (or 'are'?!) plural/listened to what I tell you …

EXERCISE 4 (pages 260–261)

1. needn't/don't need to get up
2. needn't have stayed
3. needn't have drunk
4. didn't need to call
5. doesn't need to worry
6. needn't/don't need to cook
7. needn't have bought
8. needn't/don't need to do
9. don't need to think
10. don't need to feed
11. don't need to get
12. Do I need to be
13. needn't/don't need to feel
14. doesn't need to make
15. Need/do I need to answer
16. needn't/don't need to answer
17. needn't have behaved
18. needn't/don't need to stop
19. need I/do I?
20. needn't/don't need to apologise

EXERCISE 5 (page 261)

(i)   Home Rule had never been further/so far away.
(ii) By no means was it the first time …
(iii) So unpopular was the Easter Rising that …
(iv) It was the ritual execution … that turned the tide of opinion.
(v)   It wasn't as/so expensive to be a member …

EXERCISE 6 (page 261)

(i)   I'll excuse his behaviour on account of his youth.
(ii) You needn't have gone to such trouble …
(iii) It stands to reason (that) they'll be annoyed …
(iv) … so please don't rock the boat by talking about the past!
(v)   Above all (else) I want you to be here on time …